JDA954                                    762310

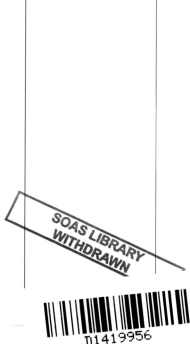

PENGUIN BOOKS
DELHI METROPOLITAN

Ranjana Sengupta has studied in London, Kolkata and New Delhi. A journalist for over two decades, she has worked in several major Indian newspapers and magazines including the *Hindustan Times*, the *Indian Express* and *Sunday*. She has contributed to *City Improbable* (Penguin Books) and *Delhi, Agra & Jaipur* (Eyewitness Guides). Her publications include *Ajanta and Ellora* (The Guidebook Company). She writes extensively on literature, travel and trends in urban life. She has lived for many years in Kuwait, Bhutan, London and Pakistan, but always comes back to Delhi.

# DELHI METROPOLITAN

*The Making of An Unlikely City*

RANJANA SENGUPTA

**PENGUIN BOOKS**

PENGUIN BOOKS
Published by the Penguin Group
Penguin Books India Pvt. Ltd, 11 Community Centre, Panchsheel Park,
New Delhi 110 017, India
Penguin Group (USA) Inc., 375 Hudson Street, New York, New York 10014, USA
Penguin Group (Canada), 90 Eglinton Avenue East, Suite 700, Toronto,
Ontario, M4P 2Y3, Canada (a division of Pearson Penguin Canada Inc.)
Penguin Books Ltd, 80 Strand, London WC2R 0RL, England
Penguin Ireland, 25 St Stephen's Green, Dublin 2, Ireland
(a division of Penguin Books Ltd)
Penguin Group (Australia), 250 Camberwell Road, Camberwell,
Victoria 3124, Australia (a division of Pearson Australia Group Pty Ltd)
Penguin Group (NZ), 67 Apollo Drive, Rosedale, North Shore 0632,
New Zealand (a division of Pearson New Zealand Ltd)
Penguin Group (South Africa) (Pty) Ltd, 24 Sturdee Avenue, Rosebank,
Johannesburg 2196, South Africa

Penguin Books Ltd, Registered Offices: 80 Strand, London WC2R 0RL, England

First published by Penguin Books India 2007

Copyright © Ranjana Sengupta 2007

All rights reserved

10 9 8 7 6 5 4 3 2 1

ISBN-13: 9780143063100      ISBN-10: 0143063103

Typeset in *PalmSprings* by SURYA, New Delhi
Printed at Chaman Offset Printers, New Delhi

*To the memory of my parents,*
*Deepali and Nirmal Chandra Sen Gupta*

# CONTENTS

# ACKNOWLEDGEMENTS

THIS BOOK HAS BEEN MORE THAN SIX YEARS IN THE making; I have worked on it, not always continuously, but always with the help of a number of people who have offered their time, knowledge, memories and advice generously and willingly. They are not responsible for its flaws, but without them this book would not exist. I would like to thank Ayesha Kagal, Ajeet Caur, Aparna Sharma, Prof. Anzar, A.G. Krishna Menon, Anuradha Roy, Bhagwant Singh, C.S. Gupte, Jayati Ghosh, J.K. Chandra, Shri Jutera, the late Jag Pravesh Chandra, Khushwant Singh, Kumkum Lal, Kamini Mahadevan, Karan Singh, Lola Chatterjee, Manish Sahai, Mohini Menon, Mandira Sen, Mahendra Vyas, Narayani Gupta, Nandini Mehta, Prita Maitra, Pandit Lila Ram, Ravi Singh, the late Sheila Dhar, Sharda Malik, Sudha Malik, Santosh Auluck, Sultana Qureishi, Sunil Shandilaya, Shehzade Bahadur, Sheema Mookherjee, Sagarika Ghose, Shaila Sathe, the Sarai centre for giving a me grant to study urban villages and Zameer Ahmad. My debt to my husband, TCA Raghavan, and to my daughters, Pallavi and Antara, is immeasurable; but for their unflagging faith and encouragement, this book would not have been written.

## PROLOGUE

THIS IS NOT A HISTORY OF DELHI; IT IS NOT AN exposition of its political structures or its economy. It is, rather, the spaces between these grand interstices where their effects are registered.

Nor is it about all of Delhi's people; I have written about the Delhi I know, that I have access to, that—if you like—I have a sense of. And my understanding of this ferocious, restless, relentless metropolis is that each of us who lives in this city carries a unique, if virtual, Delhi inside our heads: the life we have in it, the parts we are familiar with, and the parts we do not know, but nonetheless have a notion of, however inexact. This book, then, is about my Delhi, where I have lived for the greater part of my adult life, which I love, if not wholly comprehend.

**Ranjana Sengupta**

*New Delhi 2007*

# 1

## IN THE EYE OF THE BEHOLDER

WHAT MAKES FOR OWNERSHIP OF A CITY? WHAT IS it, exactly, that imbues a city's streets, stones and buildings with the resonance of belonging? What does a place have to have to bring forth identity, loyalty or pride? The notion of 'native place' has such a primal location in the Indian consciousness that professing loyalty to another territory brings with it a baggage of disloyalty to language, culture and identity. Delhi's lack of a single, overarching regional identity is often held to be responsible for its inhabitants' failure to pass the loyalty test. Cited, equally often, is Delhi's identity as a city of migrants; and then New Delhi is still considered too new; apparently a mere sixty years is insufficient to make a city a home. Yet, paradoxically, even those who complain loudest of Delhi's many and undeniable ills will rarely consider living elsewhere in India. Most Dilliwalas settle in Delhi citing professional, educational or housing reasons, explanations invariably expressed in the terminology of convenience, opportunities or finances; it is

rarely ever, affection for an environment, a way of life or
even people—the vocabulary invoked when talking of home.
Thus you have a situation where most middle-class
inhabitants of Delhi are prepared to live and eventually die
in this city, even while waxing eloquent about the lush
greenness of Kerala, the sedate charms of Chennai on a
Sunday afternoon, or the pleasures of *adda* on a Sunday in
Kolkata's Bhowanipore.

Yet Delhi, as an idea as well as a space, has not stood
still in the decades since Independence. From its stolid
imperial beginnings to the extravagant multiple universes
that make up the city today, Delhi has experienced a rapidity
of change unmatched by any other Indian metropolis. Its
economic base has expanded and diversified, from a handful
of textile mills and a very small service sector at
Independence to an ever-expanding financial and services
sector as well as numerous small-scale industries and large
industrial units. Its population, which stood at just under a
million in 1947, is today close to 14 million. It has a regional
diversity unique in India and this diversity has led to the
evolution of multiple universes within the city. Within these
worlds are varying degrees of urbanization, differing world
views and primordial loyalties, which coexist more or less
amicably, sometimes intersecting, sometimes wholly parallel.

It is one of Delhi's many discreet—if unappreciated—
charms that a single street will manifest a hundred varied
and wonderful landscapes. Take Aurobindo Marg, for
instance, one of Delhi's main arteries; thousands of people
traverse it each day but are probably unaware of the richness
of the sites they are crossing. Once called Qutub Road (after
the slave king), it begins at Safdarjang's Tomb. Safdarjang
was the prime minister of Ahmed Shah, and his son, the
Nawab of Awadh, Shuja-ud-Daula, constructed the tomb in

1754. Shuja-ud-Daula combined filial piety with frugality, and pared down expenses (a habit common among Delhi's contractors even today) by using marble stripped from the tomb of Mughal Emperor Akbar's general, Abdul Rahim Khan-i-Khanan in Nizamuddin. The road runs through Delhi's infinity of cultures: the affluent gentility of Jorbagh gives way to the shabby but smug façade of the government colony of Kidwainagar and then passes the ethnic market of Dilli Haat, opposite which is the crowded but rapidly going toney INA Market. This market is not named after the Indian National Army of Netaji Subhas Bose fame, INA standing for Indian National Airport—as Safdarjung Airport is just opposite. Aurobindo Marg then goes, via a spaghetti junction of flyovers, to the All India Institute of Medical Sciences (AIIMS) crossing, the area beneath the flyovers prettily landscaped, then to AIIMS itself, with its unique-to-India mix of cutting-edge medical research and overflowing-to-the-pavement outpatients department. After the crossing, south Delhi proper begins. Then Aurobindo Marg goes past the well-manicured frontages of Green Park and Haus Khas Enclave, crossing the cramped shops of Yusuf Sarai, haunt of all wishing for freshly ground coffee from Madras Stores, to the considerably more opulent Aurobindo Place market, opposite which is the original thirteenth-century wall of the former village of Kharera, now enclosing the offices of a private company. The road then passes the always crowded IIT Gate crossing to the remains of the twelfth-century citadel of Prithviraj Chauhan (1168-1192), Delhi's last Rajput king, who was defeated in 1192 by Muhammad Ghori, an Afghan. Ghori marked his victory by building the Qutb Minar where Aurobindo Marg ends. A thousand years of history, government dwellings, swank colonies, inexpensive shops, high-end retail emporia, regional outlets—it is all there, Delhi's amazing, eclectic mix.

Yet few appreciate this. Not the least of my reasons for writing this book was to discover the reasons behind Delhi's well-articulated unpopularity. Delhi's present, as well as its past, is inextricably woven into the perception of Delhi as a place. For instance, criticisms of Delhi are often metaphors for the dismay at the whole of India's post-Independence trajectory. Corruption, increasing social inequality or criminal behaviour is often laid at Delhi's door because the city is the nation's capital. Furthermore, Delhi's 'glorious past', its vivid, romantic history, has often overwhelmed its chroniclers. They have found the pleasures of its past so seductive, so full of the fall of empires, courtly intrigues and romantic decay, that its present appears arid in comparison.

Moreover, the past is frequently invoked as an oblique critique of the present, and different sections will invoke different pasts to buttress their own positions. Thus 'Lutyens's Delhi', the Raj, and the Delhi of the 1950s, '60s, and early '70s are invoked by the fast passing Nehruvian (for want of a better term) class as symbols of their days of glory. Those who want to evoke India's long Hindu heritage will evoke Indraprastha of the Mahabharat, or Prithviraj Chauhan. The graces of Shahjahanabad, particularly during the Mughal twilight, on the other hand, are metaphors to critique today's lack of courtesy, rampant 'Punjabification', or the vulgarity of popular culture. Some of the oft-cited grievances indicate dismay at the rise of a post-Independence non-metropolitan class, even if they are actually couched in terms of widespread corruption or administrative non-performance. Such critiques are also sometimes a means of indicating class origin. For instance, many complaints about the overt menace of Delhi's streets, or unbridled, illegal construction, can sometimes be deconstructed as a dislike of the city's changing social profile. The rise of caste-based groups, the pervasive influence of an increasingly self-confident business class, and the collaboration between the two—'an unholy nexus' in the popular press—have reduced the influence of the post-Independence ruling establishment. Thus, complaints about the growth of Delhi's politically protected criminal underclass and the growing black money economy are, on occasion, also metaphors for a social process which is national, not Delhi-specific, a function of its role as the national capital. It is Delhi's possession of a million hermetically sealed worlds spinning on their own, individual axes that has been both the city's saving grace and its nemesis. For it is possible to make any of the mud slung at it stick; somewhere in this unlikely metropolis, the villain will easily be found, usually dressed in spotless white churidar-kurta (but increasingly often sporting Armani suits or even specially woven silk sarees), sitting in a white Ambassador, pilot lights flashing.

Being the national capital is just one of Delhi's avatars; it has other identities, regional, professional, class-based, colony-based and so on, which intersect and diverge, often unpredictably. It has the pervasive government world of colonies and offices; the universities—Delhi and Jawaharlal Nehru and Jamia Millia are largely self-contained universes; it has the sub-culture of call centres, of the newer Delhis such as Gurgaon, territorially in Haryana but intrinsically a suburb of Delhi; it has the heaving, secret worlds where parallel economies and polities coexist—Govindpuri, to take a random instance—and these are apart from the regional ghettos of Bengalis in Chittaranjan Park, Tamils in Karol Bagh, Kashmiris in Pamposh. There is something for everyone here and people gravitate to the security of their own worlds, and from these protected fastnesses, roundly condemn all that is outside the magic circles of their own identities.

If the old order looks back in anguish at the lost certainties of the '60s, in the last five decades the changes in the city's ethos have been profound and probably unparalleled elsewhere in India. New economic policies have changed Delhi's social landscape irrevocably. The social trajectory of the city does, however, make its appearance in analyses of India's post-Independence history. In Pavan K. Varma's study of the Indian middle classes, for instance, tracking the change in Delhi's social vocabulary in the post-liberalization scenario, he writes: 'The removal of any stigma associated with making money has ended hypocrisy but also the need to be concerned about anything else.'[1] In a memorable passage, Varma describes a 'loo' theme party held at a Delhi 'farmhouse'—one of the opulent mansions that have come up on land still designated as agricultural—where the guests came dressed in bathroom apparel.

'Is this grand party idea just a frivolous, juvenile ripple of the affluent class? Or is there just the hint of the vulgar and the perverse? Not in moral terms . . . but in what the evening demonstrates: the unthinking acceptance of the enormous gulf that separates a tiny group of people living out, bang in the middle of a semi-rural setting, an idiom that fits in with the wild side of Manhattan . . . from thousands of people just yards away who walk a kilometre or more to obtain something as basic as drinking water."

These complex strands of dissatisfaction frequently find expression through a denunciation of what is seen as the 'Punjabi' way of life. In a glossy, coffee-table book on Delhi, marking the turn of the century, writer Khushwant Singh describes what became of the city after 1947: 'Punjabis imposed their own way of living on the city. The emphasis was on good food and ostentatious display of wealth.'[2] In the same book, journalist Madhu Jain maps the social journey of Delhi in the last fifty years. In the chapter titled 'The Happening City,' she writes about the post-Independence refugee class that has come into its own. 'Status withstood the onslaught of time, fashion and democracy. Then, however, came the brand invasion, and along with it new social ladders to accommodate the rupee- and dollar-rich classes . . . The old crème de la crème with thick silver frames and bejewelled sepia relatives . . . now sup with the corporate world . . .'[3]

If even long-term migrants long for their native landscapes, those whose families have lived in Delhi for countless generations would presumably express a deep sense of attachment to the city. Yet this is far from being the case: their loyalties are to their Delhi, a vanished, magical world of unhurried grace and honest shopkeepers. Even so established a Delhi figure as the late Sheila Dhar, singer, writer and raconteur, found little to praise in today's city. Though her recollections of childhood in the genteel environs of Civil Lines are vivid and affectionate,[4] asked about Delhi she said, 'What is it about Delhi today? It's just power, that's the milch cow. It gives you a job; it is a place where you can go for some kind of opportunities.'[5]

People who have lived their entire lives in the city ascribe their present dissatisfaction to its profound transformations after Independence. Shehzade Bahadur, who has lived all her life in Delhi, recalls her mother standing on the balcony of the family's haveli in the old city's Kayasth mohalla of Chelpuri, bargaining with a vegetable vendor standing below. She would lower a basket and the vendor would send up the produce. 'It was always good. They didn't cheat then.'[6] Similarly, Shri Jutera, a resident of Munirka village whose ancestors have lived on the same plot of land for five generations, remembers, with real feeling and regret, the beautiful sheeshum and jamun trees that once stood on his farmland, now covered by Vasant Vihar. He finds little to admire in the Delhi of today: 'It is very congested—if there's no electricity you can't breathe. All these seven-storey houses—water doesn't go up. Old Delhi, too, has got *barbad* (spoilt).'[7] The past was better—as always. These 'once was glorious' Delhi myths are evoked over and over again. Like all myths, these are perceptions based on core facts, but they are nevertheless beliefs rather than histories. They are nearly always invoked to express dissatisfaction with the present; they are triggers for a set of feelings that tap into collective memories. Among these is, for instance, the graveyard of dynasties—the subtext being that nothing of value survives in Delhi, everything rots away and declines, endings are inherent in beginnings. So, according to this school of thought, while Delhi's past was undeniably grand, its present is not. The reasons advanced are various, and depend on who is giving them.

All societies have versions of these 'glorious past' myths and they are nearly always devices to express fears about the present. In America, for instance, in the aftermath of 9/11, the safe certainties of the '50s were looked back to with yearning. David Halberstam, an American historian, believes that decade came to represent a spirit of optimism when viewed from the distance of fifty years later. He writes: 'In that era of general goodwill and expanding affluence, few Americans doubted the essential goodness of their society. After all, it was reflected back at them not only by contemporary books and magazines, but even more powerfully on television . . .'[8] This vision of a lost 'essential goodness' has entered the consciousness of some—not all—sections of Delhi's middle classes; a vision of Delhi as a safe, affluent suburb, where poverty, crime and social evils were happily invisible. In America, this nostalgia is expressed through the persistence of '50s-retro icons in films, advertising and fashion. And in an interesting sidelight on how American nostalgia becomes global chic, in Delhi every new pub, cake shop and restaurant uses such icons as old Hollywood posters and Coca-Cola ads as décor—a newly renovated coffee shop in a leisure complex even calls itself 'American Diner'. The iconic scheme is especially ironic, as the '50s in Delhi were a decade that embraced austerity and anti-Westernization.

So, every society re-invents its own past and this changes according to what it feels is wrong with the present. The past can refer to several decades, if not centuries, often simultaneously, and different parts of the past resonate differently for different sections of society. When Indraprastha and Shahjahanabad, Delhi's early avatars, are evoked, it is usually suggested that the present lacks both heroism and splendour.

Examine, for instance, the literature Delhi has generated. Literature is significant because it reflects what people think, and plays back identities that people make their own. You will find the reflections of a million small, self-contained universes, but not one real Delhi world that can be recalled with its full complement of mythology, ritual and relatives. This is why there is no great contemporary Delhi novel—Khushwant Singh's epic novel of that name deals with the city's spectacular past, not its present.[9] Yet Delhi's universes are ripe for the plucking (or writing about). Where is the three-generation Delhi Kayasth novel, for instance, with its beginnings in a haveli in the Chelpuri mohalla, with a middle section in Civil Lines and a triumphant end as a top government official in Lodi Estate? If the defining moment of today's Delhi was Partition (and few will disagree with that), despite the flowering of Indian authors writing in English in recent decades, the fictionalized refugee saga, tracking the terrible journey from Lahore, the early years of adversity in Malviya Nagar, and ending in a farmhouse in Chhatarpur, is still unwritten.

There is, however, a slew of books harking back to a more golden age, on Mehrauli where Bahadur Shah Zafar spent the monsoon season, writing poetry and hunting, the Mughal twilight itself or, more frequently, on the making of the city now reverentially called 'Lutyens's Delhi' after Sir Edwin Lutyens who designed its major buildings. This is why literature in English on Delhi is so weighted in terms of its history. Almost all of it is secular; there is an acceptance, even admiration, for all ways of life. Thus, the quintessential Delhi novel, where the city has an autonomous role that defines the behaviour of the protagonists, is Ahmed Ali's *Twilight in Delhi* first published by Hogarth Press in 1940. It is an elegy to an—even then—vanishing society, an ode to a generation that knew their world was dying. Its power lies in the deliberately nostalgic tone, the note of despair, of gentle, elegant defeat. The city is wonderfully and vividly evoked, its very streets conjuring melancholy: 'This was the street of apothecaries and hakims. With the smell the thought of death came into his mind . . . he began to think of Babban Jan. Her thought was sad and sweet, like the memory of some dear one dead . . .'[10]

This vision, this wistful sense of an irretrievably lost past, is so compelling that even William Dalrymple's *City of Djinns*,[11] an account of his sojourn in present-day Delhi, is actually all about his search for the past. This is a perfectly valid literary device, yet, sadly, the present is pitted against the gossamer allure of an older, more gracious Delhi. In this strange competition, the present is embodied by Dalrymple's

Punjabi landlady and taxi driver, who come across as venal, shallow and brash; obdurate customs officials and postmen have walk-on parts. The past is championed by a Persian scholar, a pigeon fancier, an elderly Anglo-Indian lady and other exotic and threatened species. The past, quite naturally, wins hands down. Yet, as the historian Percival Spear has pointed out, the causes of this glamorous, swashbuckling history have been as mundane as commerce, strategy and geography. 'There is nothing mystical about Delhi as the capital city of India,' he writes dampeningly in *Delhi Through the Ages*,[12] a wonderful collection of essays, many of which combine academic rigour with a vivid, anecdotal style. In the same collection, historian Narayani Gupta punctures the myth of the sad-eyed, wilting denizen of the old city with a telling phrase that has stuck in my mind for years. In the nineteenth century, the older Delhis were called 'Khandrat Kalan' or the 'Great Ruins'. Here, she writes, 'some people from Shahjahanabad dug perseveringly in the hope of turning up a hoard of coins'.[13] The past, for them, was not just an idea to be wept over, but a happy source of potential profit. Nor were accounts of Delhi's past by contemporary observers always misty-eyed or fulsome. In *Historic Delhi*, an anthology of writing on Delhi over the centuries, Val C. Prinsep, an undazzled witness to the first Delhi Durbar of 1877 when Lord Lytton proclaimed Queen Victoria as the Empress of India, writes caustically: 'The size is like a gigantic circus and the decorations are in keeping'.[14] Also illuminating the nineteenth-century Shahjahanabad as less than blissful is *The Bride's Mirror* by Nazir Ahmad.[15] This is a cautionary tale of two sisters, the saintly (and shrewd) Asgari, who reforms her gambling husband and manages his appointment to a well-paid post in Sialkot, and the wilful, spoilt (but infinitely more appealing) Akbari, who gets the fate she deserves when her trousseau gets eaten up by white ants.

If Shahjahanabad's long twilight is an endless source of delight to Delhi's chroniclers, Raj nostalgia is the alternative stock-in-trade of the 'Delhi was better once' school of literature. This continuing fascination also reflects the still deeply ambiguous feelings about the colonial period. Nationalist, even socialist, rhetoric sits comfortably alongside enthusiastic appreciation of all kinds of Raj memorabilia. Take, for instance, the redecorated Imperial Hotel on Janpath; the outside is marvellously art deco but the inside brims unapologetically with the uncle-and-nephew duo Daniells' lithographs, and chintz. Writing on the opening of the hotel's new coffee shop, '1911', named for the year of another Delhi Durbar, a highly appreciative review exclaims: 'It recreates the mystical grandeur of the past and connects it to the stark reality of the present.'[16] Social propinquity to the British is seen as a sign of 'khaandan' even today. The whole tea-on-the-club-lawns and bugles-at-sunset world of Delhi in the '30s that is the subject of so much nostalgia, is evoked by novelist M.M. Kaye in her autobiography[17], where she unapologetically outlines the sheer fun of the dinners at Akbar Road bungalows, balls at the Viceroy's House and impromptu dances to a windup gramophone in the moonlit environs of Humayun's tomb. The only Indians to appear in Kaye's narrative are servants and a few maharajahs.

Delhi during Partition has been the subject of many memoirs, most of them recording the violence, carnage and bitterness of the terrible months before and after August 1947. While the definitive English novel on Partition is still unwritten, Urvashi Butalia's *The Other Side of Silence*[18] puts on record the unheard voices of that time, 'the smaller, more invisible figures' who endured silently the repercussions of historical forces which sundered private lives. In another tone altogether, writer Anita Desai, in her *Clear Light of Day*, explores the impact of the traumatic events of 1947 on delicate relationships between siblings living in a decaying old bungalow in north Delhi which epitomizes their lives. Old Delhi here is a metaphor for wasted lives and unspoken resentments. 'It seemed to her that the dullness and the boredom of her childhood, her youth, were stored here in the room under the worn dusty red rugs, in the bloated brassware, behind the yellowed photographs in the oval frames . . .'[19]

While Partition narratives mostly speak of loss and desolation, much of the literature on Delhi written after Independence celebrates the new feel to the city, limping gamely out of the Partition holocaust. It describes the looted Muslim homes, the encampments of refugees, the totally disrupted lives; but informing it all is hope, the hope of an unquestionably better future. This conviction, that the future was a marvellous enterprise and just round the corner, which all good people could help to build, is brought out vividly by the economist, Prabhat Patnaik, writing about his time as a student in Delhi University in the '60s. He writes, 'I have a problem, like everybody, in locating the precise reasons for the general sense of euphoria. Partly, it must have been the sheer fun of being young . . .partly, for people of my generation, it must have been the absolute conviction that the world, and in particular India, was going to be a better place in the foreseeable future.'[20]

That future is still in the pipeline. The paradoxes of independent India struck British journalist James Cameron acutely in Delhi, for which he admits a 'perverse affection'. In *Indian Summer*, Cameron's account is of his first visit to Delhi in the feverish months of 1946. He remembers it as a time when 'the fading Raj was at grips with its inescapable moment of truth'.[21] Cameron's attitude, like that of many

men of his generation, is informed by his view of the first
prime minister: 'I think Jawaharlal Nehru was the most
important man I ever met . . .' he states unambiguously.
And though he was later alienated by Nehru's inability to
stem the corruption and misrule around him during his
final years, he nonetheless concludes that Nehru's greatest
quality, and one that survived to the end, was that 'he could
take the curse out of moral platitudes simply by believing in
them'. James Cameron, Jan Morris and other foreign
observers tended to see Delhi as a microcosm of India; as an
argument for and against a strong centre, socialism, big
bureaucracy—always in terms of politics or history; the
sense of Delhi as a city rarely emerges in their writings.
When it does, it is usually unfavourable. Charity has never
been Nobel laureate V.S. Naipaul's strong point, and in *An
Area of Darkness* he does not hide his dislike for the
hypocrisies of Delhi. He is contemptuous of the self-
importance of the Indian capital in the '60s. 'I could sense its
excitement as a new capital city . . . a city to which importance
had newly come . . . A city doubly unreal rising suddenly
out of the plain acres of seventeenth- and eighteenth-century
ruins, then the ultra-contemporary exhibition buildings.'[22]
Jan Morris takes the other route—the well-trodden one
immortalized by E.M. Forster—that sees India as a
profoundly mysterious, fatalistic, oriental blur. She raises
the old chestnuts of lazy officials speaking ungrammatical
English and never delivering. Delhi, and by extension India,
she concludes profoundly, 'is always as it is'.[23]

On the other hand, the perceptions of Delhi through the
'50s, '60s and early '70s, written by locals in socially
comfortable positions, are basically optimistic, even if
leavened by tart observations about pomposity and
corruption that were both beginning to set in. This world

was the location of Ruth Prawer Jhabvala's early Indian novels, but her recent writing reprises the same milieu. In her collection of short stories, *East into Upper East*, the story called 'Development and Progress', for instance, is set in the '60s and exemplifies Jhabvala's mix of fascination and distaste for a particular kind of Indian.[24] The story concerns a young British diplomat, Kitty, who falls under the spell of a brother and two sisters who live in a mansion in Civil Lines. The brother, an IAS officer, is full of the Nehruvian rhetoric of the time and Kitty is much taken with him and with the big, rambling house filled with friends, relatives and servants. Then, the story fast-forwards thirty years: one of the sisters has committed suicide, the other is embittered and lonely, and the brother is a mixture of pomposity and frustration.

The literature that has come out of present-day Delhi is often very good, but it has little to do with Delhi-specific identities; here, too, Delhi is a metaphor for India. A generation that was born expecting to rule finds that the goalposts have shifted. Sargarika Ghose's *The Gin Drinkers* is a clear-sighted, intelligent account of a younger, newer Delhi. An Oxbridge-educated generation, with idealism and ambition in unequal proportions, grapples with issues of social responsibility. They have to confront parents who are strangers and a city that has become strange to them. Coming home after several years at university, the protagonist Uma noted: 'Life was lived here over speedy generations from jhuggi to housing colony to marzipan villa in astounding succession. Intricate monuments were buried by high-rises and ancient stones breathed humbly under auto-repair shops and electricity substations.'[25] The world that Anjana Appachana evokes in *Listening Now*[26] is the quiet world of middle-class colonies. In this world of ceaselessly complaining mothers-in-law and silent, uncommunicative husbands, a world dismissed as humdrum, there is hope, anticipation and wild tragedy. Appachana gives the mundane dignity. Delhi as it was in the '70s seeps out all over this book: it was Delhi before Barista, before Archies, before my generation grew up. Appachana evokes the afternoons in the British Council Library when it was in the AIFACS building, the slow DTC buses, the bookshops in Connaught Place and the college conversations about who had 'topped their year'. Delhi in the '90s appears in Susan Vishwanathan's *The Visiting Moon*,[27] which summons the world of Patparganj housing societies, the muddy vegetable markets, the anonymity of identical flats, the ferocity of intellectual argument among the young professionals that people the area, the whole way of life that has evolved across the river. The city is a palpable presence, the universes press against each other, shape each other, but are unacknowledged—in typical Delhi fashion.

Delhi's own contemporary chroniclers are often less than kind, overcome by its ferocious, unstoppable drive toward upward mobility. This drive is expressed in various ways, one of which is architecture. Architect Gautam Bhatia has made trenchant comments on Delhi's buildings, and he observes with mordant humour a cityscape that refuses to listen to reason. In *Punjabi Baroque* he writes, 'But the Punjabi had never been satisfied with his Indian origins anyway . . . His Panchsheel Park house [was built] in his own image of a country manor, its servant's quarter a plaster replica of Chambord. A Buddhist pagoda roof, when set on a structure of Roman Corinthian columns, was seen by the Punjabi as a structure fit to provide shade to his red Maruti.'[28]

Khushwant Singh's column, 'Malice Towards One and All' in the *Hindustan Times*, has for decades monitored the whims and ripples of this extraordinary city. His monumental novel, *Delhi*,[29] has traced the chequered, romantic and terrible history of this city with characteristic rambunctiousness, but its emphasis is on the past. There is no recent portrait of the machinations of the political class, the brittle angst of the haute bourgeoisie or the arriviste post-Partition class that is soaring upwards on the wings of fashion, media or politics. While some recent fiction is set in contemporary Delhi, given the rate and scale of high-profile book launches in the capital, Delhi life today is still relatively uncharted, though Manju Kapoor and Kanika Gehlot are recent and honorable exceptions. On the whole, however, English fiction-writers have chosen not to evoke love in the lobby of Anupam PVR nor angst in the lanes of West Kidwai Nagar; and DLF's Malibu Town does not figure in the pages of an Indo-Anglian bestseller. Nor does contemporary Delhi have loyalists in literary-academic circles. In fact, the social mores of present-day Delhi are more likely to be found in research-oriented commentaries that draw an apocalyptic picture of Delhi's urban chaos. For instance, in a collection of essays on the city's political and social structures, the introduction is titled 'The Alchemy of an Unloved City'. Here, the editors boldly assert that:

> No one can doubt the fascination that Mumbai arouses throughout India, even among those who oppose much of what the city seems to represent. Similarly, Calcutta has a legendary reputation not least among its own inhabitants who are often ready to defend it with zealous affection. No such loyalty and affection is found amongst the inhabitants of Delhi who are usually indifferent or actively dislike the city in which they live. With the exception of a few chasers of djinns, of the writer Khushwant Singh, some descendants of long-established Delhi families and a smattering of others (including some

of the collaborators of this book) *hardly anyone is ready to declare a passion for Delhi . . .*[30] [emphasis mine]

This is quite a claim, not least because the editors apparently imply that a passion for Delhi is not only rare, but also confined to a certain literate and/or well-established section of the city's inhabitants. Such an assumption is not confined to the editors of this book of uniformly well-researched and illuminating articles, but part of a universal mythology about Delhi which is accepted unquestioningly as fact.

The emotional life of the city is recorded daily, and in detail, in newspapers and glossy magazines, but we still do not have a definitive novel about the inner lives of the fashion frat, for instance, or a diary of the life and times of the Bridget Joneses of Rohini or Gurgaon, nor an account of the journey from DDA flats in Vasant Kunj to the Miss Universe pageant in the Philippines, a journey Indian beauty contestants make with a fair degree of regularity. Frivolous, self-indulgent and irrelevant, the literati will exclaim, but this is the nitty-gritty of Delhi life, every bit as stark as alienation in a resettlement colony—but no one has written about that, either. Somewhere, there are invisible rules governing what should be written, what makes a valid story, and what will sell, and writers in Delhi appear to heed such messages unquestioningly. Being in the national capital gives an unnecessary burden of false gravitas to potential writers. The siren calls of recent politics, social inequality and historical trends fetter their imaginations.

It is acceptable in Delhi to explore Page Three and popular culture generally through exhibitions or op-ed articles, which provide the requisite anthropological distance. But to plunge right in, to immerse yourself unreservedly in that world, is to accept that it is as valid as your own, and this will never do. This will disturb the hierarchies, set in stone, that have governed English-speaking intellectual life in Delhi since well before Independence. This conflict is most visible in the media. The realities of circulation and ratings have led to popular culture in the form of showbiz, soaps, songs and gossip getting more and more column space and airtime. The intelligentsia has watched its own previously unbreachable bastions crumble. They have turned to history to political analysis to heritage, anything that will strengthen their position as the sole interpreters and inheritors of this anarchic, untamable city with its untrammelled, extravagant aspirations.

Yet Delhi is not a city that lends itself to analysis from one quarter alone. More than any other Indian metropolis, because of its lack of a single culture, because of its lack of a stable population, because of its different masters, Delhi is a city that is simultaneously many things to many people. It continuously evolves, mutates and reinvents; different Delhis coexist alongside one another, often wildly disparate, even contradictory. Looking merely at the outward forms— architecture is one example—it is possible to see structures four hundred years apart, wall to wall with each other. Within a single neighbourhood, a wide variety of styles, drawing inspiration from iconography as varied as the Renaissance to Californian to Rajput, will abut each other on a single street, testimony to their owners' unfettered imaginations. 'Reading' these forms, gives an indication of the city's aspirations, the nature of the identity it wishes to have. The one persistent identity Delhi has always had is that of power, which has been its unique selling point for centuries. Forts and bhavans (the latter are modern-day forts, contemporary citadels of power and equally hard to access) pepper Delhi's landscape; government colonies, shabby, peeling, but nonetheless possessing an indefinable air of self-confidence, are small, self-contained islands all over the city. The texture of middle-class life that evolved in these government colonies after 1947 was subtly but significantly different from that in the colonies set up by private developers and group housing societies. It was in these private colonies that the social architecture of the local market, the colony club, the neighbourhood park, became an inevitable signifier of middle-class urban living; so much so they were largely replicated—sometimes more opulently— in the newer Delhis that came up across the river and in Gurgaon. These new developments adhered to that basic Delhi impulse—followed for centuries—of reinvention. Unlike many other ancient capitals, Delhi does not have a core which gets rebuilt and expanded. Delhi's conquerors have always built themselves new capitals, usually within a few miles of the previous one. It was only after 1947 that Delhi's newest rulers stayed put, but population pressures led to an inexorable expansion first southwards and westwards, then eastwards across the river. The expansion ate up the surrounding agricultural land but the villages remained, enfolded by urban development. The villages retain their old topographies—the winding lanes, the chowks (squares)—and much of their original populations, not necessarily out of choice, but because of the regulations governing 'laldora' (red string), the land on which the village stands. The dwellers are urbanized, but the look remains largely rural. Recent transformations of some of them into high-end retail outlets have, in fact, turned their 'rustic' look into an asset. This evolution indicates the extent of the changes in Delhi's culture over the last half-century.

From a small town weaned on a strange mix of imperial pomp and Gandhian austerities, it is today a ferocious metropolis, home to a million disparate universes, virtually all of which have abjured the mantras of austerity. Delhi's aspirations are now unbridled, whether expressed through bacchanalian weddings, faux chateaux house designs or deluxe masala paneer pizza. At the same time, being the nation's capital, the patronage of classical culture is part of the national agenda and the political culture has negotiated an amicable relationship with it and with the popular culture of the streets. The city's social spaces have evolved to accommodate the myriad universes, the malls and the multiplexes being but the latest additions. Through it all, during the sixty years of the post-Independence period, Delhi's trajectory has been heavily influenced by the 'refugees' (though 'evacuees' is, in fact, a more accurate term) whose relentless drive to regain their lost positions has transformed the social and physical landscape of the capital. The result is the sprawling, restless megapolis we see today. Ultimately, there are a million Delhis even if the beholder's eye can see only one.

# 2

## THE IDEA OF NEW DELHI

TODAY'S DELHI IS NOT THE LINEAR DESCENDANT OF the cities that rose and fell on this irregular plain between the river and the ridge. Its real ancestor is New Delhi and its real beginning is no earlier than 1911. While its ancient ancestry, the ebb and flow of empires, sackings and phoenix-like resurrections are part of its oft-expressed mythology and have provided much grist to poets and guidebooks alike, the truth is more mundane—and recent. If we want to trace the social conventions, the iconography and the hierarchies that we take for granted and set so much store by, we need to go back to the idea of that new capital and what that idea sought to express. For it was here that so many of the practices of today were set in stone; quite literally, scored in the ground. And as so much of our thinking is conditioned by the physical structures around us, we need to lift the stones, one by one, and see what lies beneath.

≈  ≈

In the immediate aftermath of Independence the Raisina
Hill complex and the other structures of colonial Delhi were
regarded as useful, readymade spaces for the work of the
new Indian government. While some new public buildings,
built in the 1950s and '60s, followed (after a fashion) the
Lutyens mould—the Supreme Court, for instance, or the
National Museum—others were consciously radical
departures from this style: Shastri Bhavan is one instance,
the Ramakrishnapuram complex another. Lutyens's Delhi
was not then a cult; its symbolic significance was not
consciously accessed; if anything, its associations with the
recently departed British were a little embarrassing. Post-
Independence architectural styles favoured Modernism,
considered most suited to the prevailing ideology of socialism
and national liberation. The immediate past, when evoked,
was in terms of the freedom struggle, not empire.

Things have changed greatly over the last six decades.
Even before the advent of liberalization came the jettisoning
of both the socialist past and the rhetoric of anti-colonialism.
In the slipstream came the renewed acceptability of imperial
iconography. Among the reinstated were Edwin Landseer
Lutyens and the look he invented for the new capital.
Today, pink sandstone has become the near mandatory
architectural façade for new structures—public and private.
This has also been accompanied by much forelock-tugging
to a space known reverentially as 'Lutyens's Delhi'. The
process has also involved the elevation of Lutyens to near
canonical status: a grand visionary, just a little below Shah
Jahan in the builder stakes. The irony is that Lutyens held
Indian architecture to be ugly and lacking in intellectual
rigour; in fact he did not believe that an Indian architectural
tradition existed at all. Interestingly, the veneration for
Lutyens does not include every building in the New Delhi

Municipal Committee zone. Some buildings are considered more 'Lutyens's Delhi' than others. Witness for instance the debate about New Delhi's bungalows. Lutyens did not design any of these; they were largely the work of Robert Tor Russell, chief architect to the Government of India, who also designed Connaught Place. Yet the preservation of each and every one of these largely repetitive structures on roads south of Rajpath in the name of Lutyens's Delhi, is a powerful battle cry. Meanwhile, bungalows in Rouse Avenue, dating to the same era, are being razed without any of the public anguish about our sad lack of respect for the past which usually accompanies onslaughts on Lutyens's Delhi.

The bungalows earmarked for Indian officials were built to a different, supposedly more 'Indian', design. The higher ranks of British officials occupied houses in areas such as Kushak Road, Race Course Road and so on. Post Independence, these distinctions continue to be observed. Ministers, MPs, judges, generals and (very, very few) secretaries occupy bungalows in the heart of the Delhi Imperial Zone and it is this section that is often the most vocal about protecting the 'bungalow zone' in the name of heritage. But the bungalows on the north side have no champions, despite dating to the same era; they are a reminder that those who live in 'Lutyens's Delhi' today, would not have been allowed to live there sixty years ago. So a kind of selective nostalgia is being invoked. The Lutyens cult routinely invokes history to establish its acceptability. History, though, is not nostalgia, and we have to ask if the 'Lutyens's Delhi' mindset represents a philosophy that we need to get nostalgic about. Moreover, we need to examine the ways through which symbols of imperial domination have been turned into symbols of legitimacy by today's rulers and the impact that this has had on the urban imagination of New Delhi.

The story of New Delhi, *this* New Delhi, begins appropriately enough on 17 June 1911 in a memorandum written by John Lewis Jenkins, 'member home' in the Viceroy's council. Considering the momentous consequences, Jenkins's obscurity is surprising, yet, given New Delhi's subsequent history, it is quite fitting that its genesis was inside a civil servant's head. Jenkins wrote to the Viceroy, Lord Hardinge, that moving the capital from Calcutta to Delhi would 'be a bold stroke of statesmanship, which would give universal satisfaction and mark a new era in history'. Thus, from its very inception, New Delhi's fundamental purpose was to showcase imperial power; it was never a necessity; it began life as a crowd- pleaser for the Indians and was sold in Britain as a grand imperial gesture.

The notion was enthusiastically supported by the 'finance member' of the Viceroy's council, Sir Guy Fleetwood Wilson, who mooted the idea of 'an enclave on the lines of Washington'. His estimate for this enterprise was five million pounds; which he later reduced to four million. It ultimately cost several times as much but was about as accurate an estimate as most financial experts give when they want to push an idea. Lord Hardinge, too, was taken by the idea. King George V and Queen Mary were to visit Delhi and a grand imperial durbar would be held to mark their coming. Hardinge was looking for something big, something significant enough to justify the gigantic *bandobast*, expense and expectation that the royal presence would generate. On 25 August 1911 he wrote a memo to Lord Crewe, the Secretary of State in London. It was titled, 'Transfer of the Capital to New Delhi'. Crewe was enthusiastic; a brand new capital would, he felt, be a suitable sound bite for George V to announce in the presence of the assembled dignitaries at the durbar. Crewe wrote, in appropriately stentorian phrases: 'To the races of India for whom the legends and the records of the past are charged with so intense a meaning, a resumption by the paramount Power of the seat of the venerable Empire should at once enforce the continuity, and the promise of the permanency of British sovereign rule over the length and breadth of the country.' It was official: New Delhi was on.

All kinds of post-facto justifications were rolled out once the announcement was made. Suddenly, Calcutta was too far. It was too swayed by radical Indian influences and, at the same time, too captive to the conservative British merchant lobby. Moreover, the recent decision to rescind the partition of Bengal was viewed as something of a comedown for the British; it was felt public attention would be diverted from the rollback by this announcement. The official spin was that the presence of both the Viceroy of India and the governor of Bengal in Calcutta led to administrative confusion. Privately, they said that the thirty-two Indian members of the Viceroy's council (out of a total of sixty-two) would be better off in Delhi, at a safe distance from unsuitable nationalist influences. Furthermore, it was felt that the move would please the Rajputs and the Muslim community; the latter, apparently, because 'the idea of Delhi clings to the Mohammedan mind'. Finally, it gave the Viceroy, Lord Hardinge, the opportunity to ensure that his name would be immortalized as the man who brought a new imperial capital into being. (In the event, his name is barely remembered today.) Lady Hardinge Hospital which began life as Lady Hardinge Sarai, a resting place for travellers, was built by the vicereine to give thanks for her husband's survival from an assassination attempt in 1913; it became Sucheta Kripalani Hospital in 1977, and Hardinge Bridge is called Tilak Bridge today.

Despite Lord Hardinge's backing, the decision to abandon Calcutta inevitably generated controversy. Though the transfer of the capital had been periodically canvassed over the previous fifty years, it was immediately apparent that this time it was serious. The Calcutta lobby was particularly irate and envisaged many worst case scenarios including *The Statesman*'s descent into a local paper and an irreversible decline in the city's clubs. In the event, both prophesies came true. Notwithstanding these apocalyptic visions, however, the Delhi idea gathered momentum, and easily withstood rival bids from all over India including, for instance, Sagar in the Central Provinces. The people of Sagar claimed the town was more central than Delhi and had a permanently mild climate which would obviate the annual move to Simla. The last alone was reason enough to reject Sagar; after all, who would want to give *that* up? Delhi was elected unopposed, so to speak, helped in no small measure by history.

Lord Crewe observed approvingly, 'The ancient walls of Delhi enshrine an imperial tradition comparable to Constantinople or that of Rome itself.' Thus, before the name, the actual site or architect had been selected, the tone was set. It was to be imperial, imposing, immortal, a fitting monument to Britain's idea of Empire. And though, subsequently, there was much clamour over the choice of an architectural style—whether European classical, Indo-Saracenic or Mughal—the fundamental appearance had been established and articulated. New Delhi's legitimacy was underpinned by symbolic references to earlier imperial cities on the site. In this scenario, the British were the final and greatest of Delhi's conquerors, right up there in the neon lights with the Khiljis, Lodis and Mughals. The references to Rome and Washington were not fortuitous; there was an instinctive, universal notion of how the new capital would look. This 'look' is called the Grand Manner. It is, writes the urban historian Spiro Kostov, 'an urban grandeur beyond utility, beyond pragmatic considerations . . . whether it is ancient Babylon or Nazi Berlin. And its instruments are heroic scale, visual fluency and the luxury of building materials'.[1] The basic components of the Grand Manner have been very succinctly summarized by Kostov and are worth quoting in full:

> The Grand Manner is not the currency of little towns. It is neither practical nor modest. Perceived as an expansive pattern of sweeping vistas, its relation to topography and prior urban arrangements is arbitrary, its effects often grandiloquent. Typically, behind designs in the Grand Manner stands a powerful, centrist state whose resources and undiluted authority make possible the extravagant urban visions of ramrod-straight avenues, vast, uniformly bordered squares, and a suitable accompaniment of urban buildings. This is, in fact, a public urbanism. It speaks of ceremony, processional intentions, a regimented public life. The street holds the promise of pomp: it traverses the city with a single-minded purpose and sports accessories like triumphal arches, obelisks, and free-standing fountains. All this architectural drama subsumes the untidiness of our common routines. Shielded by our spacious envelopes, most of us continue to manage our plain existence, ready to gather into attendant crowds when the high business of the Grand Manner city needs its popular complement.[2]

All cities are repositories of power in varying degrees, but when power and its physical, tangible manifestation is the significant issue, this has, historically, been expressed through the Grand Manner. Such cities do not naturally or organically develop; they are made. Writes Kostov:

Cities designed in the Grand Manner employ conventions that make power physically manifest. They do so in the structure of urban space and the full panoply of fittings that gives it substance. Theirs is an idealized urbanism, a dissembling order that subsumes reality. There is much in the Grand Manner that is real, which is to say much that is uncomfortable. It must be concealed. The staging of power is a matter of managing appearances. The managers have a choice audience in mind, an impression they wish to create for it and a visual language that can bespeak in proper measure, regimentation, pomp and delight.

Lutyens himself was a convinced votary of this idea. He wrote, 'Architecture, more than any art, represents the intellectual progress of those in authority.'[3]

Thus, from the moment Jenkins wrote his memorandum, the appearance of the new capital was settled; there remained the choice of architect and the style. Despite all the hype surrounding him now, Lutyens was not the immediate, obvious or unanimous choice for this grand plan. Lutyens got the job partly because he was a prominent establishment architect designing country houses for the rich, and partly because he was involved in London's fashionably progressive Hampstead Garden Suburb project. He was also the best networked: his wife, Emily, was the daughter of a former Indian Viceroy, Lord Lytton. In fact, a competition was mooted in the initial stages, which led the then Viceroy, Lord Hardinge, to suggest that it should be open—at least formally—to Indian architects: 'The door must not be shut in their faces . . . it satisfies their vanity, and can do no harm.' Ultimately, the competition idea was given up as too expensive, and Lutyens was, along with two others, J.A. Brodie and George Swinton, appointed initially to the Site

Planning Committee, the body which was to decide the specific location.

This took time to settle. The site had to allow for a sufficiently imposing set of buildings, be on a suitably elevated setting, surrounded by a large amount of clear, unhindered space. Unlike Baron Haussmann's redesign of Paris in the nineteenth century, which involved much ruthless bulldozing and razing of existing buildings and streets, New Delhi was built on open fields and scrub; the occasional village which got in the way was removed, the villagers were compensated and resettled elsewhere—many in what is now Bhogal (near today's Jangpura). Before that could happen, however, various entrenched anxieties about India had to be allayed first. It was widely believed, for instance, that the Jamuna plain was mosquito-ridden and injurious to British health. Since their majesties, using specially made amethyst-studded silver trowels, had laid the foundation stones of the new capital at the site of the Coronation Durbar in north Delhi, near today's bustling Mukherjee Nagar, that area came under serious consideration first. Ultimately it was felt to be too small and, more significantly, too close to what the British regarded as the unsanitary Old City.

Underlying the idea of a new imperial capital was the unshakable British conviction that traditional Indian cities were dirty, unhealthy and inherently lawless. The cornerstone of the imperial idea was that it imposed a clear-cut rationality on the chaotic, teeming mess of India. 'We must let him [the Indian] see for the first time the power of Western science, art and civilization,' wrote Lord Stamfordham, George V's private secretary. The British sought, by their rigid geometry, their grids, diagonals, and hexagons to impose a sense of order and control. Raj literature is full of these differences—

Paul Scott's evocation of the fictional Mayapore in *The Jewel in the Crown*, or E.M. Forster's *Passage to India*, for instance, vividly evoke the native town with its swarm of congested streets, opposed, quite consciously, by the neat, calm, well-defended streets of the Cantonment and the Civil Lines. In such novels, the former gives off an indefinable whiff of simmering danger; the latter of carbolic soap and a solid, if stolid, sense of order.

So north-west Delhi was rejected; the area of the present Cantonment was a leading contender for a long time and was, initially favoured by Lord Hardinge. This, too, was ultimately ruled out, partly because the area was thought to be malarial; and partly because it was feared that even if the Government House, the proposed heart of the capital complex, were constructed right atop the Ridge, it would still not be sufficiently visible from all parts of the new capital. The use of heights is central to the Grand Manner. It positions important buildings, physically and symbolically, above the humdrum of everyday existence, and the elevation also provides for a sufficiently imposing approach. This consideration was absolutely critical to the entire project. Lord Stamfordham warned the Viceroy, quite categorically, that the new Government House 'must on no account be dwarfed by Jama Masjid or the Red Fort'. Ultimately, Raisina Hill, surrounded by flat ground, proved ideal. It was also near Purana Qila, thus neatly providing the needed symbolic connection between the British and previous empires. Like most politicians, Hardinge took the credit for this choice. He even recorded his moment of triumph. Hardinge, and the then chief commissioner of Delhi, Malcolm Hailey (he of Hailey Road fame), had gone to look for a suitable site. Hardinge recalled: 'We galloped over a plain to a hill some distance away. From the top of the hill there was a magnificent view embracing old Delhi and all the principal monuments situated outside the town, the Yamuna winding its way like a silver streak in the foreground at a little distance. I at once told Hailey; "This is the site for Government House." He readily agreed.'[4] Of course Hailey agreed; few civil servants would contradict the head of his government. Hailey's acquiescence was just the first of several million such actions that were to take place on Raisina Hill in the decades to come.

By positioning Government House on the crown of the hill with the two Secretariats just below, a strong imperial statement was being expressed. The Imperial Delhi Committee, set up in 1913 to oversee the building of the new capital (headed, incidentally, by Hailey), noted approvingly in its report, 'The imagination is led from the machinery to the prime moving power itself. Government House is the keystone of the rule of the Empire over India; this is the place of Government in its highest expression.'

If Government House had to be on a higher elevation to everything else, then the rest of New Delhi followed the same formula. The residential plans were drafted by the romantically-named Geoffrey de Montmorency, secretary of the Imperial Delhi Committee. One of the problems dogging the planners was that vast stretches of the ten-square-mile of space earmarked for the new city needed to be filled. Nothing demonstrates more clearly the difference between a city built with a purely ceremonial-political purpose and one that grows and stretches naturally as its functions become more complex. The task of enumerating the future residents of this imperial suburb was assigned to de Montmorency. He placed all the bureaucratic biggies as close to the Raisina Hill complex as possible, and the rest of government went in concentric circles from the centre to the peripheries.

Indian officials were largely segregated in small plots at the edge of the European city. Lutyens embraced de Montmorency's formula with enthusiasm, christening the serried ranks of officialdom with the political incorrectness which was allowable at the time, as 'fat white', 'thin white' and 'thin black', depending on race and seniority. He did not have a category for 'fat black', presumably because the thought that senior Indian government officials existed did not occur to him.

Thus, Government House occupied the highest position, flanked by the Secretariats, with the broad plaza of Central Vista at the base of the hill. Immediately to the south were two-storey houses, the quarters of the members of the executive council. The commander-in-chief's house (now Teen Murti Bhavan) was directly south of the Secretariats; while the Club was south-west of the Viceroy's House, at an easy distance for both British civil officials and the higher ranks of the military to get to. The seniormost gazetted officers were housed in sprawling, single-storey bungalows slightly more to the south, the joint secretaries fanning even further southwards; lower ranking administrators, that is deputy secretaries, under secretaries, registrars and superintendents, were placed west of Janpath, between the railway station and the Secretariats, followed by the higher ranks of European clerks. North of Rajpath in Allenby Road (now Bishamber Das Marg), near the Gol Dakkhana, for instance, were officials from the Posts and Telegraphs, the Supplies department, or the New Delhi Municipal Committee (NDMC). To the north of Connaught Place, in Rouse Avenue, were houses built round an inner courtyard or *angan*, to fulfil what the British planners decided were the needs of Indian officials. While the lower ranks of Indian clerks were positioned even further away, at the northern-most rim of the city was the area allocated to peons, *dhobis* and sweepers. Nearer the centre, the major princely states were given space at the eastern end of Kingsway (now Rajpath). Affluent Indians, including the smaller princes, were also allotted plots, along the roads leading out of Connaught Place, on Curzon Road (now Kasturba Gandhi Marg), for instance.

It was here that one of Delhi's leading businessmen, Lala Shri Ram, built an imposing classical mansion; today the *Hindustan Times* building stands on the site of Shri Ram house. Favoured Indians were also encouraged to buy plots on what was then the outskirts of the city near today's Lodi Road. Delhi's first apartments, Sujan Singh Park, were built in that area by Sir Sobha Singh, New Delhi's leading contractor. Businessmen, British and Indian, were allowed into New Delhi, but kept at some distance: the purpose of the new capital was unambiguously government.

Not coincidentally, hierarchies such as these, expressed in spatial terms, are found in Hanoi, built by the French, Manila, built by the Americans, and in Lusaka, built by the British. Allocations by minutely specified gradation are a common feature of all colonial cities. New Delhi, however, refines the distinctions of race and rank to an unprecedented degree. The address not only conveyed professional status, but also the size of the house and garden, the width of the road and whether the official was British or Indian. The concentric principle was, however, not new; it was a virtually universal feature of European towns since towns began and this was a notion that was exported to the colonized world in the seventeenth and eighteenth centuries. In several South American and New England towns, for instance, the powerful lived within the secure centre and the poor set up house on the outskirts. In India, things worked a little differently with the prevalence of caste *mohallahs* or, as in

Shahjahanabad, where each noble household had its retainers living in close proximity.

If New Delhi borrowed its ideas of grandeur from Europe, other European ideas also found expression in the new capital. Lutyens was greatly influenced by the 'garden suburb' movement then fashionable in British urban planning. He had designed the church in London's Hampstead Garden Suburb and he and his fellow planners—Herbert Baker and Swinton Jacob—felt that the empty acres of the new capital could well be filled with stretches of ornamental lawn and garden. In fact, Sir Harcourt Butler, member of the Viceroy's council, noted helpfully that if a sufficient number of trees were planted, the empty spaces between the important buildings would not show up. Due to this extensive planting, today Lutyens's Delhi has a high ratio of open space—one open acre to every ten built-up ones.

While the oft-expressed ideal for the new capital was Rome (not, significantly, Canberra or Pretoria—which were the obvious comparisons, and contemporary to boot), the layout was borrowed from Washington DC. Raisina Hill was regarded as a putative Acropolis or Palatine Hill, but many of New Delhi's features echo the American capital. The treatment of topographical features and the way they were utilized to make symbolic statements about public buildings, was one which New Delhi's planners embraced. The most obvious example is the Mall in Washington DC, with the Capitol at the head of the long green band and the Lincoln Memorial at the opposite end. This is echoed by the verdant expanse on either side of Rajpath with lawns stretching between Rashtrapati Bhavan and India Gate. Urban historian Robert Grant Irving relates this clinching story: 'On visiting the American capital in 1925, Lutyens told his wife, frankly and without false modesty, that he thought the plan "was not as good as Delhi or as fine.'"[5]

Washington DC's planner, Pierre Charles L'Enfant's own conception was influenced by the grand daddy of all grand and planned towns, and the prototype of the Grand Manner in the last two centuries: Versailles, in France. Versailles was based on the premise of absolute power, which explains its appeal for the likes of Hitler and Mussolini and several colonial powers; its very layout showcased domination. Common to all Grand Manner cities of whatever period or continent is geometric uniformity. This slotted in neatly with Edwin Lutyens's own preference for the equilateral triangle and the hexagon. His plan for New Delhi had all the broad processional avenues that radiated out from Government House at uniform angles of either sixty or thirty degrees. There was both a theatrical and a practical consideration: absolutism is prone to fear popular protests. While some avenues were earmarked for spectacular military displays, their breadth also provided easy access routes for the same military to be rushed to trouble spots. Haussmann's elegant Parisian boulevards doubled as 'anti-riot' streets linked to the city's major barracks and police stations. This same consideration underlay the British decision to raze the area of Shahjahanabad near the Red Fort after 1857. 'In Fascist rhetoric,' writes Kostov, 'la linea diretta [the straight line] is a metaphor for resolute decision making—the straight line does not lose itself in the meanders of Hamlet-like thought.'[6]

In the colonies, this organized, radial and grid layout symbolized not just urban European notions of the city, but expressed the idea of the superiority of Western rationalism in concrete form. The geometry, the deliberate patterns and above all the straight streets were making a point. The

British wanted their new city to symbolize men supremely in control of their own environment, a conscious departure from what they saw as the congested, chaotic environment of Shahjahanabad in particular, and most Indian cities in general. The wide plazas and straight avenues were necessary to showcase civilizational superiority. This impression was enhanced by specific classical schemes: triumphal arches, for instance, and ramps. India Gate was known in pre-Independence New Delhi as the All India War Memorial Arch and commemorated the names of those who died in the First World War. It was designed by Lutyens, who had had much experience in designing such memorials. He designed the Cenotaph to the Great War's dead in London's Whitehall and was commissioned by large numbers of his clients in Britain to design memorials for their sons who perished on the western front. The symbolism of the Arch has always been appreciated: at the time the Viceroy, Lord Chelmsford, felt that it expressed the 'ideal and fact of British Rule over India'. Today, India Gate remains the focus of patriotic ceremonials centred on the eternal flame and the Unknown Soldier, both symbols borrowed from elsewhere, but which serve the purpose of elevating the notion of the state into a mystic realm, thereby legitimizing its demands of sacrifice and duty from common citizens.

Similarly, a column in classical architectural lexicography celebrates victory (think Qutb Minar) or domination. Sketches by Lutyens show he had Trajan's column in Rome in mind when he designed the Jaipur column in the forecourt of Government House. Again, the fact that today the column, and Rashtrapati Bhavan as a whole, are held to represent national sovereignty, demonstrates how the icons of a well-thought-out imperialism have been adapted to legitimize another order altogether. This is also true of the Raisina Hill complex and the wide plaza of Vijay Chowk. Their use today is to showcase the military prowess of independent India on Republic Day; yet they were conceived to symbolize the permanent domination of the British over India. The transition has been virtually seamless.

In the end the commotion over a suitable architectural style for New Delhi, though accompanied by much sound and fury and trenchant official noting, was a minor discourse. The basics of the Grand Manner and the notion of an architecture that conveyed the idea of domination had been settled without argument. There was, in fact, a universal acceptance of the scheme; it remained only to decide the nature of the embellishments, the icing as it were.

Here, the debate ranged over whether the look should be Indo-Saracenic, Mughal, Rajput or pure Renaissance Classicism. Lutyens was firmly in favour of European Classicism mixed with a touch of Jacobean solidity—basically the style of his English countryhouses. He had great contempt for Indian architecture, which he viewed as merely 'the random expressions of mushroom dynasties' and without any intellectual foundation. He was a man who looked to Athens, Rome and Christopher Wren for inspiration throughout his career. He found Mughal architecture 'cumbersome, poorly coordinated and tiresome to the Western mind'. He conceded that there was some attractive detailing, but these he ascribed to Italian influences. When he was planning the city, he found the numerous ruined mosques, tombs or citadels that got in the way of his geometric street plans, 'uncared for nuisances'. He likened the domes of Delhi's mosques to turnips. He believed Hindu architecture was merely 'veneered joinery'—in other words, over-decorated and without a scientific basis. In a letter to Herbert Baker (with whom he was still, in 1912, good friends), he outlined a comic little scenario on Hindu architectural construction: 'Set square stones and build childwise . . . before you erect, carve every stone differently and independently with lace patterns and terrifying shapes. On the top, build over-trabeated pendentives and an onion.' This was a man who saw architecture as a study of geometric proportion, the 'entasis' established by the ancient Greeks. This refers to architectural principles in which a structure's horizontal surfaces were parts of parallel spheres 1801 feet and eighteen inches in diameter, and all its verticals converge at a point 1801 feet and eight inches above the centre of these spheres; Lutyens applied these principles most famously when designing the Cenotaph in London, a memorial to the soldiers who fell in the Great War, which was built in 1919.

Hardinge, uneasily aware that Indian revenues would be footing the bill for New Delhi and conscious of the need to keep Indian public opinion quiescent, suggested a mix of what he called the Palladian and the Pathan. King George V had a marked preference for the Mughal. Everybody had an opinion, and though there was little controversy about the necessity of a fundamentally European style, there were some differences over which one. Suggestions included the English and the Italian architectural styles. This last had many adherents as it was felt that Italian architecture was suited to places with brilliant sunshine. There were others who advocated the Hellenistic, buttressing their preference by citing Alexander the Great's influence on Indian art by way of the Gandhara school. Others wanted pure Roman. Herbert Baker was more amenable to Indian motifs, and felt the generous use of colonnades and columns would satisfy everyone and at the same time be sufficiently classical. In the end, it was a pastiche of Western classical architectural form and proportion, with Rajput and Mughal embellishments. And these were lavish. Rashtrapati Bhavan has, for instance, a full complement of lotuses, cobras, elephants, sacred bulls and bells carved onto its surface.

New Delhi was inaugurated in 1931, way over budget and timeframe. The British left permanently sixteen years later. Today, because of the great reverence surrounding it, few actually look at the great Raisina complex critically. The monumentality, the high 'classical' reputation, the inevitable appearance in all the guidebooks and the hype surrounding Lutyens, prevents these buildings from real evaluation. Yet, from some angles, the Secretariat buildings look like two giant bricks of strawberry ice cream sliding majestically down the Raisina slope. The two watchtowers in front stick out like two thumbs (literally) and, as far as can be ascertained, have absolutely no function except as a perch for the trumpeter during the annual Beating of the Retreat ceremony (which commemorates the ritual of lowering the flag to the notes of a bugle; a ritual which took place every sunset in the 'farflung outposts' of the British Empire and one which is much evoked by Empire nostalgists). The domes are seriously over-ornamented (they are said to be inspired by St Peter's in Rome), and the baroque style sits uncomfortably with the carved elephants and the elaborate Mughal-style *jaalis*. Most offensive is the legend, selected in 1925 and carved on an arched gateway of North Block, which articulates the imperial message a little too clearly for post-Independence sensibilities: 'Liberty will not descend to a people; a people must raise themselves to liberty; it is a blessing which must be earned before it can be enjoyed.'

As to Rashtrapati Bhavan, the dome has a disproportionately high drum in relation to the building it surmounts. Lutyens increased the height because the gradient of the hill obscured the view of the building from Central Vista. His celebrated fight with Baker—his 'Bakerloo' as he called it—was over the angle of the ramp leading to Rashtrapati Bhavan, and is a highlight in the chronicles of 'Lutyens's Delhi' and oft quoted by Lutyens literati. Lutyens, for all his geometry, discovered the problem too late and could not convince the government, already embarrassed by the time and money spent on the new capital, to relay the road. In the end—as Raj romancer M.M. Kaye quotes Lutyens as telling her in the 1930s—he was forced to increase the height of the drum supporting the dome to ensure an at least partial visibility.[7] Compare the dome of Baroda House, also designed by Lutyens, to that of Rashtrapati Bhavan and the disproportionate height of the latter's drum will become obvious.

New Delhi was built to be an unambiguous statement of imperial purpose. By the time the new capital was inaugurated in 1931, that purpose had lost conviction and had only a decade and a half left to run. In hindsight, it is easy to say that by their very nature, such grandiose imperial schemes, with no other function than to project imperialism, are in themselves suspect; dead giveaways that British rule in India was floundering, was scrabbling to appear confident and purposeful, when in fact their own conviction in their imperial destiny was ebbing. Architectural historian Robert Grant Irving wrote: 'The capital India's rulers planned, now stands as a monument to their belief in ordered governance and with that elusive, but keenly sought goal, progress.' Few will believe today that building a city—no matter how carefully calibrated the angles of its avenues, the proportions of its facades and systematic allocation of space to its administrative ranks—will lead to the alleviation of poverty or even the dissemination of a scientific temper. Irving observes: 'The founders' faith [was] that art and life as they ought to be can be reached in this world and ideas can be translated into practice.' Some seventy-five years down the line, it is hard to credit such virtuous aspirations. The employment of the Grand Manner, the preoccupation with height for government buildings, the fantastically careful ranking by race and status, all work against this conception. The conviction in the superiority of Western science and civilization was a product of the age, but its logical accompaniment was that Indian science and civilization was inferior, if it existed at all. To celebrate these principles *today*, as well as an architect who shared these sentiments, is puzzling.

What impact has this kind of city architecture and planning had on our post-Independence selves? Today, the regalia, so to speak, of imperialism is being used to confer legitimacy on present-day regimes. It is not just that they are occupying the same space, but that space itself has become a symbol of office and is invoked with the same sense of history and pageantry as when the British invoked the Mughals, Lodis and Tughlaqs to buttress their position as the unquestioned rulers of the Indian empire. It is as if, given enough time, the political subordination implicit in colonialism has somehow been leached out, leaving its ornaments with a kind of neutral power. By buying into all the accessories—the regimented housing, the use of Rajpath and Vijay Chowk for impressive military displays, the swashbuckling pageantry surrounding the Unknown Soldier at India Gate—the symbols of the past have all survived into the present and are being used for much the same purposes. By elevating the whole of Lutyens's Delhi into a sort of sacred monument, the broad streets and huge parks and large compounds that characterize this space are being imbued, unwittingly or otherwise, with a sense of 'rightness'.

Ultimately, this has had an enormous impact on the urban bourgeois imagination. It is seen as the identification mark of the affluent. When new enclaves come up on the edge of today's city, many aspects of Lutyens's Delhi are being replicated: pink sandstone facades, broad, tree-lined streets laid out in a grid pattern and the service personnel tucked away in well-hidden quarters. Equally obvious is the continuing organization by rank and status and the consequent separations of those with power and those without. The celebration of 'Lutyens's Delhi' may be couched in the vocabulary of heritage, architectural aesthetics and history, but the values it asserts—consciously or not—are those of regimentation, hierarchy and exclusion. It embodies a fear of organic urban growth, of the poor, indeed of everyone outside the tight circle of the privileged; of diversity, creativity and irreverence—everything, in fact, that makes a city vital, unpredictable and innovative.

# 3

## THE MAKING OF NEWER DELHI

IF NEW DELHI WAS THE CAPITAL OF BRITAIN'S Indian Empire, post-Independence India created *newer* Delhi, a new capital, but one perched securely on the foundations of the older one. Its purpose was to showcase the new nation's commitment to modernity and development. A well-established belief of that time, and one advocated by Jawaharlal Nehru, India's first prime minister, was that creating an egalitarian, progressive environment would lead to an egalitarian and progressive society. 'The nationalist state,' the historian Sunil Khilnani has written, 'took up residence in the city, and it was here too that the Nehruvian ambition to modernize and develop Indian society was scripted and broadcast, radiating outwards to the villages'.[1] Naturally, this impulse was at its most profound in regard to Delhi. C.S. Gupte, former chief planner, Government of India, vividly remembered the personal interest that Nehru took in the details of the new capital's plan. As a member of the Town Planning Organization, Gupte was involved in the Interim General Plan, prepared in just six months and presented to a Cabinet committee which included, apart from the prime minister and the cabinet secretary, India's long-serving External Affairs minister, Sardar Swaran Singh, the Education minister, Maulana Azad, and his adviser, Humayun Kabir. Gupte recalled: 'The Cabinet secretary said we had ten minutes to explain everything. The prime minister intervened. He said, "No, no, take your time."'[2]

This commitment to a planned urban process, this conviction that controlling the physical aspects of the urban landscape could transform people's minds, led to two developments that have created the Delhi we know today. The first was the formulation of the Masterplan with its emphasis on the rigid segregation of the city into residential, commercial and public areas. The second was the adoption of Modernism as the near-official architectural style for most of the capital's new constructions. These matchbox buildings with their distinctive protruding slabs of concrete were meant to represent a complete break with all past architectural ideas, showcasing an unfettered, uncompromising contemporary feel. If today the encroachments, illegal constructions and mushrooming markets show the limits of the Masterplan's effectiveness, Modernism's peeling and shabby buildings appear to exemplify the old austerities of the immediate post-Independence era, a kind of Soviet-era drabness, a look now regarded as both unfashionable and impractical.

It was not meant to be so. While planning Independent India's new capital was a matter of urgency, it was undertaken with great seriousness. Within hours of Independence, the authorities were faced with two formidable tasks: one was the accommodation of the four *million* refugees from Pakistan; the other was the need for new government offices and housing for the increasing numbers of officials that the independent nation required. Moreover, professionals were flooding in from all parts of the country, attracted by the new opportunities; they too needed houses. Migrant labour started flowing into Delhi. There was an explosion in the population of the city. New Delhi was not constructed for this. As Delhi's *Gazetteer* observed, in typically measured periods, 'The even tenor of New Delhi's slow growth was disturbed in the wake of Partition and [by] other factors. The population of the twin cities shot up from 6.95 lakh in 1941 to 14.37 lakh in 1951 . . . Settlements were hastily improvised, and urban development was in the first few years highly irregular and haphazard.'[3]

The government's solution was to set in motion the development of a Masterplan to establish the parameters of Delhi's development in the foreseeable future. Approved in 1962, it had a defining impact on the new capital. Santosh Auluck, former member of the Town Planning Organization, was associated with the process from the inception and had a grandstand view of the Masterplan's early development. He maintains the basic principles were sound: 'The idea was not to develop colony by colony, but zone by zone. The thinking was that each zone should be self-sufficient—have its own social, educational and health infrastructure.'[4] Each zone had its own Zonal Development Plan but conformity to the pattern has been hard to implement and even harder to sustain. Within a decade, it was estimated that twenty-five per cent of the city's land and fully forty-five per cent of the buildings were not in accordance with the Plan.

Viewing Delhi's development today, it is easy to criticize the planners for the evident unviability of some of their proposals. But it was also a laudable attempt to prevent

speculation in land prices, the concentration of land in a few
hands and to curb the unscrupulous actions of land mafia
that were profiteering from the uncontrolled growth of the
city. Yet land mafia thrive, and the natural trend of urban
development in India has never been segmented by function.
Within weeks of the first houses being occupied in a
residential colony, small shops come up to supply daily
necessities; *jhuggis* mushroom to accommodate the domestic
labour. Razing such structures, the authorities' typical
reaction to the problem, causes hardship and moreover
works only temporarily. In 1962, for example, there were an
estimated 110 unauthorized colonies in Delhi. All those
established before 1967 were regularized in 1969; in 1990 a
survey found 900 unauthorized colonies and over 1,000
unauthorized markets—containing a quarter of the city's
population. It was not as if the planners were unaware of
the situation: the second Masterplan had warned that if then
prevailing trends continued, fully eighty per cent of the
city's population would reside in such colonies, but, as late
as 1976, Delhi's *Gazetteer* observed in regard to the
implementation of the Masterplan, 'The location of industries,
commercial centres, residential colonies, educational
institutions, etc. were all mapped out . . . the new slums that
were cropping up were to be liquidated (*sic*).'[5]

Recent newspaper reports indicate there are as many as
1,600 unauthorized colonies in the capital, home to at least
30 lakh people, who are without the basic amenities of
water, sewerage and power. The Delhi government has
promised to provide these facilities, and a substantial number
of these colonies will doubtless be regularized eventually.
But the point is, since the '60s, while the numbers have
increased exponentially, the situation remains the same.

The first Masterplan had envisaged the development of

ring towns round the capital which would draw migrants away from the capital, but this scenario failed to materialize. To this day planners have failed to make provision for the fact that poor migrants in search of a livelihood will inevitably be drawn to Delhi in the absence of any other means of survival in their native places; furthermore, their presence in Delhi will inevitably become a political issue. Regularizing colonies creates vote banks that no political party can afford to ignore. Similarly, the plan's somewhat inflexible strictures with regard to land use, floor area and so on, have led to rampant violations which, in turn, lead to corruption. Those who can afford to, simply pay their way out. There has come into existence a self-perpetuating cycle of regulations, violations and payoffs. The losers are the poor, the law-abiding, and—ultimately—Delhi.

By the time the Masterplan was approved in 1962, the capital's planning process had already been through more than a decade of committees, commissions and authorities: the Central Coordination Committee for the Development of Greater Delhi had been set up as early as 1949 and had recommended that a committee be set up to identify suitable development processes for the new capital. This—the Birla Committee—recommended the establishment of a single planning authority and duly, in 1955, the Delhi Development (Provisional) Authority came into being. The Masterplan itself was formulated by the Town Planning Organization, instituted in 1956, which was given the brief of, first, putting together an Interim General Plan for Greater Delhi and, eventually, the Masterplan for the entire capital region. The following year, in 1957, the Delhi Development Authority (DDA) Act was passed and the DDA, the agency which was to oversee the development of Delhi according to the forthcoming Masterplan, came into being. Two years later, in preparation for this, and in order to control spiralling land prices, speculation and haphazard land use, the government acquired all vacant urban land under the Land Acquisition Act 1959.

The proliferation of bodies established to look after Delhi's environment has proceeded apace. In 1971 the New Delhi Redevelopment Advisory Committee was set up; in 1974 the Urban Art Commission was instituted to preserve and develop the aesthetic and environmental quality of Delhi, and 1985 saw the establishment of the Delhi Capital Region Planning Board. Clearly, if urban development could be measured by the number of boards alone, then Delhi has absolutely no problems. Yet in many ways, the plethora of such bodies and the provisions of the Masterplans, including the latest one, indicate the fundamental confusion over the nature of Delhi's urban environment: some sections desire a manicured middle-class enclave on the lines of American suburbia, but the realities of India's urban development indicate a more multifunctional, less tidy, entity. As early as 1908, the Whitehead Report on Shahjahanabad was condemning it for being 'a useless maze . . . of hovels.' The British associated congestion with squalor and squalor with subversion. They were convinced that if the native population were settled in neatly gridded, broad streets, they would become placid and acquiescent subjects of the Crown. Such calculations were inevitably part of a colonial mindset; it is, therefore, surprising to find the 1962 Masterplan echoing much the same sentiments. It found the old city to be congested, filthy and fundamentally lacking in exclusive land use, without open green spaces, and 'socially and culturally stagnant'. Its recommendation was to move *forty-five per cent of the population* outside the old city (emphasis mine). In the event, the residential population of

Shahjahanabad has decreased substantially, though not in ways that the 1962 Masterplan envisioned. Much of the old city is now occupied by retail outlets and small manufacturing units; while the day population remains high, the residential population has actually declined. For pre- and post-Independence planners alike, cities were required to be well-regulated middle-class enclaves, with a separation of work and home. Nearly five decades after the 1962 Masterplan, this has not happened.

The 2021 Masterplan states that 'the cornerstone for making Delhi a world-class city is the planning process itself and related aspects of governance and management'. Absent from this self-congratulatory assertion are the inhabitants of the city whose definitions of what would make for a 'world-class city' often differ radically from the planners', governors' and managers' views. Delhi's role as the capital exacerbates the situation as ambitious 'prestige' projects—the forthcoming Commonwealth Games in 2010 for example—require investments that do not necessarily prioritize the average citizen's needs. The argument that it will all ultimately improve the city cuts little ice with those whose houses are just feet away from proposed elevated sections of the Metro, or those who travel on roads made impassable by the construction of the new bus corridor.

Moreover, different segments of the population have different, often conflicting, priorities. Take the Yamuna Satyagraha, a group opposing the construction of the Commonwealth Games Village on the Yamuna flood plain. They express their anguish at the fate of the river, the loss of natural habitat for wildlife, and other clean, green issues, by tying rakhis to soon-to-be-chopped-down trees. The residents of Tri Nagar in north Delhi, on the other hand, are on the opposite side of the green spectrum. This area is one of forty-two residential localities in Delhi which actually contain more industrial units than homes. Most houses have a small manufacturing unit on the ground floor, while the owner and family live upstairs. When the Supreme Court had ordered the closure of all such units and their relocation in designated industrial zones, the decision was fiercely contested by owners and workers alike, who saw their very livelihood in jeopardy. Their pressure on local political leaders resulted in a decree from the state government that areas where such units comprised more than 70 per cent of the housing would be exempted. Moreover, the designated area—the Bawana Industrial Area—was neither large enough, nor yet fully developed enough to accommodate such a large number of units. There are over 1,25,000 manufacturing units in Delhi and the political argument was that residents of such heavily industrialized areas were all dependent in one way or another on the units. The benefits of cleaner air and streets were—for them—not sufficiently persuasive.

The same ground-level realities were behind the decision to allow mixed land use in areas previously designated as wholly residential, and to freeze MCD's demolitions of commercial constructions in violation of zoning by-laws for a year, while the issue was studied (inevitably) by a committee. Now, commercial and professional establishments are allowed to remain in residential areas if they are on main roads and if enough parking space is available. These establishments include shops, offices, nursing homes, primary schools, banks and so on. Given the number and volume of establishments that have functioned and flourished openly in every street of every residential locality in Delhi, the fact that they were, in fact, illegal, came as a surprise to many. The conflicts between different interest groups cannot be resolved by one, overarching document like the Masterplan. The continuing battles for Delhi's soul are being played out on the streets, in the courts, and in the media.

The sole implementing agent of the Masterplan is the DDA, frequently an object of great odium among the public at large. It is a hydra-headed monster involved in nearly every aspect of Delhi's urban development and considered— justly or otherwise—responsible for most, if not all, of Delhi's ills. Its monopoly on land has led, it is widely claimed, to unbridled speculation by criminal land mafia; its house construction is held to be poorly done and even more poorly maintained. The authority has an unenviable reputation for corruption and the popular belief is that it has neglected its planning brief and concentrated on construction because the latter is more profitable. Yet, undeniably, the DDA's sheer size and near monopoly have made it responsible for the largest number of developments in Delhi, and its self-financing schemes for higher- and middle-income groups have certainly facilitated home ownership for large sections of the Delhi middle class— though whether this is its primary purpose is open to question. Moreover, as both C.S. Gupte and Santosh Auluck have pointed out, when DDA started out, it was stepping into completely uncharted territory with limited financial resources. Therefore one obvious way of raising funds was to construct buildings and then sell them. Both issues informed the DDA's early approach to markets. Auluck recalled, 'We did not know initially how commercial areas should be developed. We started by selling three-metre-by-three-metre plots for convenience (i.e. local) shopping centres. These were garage-type things and were not very good. Then people started looking at the whole idea afresh: instead of a small plot along a street, we thought of a plaza. It was a learning curve.'

～  ～

While the planners were evolving strategies for Delhi's urban development, architects were designing a new built environment for the new capital. Architecture is among the most visible expressions of a society's aspirations, and, in Delhi, from the time the founder of the Delhi Sultanate, Qutubuddin Aibak, built the Qutb Minar in 1192 to mark his victorious conquest, it has always been a significant political statement. The brick, steel and stone is the public face of a city: 'This is who we think we are', or more accurately, 'This is what we would like to be.' In newer enclaves like Gurgaon, the subliminal message includes, 'This looks like where we would like to be.' Examining the architecture of a city like Delhi is to be confronted by a cacophony, a confused and raucous babble, a million voices. What is the architecture of Delhi? Is it the serried rows of government housing, or the ice cream castles that line Ring Road from Lajpat Nagar to New Friends Colony? Or is it the futuristic buildings of Gurgaon or even the trademark 'highbrow' architectural constructions—Delhi has plenty of those—the minimalist Institute of Immunology, for instance, or the steel-and-plate-glass Life Insurance Corporation (LIC) building in Connaught Circus? Or is it the extraordinary statements made by the giant marble temples of Chhatarpur? They are all, in their own way, undeniably expressions of Delhi and the directions it wants to take in the twenty-first century.

It was not always so. Before 1947, Delhi's buildings followed sequential architectural trends. The Tughlaqs, the Lodis and the Mughals left their mark building-wise. Instances of late Mughal architecture are still visible all over the city in the form of cusped arches and *jharokas* in the old villages or in the exaggeratedly onion-shaped domes, such as in Safdarjang's Tomb. The British introduced classical

styles in the early nineteenth century, the first time that
architectural inspiration was completely imported, and this—
the importation—was a trend that continues to this day. St
James Church, the Residency (built around the seventeenth-
century library of the Mughal emperor Shah Jahan's son,
Dara Shikoh), and Metcalfe House, erected in the 1830s by
Thomas Metcalfe, the British Resident of Delhi, are all
examples of the classical style. In the late nineteenth century,
the Victorian Gothic style of architecture came to India—an
assemblage of turrets, spires and arches that pepper the
public buildings in the Presidency towns of Madras, Calcutta
and Bombay. Delhi's only example of this is the Mutiny
Memorial, a spiky bit of Victoriana that crowns the Ridge
near the university. In time, British engineers added
decorative embellishments—taken from what they regarded
as Indian architectural motifs—to the Victorian Gothic style,
and this marriage was the first such synthesis of European
and Indian architectural styles. It came to be known as the
Indo-Saracenic style.[6]

It can be argued that this was the precursor of what
Delhi architect Gautam Bhatia has termed 'Punjabi Baroque'.[7]
In its heyday, nearly every railway station, high court and
university built in the '20s, '30s and '40s of the twentieth
century was constructed in this style and came with a
complement of pointed arches, cupolas and domes. When it
began it was thought to be extremely radical, including as it
did architectural motifs from the subcontinent when the
prevailing British view of Indian aesthetics was that it was
'degraded' and 'corrupt'. But more significantly, it was also
an assertion of the permanence of the British presence in
India. Constructing public buildings, whether Residencies
or offices, was in itself an indication that they were here to
stay; including 'Indian-style' motifs in the architecture

showcased the nature of their intention. The Indo-Saracenic style has survived in only one building in Delhi, and that is the old St Stephen's College near Kashmiri Gate. Built in 1890, and designed by Samuel Swinton Jacob, it is now one of the offices of the Election Commission.[8]

While before 1947 the pre-colonial past was used by Indian architects to call attention to a nationalist identity, after Independence Delhi's architectural vocabulary changed radically: Modernism burst like a thunderclap over the new nation. Modernism has many critics, not least in Delhi where its less inspired constructions mar the skyline with their square and bulky appearance; yet the style has been described as 'the greatest efflorescence of Western genius since the Renaissance'.[9] Contemplating, for instance, the grungy, unkempt Auditor General's (AG) office near (Tilak Bridge) ITO, it is hard to believe that the intellectual rationale underlying the building's style represented a complete 'rejection of history and tradition and a belief in the power of industry and in the machine'. Modernism rejected ornament and decoration (this is certainly true of the AG's Office and most Modernist Delhi buildings) and in India the style was enthusiastically embraced by a new nation seeking to establish itself as progressive and forward-looking.

In the euphoria, no one apparently noticed that this was imperialism of another kind, a wholesale borrowing of ideas that originated in another culture, for another culture and implemented most enthusiastically in a post-World War II Europe which wanted to banish the grand triumphalist posturings of Fascism forever. At the time the style seemed refreshingly blunt and unadorned, the emphasis on utilitarianism a welcome departure from the fuss and pomposity of the Lutyens-Baker school of imperial architecture.

Many Indian architects of the time had studied in America and Europe and had imbibed Modernist ideas as gospel. Men who were to establish the face of Delhi—and they included such architectural luminaries as Habib Rahman, Achyut Kanvinde, M.N. Jogelkar, Mansingh Rana, and C.S.H. Jhabvala—believed as firmly as the new political establishment that Modernism was the route to modernity. A minority were, however, following other paths. Walter Sykes George, for instance, who came to India in 1911 to work in Herbert Baker's office, designed Sujan Singh Park, St Thomas' Church and the new St Stephen's College using an exposed brick technique which was both innovative and a decisive move away from Lutyens's endless pink. But it was Modernism that was the flavour of the season—or rather, as it turned out, the flavour of the next four decades— and became the official style for post-Independence Indian cities.

Modernism has certain distinctive characteristics: the use of reinforced concrete, horizontal massing, recessed windows and the liberal use of concrete fins on building facades; free-standing staircases and cantilevered porches are elements which most Delhi residents recognize without even knowing it is a specific style.[10] Any main street in Delhi will yield at least two Modernist buildings, probably more. This is the look we identify with large government offices, schools and auditoria built through the '50s, '60s and '70s, many of them appearing ramshackle and derelict today. It is a toss-up in which proportion the climate or the lack of basic maintenance is responsible. Lately some prestigious buildings of the Central Public Works Department (CPWD) employ other styles, but the majority of its initial constructions follow Modernist blueprints. Shastri Bhavan and Udyog Bhavan, built in the '50s, are early examples, as is the aforementioned AG's Office near ITO. The latter was designed by Habib Rahman, who was chief architect, CPWD, in the decades after Independence. Rahman also designed the multistorey flats in Ramamkrishnapuram, the World Health Organization's headquarters and, in 1954, Rabindra Bhavan.

It shows the extent of Nehru's involvement in the details of architecture that he rejected Rahman's first design for the latter as 'not being in the spirit of Tagore'. Rahman was an immensely talented architect, and if some of his buildings look cumbersome today, it is not because of any flaws in their design but because aesthetics have changed. He also designed the austere, elegant mazar of President Fakhruddin Ali Ahmed, barely noticed in the rush of Parliament Street traffic that surrounds it today, which is among the most remarkable pieces of modern architecture in Delhi.

While Modernism was sweeping all before it, there were some faint stirrings of revivalism, efforts to project what was thought to be an 'Indian' look. In many instances this was confined to adding a cupola or two or some stucco embellishments. The Ashoka Hotel built in 1956 sported jharokas cantilevered out at its four corners. This was said to be at Jawaharlal Nehru's instigation as it was felt that some 'Indian elements' were necessary in the government's first prestigious hotel; but the jharokas look like—as they indeed are—afterthoughts, and serve no discernible purpose unless as a point of exit for desperate guests driven to suicide by the dilatory nature of room service. Vigyan Bhavan, built by R.I. Geholote in 1955, works rather better. Symbolizing the importance of secularism, it combines Buddhist, Rajput and Mughal architectural elements. Thus it has a Buddhist *chaitya* façade, a *jali* and a *chajja*. Despite the anti-colonial feeling of the time, some post-Independence buildings were in the Lutyens mould—whether successfully or not is moot. The Supreme Court, designed by G.B. Deolalikar, the first Indian head of the CPWD, is one such, though critics have pointed to the disproportionate thickness of its pillars. The National Museum, built in the '50s, is a more faithful 'replica' of the Lutyens look, according to some.

Yet even in the '50s and '60s, Modernism was not the sole architectural narrative. American architect Edward Darrell Stone designed the American Embassy in Chanakyapuri in 1952, and the Indian referent of the pierced *jali* screen and the classicism of the slender pillars were widely appreciated by contemporary Indian architects. Stone was not the only American architect working in India. Joseph Allen Stein first came to India in 1952 to teach at the Bengal College of Engineering and set up an architectural firm in Delhi three years later. His design for the India International Centre near Lodi Gardens in 1962, and for Triveni Kala Sangam near Bengali Market some years later, have weathered time and trends with grace. Stein also designed the Ford Foundation building in 1981.

As gentle and organic in shape is Mansingh Rana's design of the Jawaharlal Nehru Library in 1969, the most comfortable library in Delhi, standing in the grounds of Teen Murti Bhavan, itself a '30s building designed in the Lutyens style by Robert T. Russell for the commander-in-chief of the army. Rana's design blends effortlessly with the surroundings without losing its own contemporary character.

Such departures were, however, rare. All through the '50s, '60s and '70s, Modernism or its mutations ruled. The Indian Institute of Technology campus, designed by Jugal Kishore Choudhury, came up in 1964; Kanvinde designed the Jawarharlal Nehru University (old) campus in 1973. An offshoot of Modernism called (apparently without irony) Brutalism, saw virtue in starkness and honesty—revealing the source materials and structure, and severely eschewing all adornment. Akbar Hotel and the Sri Ram Centre were both designed by Shiv Nath Prasad in 1969. While the layman's eye can certainly perceive the innovation in the gravity-defying Sri Ram Centre, the concrete slab of Akbar Hotel (now Akbar Bhavan) has little appeal. Many people thought quite seriously that a stay order, union trouble or bankruptcy had stalled the completion of Akbar Bhavan, realizing only much later that the scratched and pitted concrete finish was deliberate. Those who have worked there testify to the high temperatures reached within the concrete and plate-glass structure during frequent electricity failures. Another Brutalist building, the mammoth Inter-State Bus Terminus (ISBT), came up in 1971 and was the work of architect Rajinder Kumar. Today, most of these buildings look squalid and ugly.

Brutalism has, however, always generated controversy. According to architectural historian Tom Dyckhoff: 'Brutalism's chief apologist Rayner Banham wrote in the '50s how, even then, people "complained of the deliberate flouting of the traditional concepts of photographic beauty, (and) of a cult of ugliness".'[11] To ask the Delhi public to take on board such esoteric considerations, and that too in the '60s, was probably unrealistic. At any rate, they were not asked; so in some cases with their consent, mostly without, the Delhi skyline, as we know it today, was taking shape.

～ ～

Where the Masterplan and Modernism dovetailed was in the advocacy of zoning, which entailed the separation of the residential structures from other urban functions. Early residential colonies in Delhi were planned as rows of plots along a street. Not only were the oldest private colonies—for instance, Jorbagh, Sundarnagar and Golf Links, as well as parts of the Western Extension Area and Karolbagh—laid out in this manner, the private residential streets of Kautilya Marg, Aurangzeb Road and Prithiviraj Road followed the same pattern. These dwellings were departures from traditional houses in the old city which were built to the street and comprised several floors. New Delhi's houses, by contrast, were bungalows—a single-storey unit set in a large plot, known in architectural vocabulary as the 'Colonial Vernacular style'.

The bungalow has had a colossal impact on Delhi's urban imagination. It was the residence of choice when New Delhi was built, and its size and location became a critical indicator of the occupant's rank and status. The bungalow was not just architecturally different; the secret of its underlying attraction was that the occupants had 'modern' lifestyles; in other words, they were perceived as possessing power and status. This form of housing evolved over a century-and-a-half in colonial settlements all over the country and consisted of a single-storey building with verandahs on all four sides and rooms which opened off a central hall. The kitchen was usually in an adjacent outbuilding and the servants' quarters at some distance. The whole was contained within a large compound that also boasted a large front lawn and a driveway. Regional differences were enormous—pitched roofs, flat roofs; high plinths, low plinths—but the essentials remained the same for more than 200 years. Bungalows were the standard type of housing in cantonments and Civil Lines across the country, and Delhi was no exception.

The idea that a suitable house should stand in the middle of an open private space, separated from the street and other houses by gardens and walls, was a radical departure from indigenous urban houses which were contiguous to the street and to each other. Traditionally, the street was an integral part of an Indian house and the sequence of public to private space within the house was a function of distance from the street. For instance, the street was considered wholly public, while the steps, verandah and doorway were quasi-public, where all interactions with those not completely familiar to the household or of unknown social status took place. The sitting areas within the house were quasi-private and the living quarters entirely private. These were universally understood gradations, and reflected the interface of the family with the rest of the world. The open space in indigenous architecture was supplied by a courtyard inside the house that provided light and ventilation to inner rooms. This style of building had characterized urban settlements in India for millennia, but in just 200 years the bungalow changed the middle-class urban mindset irrevocably.

Middle-class houses in pre-Independence Delhi had followed certain basic culturally defined patterns: bathrooms and kitchens were kept as far apart as possible and bathrooms usually had a separate entrance for the cleaner. This pattern persisted for some years after Independence, but some small but significant changes came into being as lifestyles changed. 'Western-style' toilets became popular, as did kitchen counters with the advent of gas stoves and cylinders. With space increasingly at a premium, the entrance verandah disappeared and multiple entrances to bathrooms became a thing of the past, indicating a weakening of the hold of caste taboos of pollution and purity in some urban situations at least. Increasingly, middle-class housing was constructed on a 'drawing-dining room' and one or two bedrooms-'with attached-baths' pattern.

If this was the commonly followed internal pattern, the outside of houses was squarish, with recessed windows and horizontal markings, a style that has been called 'streamline modern'; in the '60s, when there was a boom in private house construction, this was the preferred style and the houses from that era can be identified by the slightly rounded corners that were much in vogue then. This came to be identified, according to A.G. Krishna Menon, eminent Delhi architect and head of the TVB School of Habitat Studies in the capital, as a recognizably 'Delhi' style.[12] Neat and symmetrical, this style was the standard in the older New Delhi colonies, from 'posh' localities, to refugee colonies, to developer colonies like, for instance, Haus Khas, or group housing colonies such as Defence Colony. But, from the '80s, according to Menon, a reaction to the long decades of State-imposed austerity and control set in, and private house-owners began to rebel. To this one can add the surge in disposable incomes, sojourns abroad and a growing self-confidence among the new generation of house-owners in the validity and suitability of their own taste.

The form this rebellion took was an architectural concoction where random architectural features from Europe and America were blended together to create highly individual house facades. This was about as far from the bland, utilitarian Modern style that you could get, but the inspiration remained Western. This trend has been the source of many regretful reflections on the philistinism and lack of aesthetic sensibilities in the newly affluent. The new houses unapologetically combine pitched roofs covered with Mangalore tiles, with chajjas, balustrades, Dutch gables and even the occasional spire. Joseph Heinz, a German architect based in the capital, brought the techniques of crested mouldings, medallions and other trimmings into the Delhi architectural vocabulary during the '60s and '70s. Subsequently, during the '80s and '90s, there was a revival of interest in the house styles of Rajasthan, and this resulted in the incorporation of corbelled arches, carved brackets and jharoka-style windows into house frontages, which are often faced with either pink or buff Dholpur marble. Rather than viewing this as a terminal nosedive for all aesthetic standards, A.G. Krishna Menon feels it might be more useful to regard it 'as an emerging hybrid, a product of globalization', which finds reflection not just in architecture but in all aspects of Indian urban life.

The discourse between committed architects and between the general public and their contractors has, however, remained largely parallel. It is not a dialogue and the two groups simply see each other as objects of pity. Architects continue to debate whether a contemporary 'Indian' architecture exists, and if so, what it comprises. Among them are advocates of particular regional architectures, champions of local, low-cost, environment-friendly materials, and so on. Simultaneously, but separately, the wider house-building or buying public happily follows its own predilections.

With growing pressure on land and rising construction costs, independent house development became increasingly impractical. Newer group housing societies in the late '70s opted for low-rise apartment complexes instead. In designs for DDA colonies, beginning from Munirka in the '70s, the flats were laid out in a series of interconnected courtyards and public parks. In the designs for the Asiad Village, built to accommodate the international athletes for the Asian

Games of 1982, and later Yamuna Apartments, Tara Apartments and Press Enclave, a conscious attempt was made to bring the outside closer to the house. Moreover, the idea of apartment-living was relatively new to Delhi— unlike, say, to Bombay—so not only were the architects dealing with a new form of residence, they were attempting to reverse the isolation of house-in-compounds feature of plotted development, and work out something entirely new. Some of Delhi's eminent architects were involved: Raj Rewal was the architect of the Asiad Village, Charles Correa designed Tara Apartments while M.N. Ashish Ganju designed Press Enclave, all within schema which incorporated the surrounding landscape. Yet, these developments, while internally integrated, are not, in fact, accessible to the street which is separated as firmly as before from the houses by a forbidding compound wall.

The more recent housing developments in south Delhi and the surrounding New Okhla Industrial Development Area (NOIDA) reflect the growing self-confidence of the buying class, who have well-defined ideas of the kind of residence appropriate for their needs. That it is not what the State persists in thinking is suitable, is amply evident if one examines the reinvention of Vasant Kunj, a south Delhi colony constructed by the DDA, by the people who bought houses there. The inevitability of such transformations is well established: for instance, an article in the *Indian Express* reports on a company that boasts they 'can turn any DDA flat into a bungalow'.[13]

Nearly every flat in Vasant Kunj (there are 10,000 in the colony) has re-done its frontage in marble or slate, added balconies and balustrades, and some have managed to accommodate up to two extra bedrooms by enclosing balconies or other open space within. Yet, officially, only seven or eight specified alterations are allowed. That this scale of renovation is virtually universal shows that the rules do not reflect people's real needs and that such practices are now within a quasi-institutionalized framework which the system has learnt to unofficially accommodate—doubtless to the mutual benefit of house-owner and authorities alike. Cynics maintain that well-publicized demolition drives target only a few flagrant violators and simply increase corruption. The cost for minimum alterations (that is, over and above the usual woodwork or finishing) can easily reach Rs 50,000, and according to the *Express* article, most house-owners spend an average of Rs 5 lakh.

But what of the poor, the people euphemistically termed the Economically Weaker Sections in Delhi's government publications? Which architectural style has been allotted to them? The answer is that most of the enormous quantity of construction that has taken place in the last fifty years has passed them by. Other than resettlement colonies, little has been done for these sections. The really poor in the squatter colonies build shacks from abandoned bricks and any material they can find—asbestos sheets, plastic sheets, corrugated iron sheets. In fact, it is the failure to provide housing for the weaker sections in sufficient quantity, and of an acceptable quality, which is the real failure of post-1947 planning in Delhi.

The State's patronage of architecture was unprecedented in the post-Independence capital. High-profile projects that were constructed from the '50s to even the '80s provided Delhi architects with the opportunity to build on a scale that was unmatched in the rest of the country. In its early decades, the CPWD had a line-up of the most qualified and talented architects in the country and they were handed enormously prestigious projects, but none—or very few—

involved housing for the poor. Jawaharlal Nehru's belief that it was possible to build—quite literally—a more egalitarian society was evidently misplaced; six decades of planning and state-sponsored architectural projects later, this has not happened.

The general public acquiesced for a while and then let the architects get on with Brutalism or Empiricism and built the kind of houses they desired in the styles they preferred. When they wanted a middle-American city, they built one in Gurgaon. It is true that Delhi's newer architecture is a series of borrowed ideas; but equally, in the very hybrid nature of those ideas, is a class—even if not a society—that is asserting itself and building itself the environment it wants, even if this goes against the tenets of architectural purity, uses environment-unfriendly materials and invokes intellectual ridicule. These styles, labelled by the architectural community as Modern Indian Vernacular, may be a pastiche of elements seen on holidays, in movies and magazines but are an authentic personal statement all the same. The pioneering planners and architects of the post-Independence generation believed that they were agents of change, yet whether the layouts they created for the city or the buildings they built were suitable for the climate, the prevailing levels of maintenance, and the needs of the people who would use them, were not questions that were asked—or at least not publicly. Nor was it considered necessary to take the general public on board for projects that would ultimately impinge on their lives.

The intentions were overwhelmingly good; the problem is that the idea of moulding the development of a whole city is apparently so irresistible that nearly all planners are prey to its seductions. Peter Ackroyd, writing of British city-planner Patrick Abercrombie's enormously influential plans for the redevelopment of London after World War II, observed, '[Abercrombie] had prepared two proposals, the County of London Plan and the Greater London Plan, which would lend London "order and efficiency and beauty and spaciousness" with an end to "violent competitive passion". It is the eternal aspiration, or delusion, that somehow the city can be forced to change its nature by getting rid of all the elements by which it had previously thrived.'[14]

# 4

## REFUGEES: DELHI'S LAST CONQUERORS

ON SUNDAY MORNINGS AT ELEVEN, A SMALL CROWD gathers at an old bakery in the market opposite Deshbandhu College in Kalkaji. This is when freshly baked biscuits are brought out of the ovens in the soot-laden kitchen at the back. Inside, the air is warm with the smell of *atta* biscuits, *nankhatais*, small pound cakes, and buns sticky with lurid green and red candied fruit. These, alongside pastries topped with pink butter icing, are lined up in large black tin trays on the scratched and chipped marble counter. The shop is a local secret; the customers loyal, but comparatively few. Its owner was a refugee from west Punjab and the shop, allotted by the ministry of rehabilitation, has supplied the biscuit needs of the neighbourhood for over five decades. When ovens were rare, regular customers routinely brought flour, sugar and vegetable oil from home to be baked into oily pound cakes, delicious when fresh, tooth-breaking after the second day. It was a family enterprise, but the present generation is not interested in the small profit margins the bakery offers. Commercial real estate prices have skyrocketed in south Delhi and renting out the space brings in several times the money. Anyway, like the rest of their generation, people prefer packaged biscuits, black forest cakes and tiramisu from upmarket patisseries.

The bakery is surrounded by other small shops: general merchants selling an idiosyncratic mix of satin ribbons and *naras* alongside open sacks of chillis and *dals*; electrical repair shops with antique mixies lined up on the counter, and drycleaners promising same-day service. These are still open for business, but they too will be displaced sooner rather than later by the unstoppable tide of 'Archies' or upmarket sanitaryware specialists or branded boutiques that have replaced the old *kirana* stores of Kalkaji's main market to suit the needs of the increasingly prosperous neighbourhood. Yet, this is not a sad story; this is, in fact, a happy ending, the triumphant finale of the rags-to-riches refugee saga that has been playing out in Delhi for nearly six decades.

If today's Delhi had a defining moment, it was when refugees from areas that were to become the new nation of Pakistan started flooding into the sedate capital city before and after 15 August 1947. In a matter of decades they became the driving dynamic behind the enormous transformation of Delhi from its stolid imperial identity of 1947 to the brimming, prosperous, ferocious city of multiple universes it is today. The dispossessed, bewildered and often desperate people, whose pasts had been torn from them and whose future was totally uncharted, have become the inheritors, if not the perpetrators, of the gleaming chrome and glass malls, the serried ranks of exotic restaurants and the marble and Dholpur stone mansions of contemporary Delhi. This Delhi has, in fact, been invented by the refugees, and while this is rarely disputed, the refugee experience is relatively unexamined today. The blood and horror of the Partition narrative is so dramatic that it has drowned out the post-1947 story of the settlers. It is almost as if the second and third refugee generations are only too anxious to forget the hardships, austerities and self-denial of their forebears; they much prefer the present. The post-1947 refugee experience, if accessed at all, is always in terms of the success stories, the relentless hard work deservedly rewarded by prosperity and success.

Delhi accommodated some 496,000 of the 4.75 million refugees who had left their homes in West Punjab, Sind and the North-West Frontier Province. In the space of the two months leading to Independence, Delhi's population had doubled. Refugees started to arrive before August 1947 and continued to arrive until well into late 1948. Some went first to other towns in north India but settled finally in Delhi. Most were urban dwellers—largely from Rawalpindi, Lahore and Multan—for whom Delhi represented better employment opportunities; moreover, many had relatives there who would help them settle down. Unarguably, Partition and Independence changed Delhi's demographic profile radically: a town which had a population of 6.95 lakh in 1941 swelled to one of 14.37 lakh by 1951. An estimated 3,29,000 Muslims had left the Delhi region: in 1947 the Muslim population stood at a mere 99,501, but it grew to 1,55, 453 by the end of the decade, an increase of 56 per cent. Sikhs, who were a mere 0.64 per cent of the population of Delhi in 1901, had grown to 7.7 per cent of the population by 1961.

The new leaders of the new capital had to come up with viable ways of handling this explosive increase in the number of inhabitants, even as they assumed control of the nation. While on the one hand, a whole generation wept as the tricolour was unfurled for the first time, there was a simultaneous awareness that this emotional tryst with destiny was taking place in a crammed and volatile city. Three large refugee camps had been set up at Kingsway Camp in north Delhi, Tibia College in east Delhi and Kalkaji in the south. Kingsway Camp was the largest and its population doubled between January and April 1946; at its peak, 30,000 refugees were accommodated there. Another 45,000 were placed in seven townships across Delhi, including Tis Hazari, Bela Road and Anand Parbat. Some 5,500 were camped in the Purana Qila. The numbers were such that any available structure—barracks, gurdwaras, temples and school buildings—was pressed into service. Even the Wavell Canteen became home for 800 people. Empty government flats, such as those of Lodi Colony, constructed for American and British airmen billeted in the 'chummeries' there during the war, were occupied by refugees with nowhere to go. Some simply found place on any unoccupied piece of land— on the pavements of Chandni Chowk, for example, or in the gardens of Qudsia Bagh.

Khushwant Singh remembers the elegant arcades of Connaught Circus crammed with the *bistars* and trunks of the homeless—any sheltered spot became a home. C.S. Gupte, former chief town planner and in 1947 a member of the Town and Country Planning Organization, described the utter desperation of those times. Some refugees had set up house in the ditch that abutted the old city's walls. Since it was a grey area, claimed neither by the Municipal Council of Delhi (MCD) nor the New Delhi Municipal Committee (NDMC), this occupation lasted a long time. The ditch, said Gupte, who is still appalled after over five decades, was filled with animal carcasses and the uncleared rubbish of years, but it became a home for many refugees who were grateful for the space.[1]

If the refugee influx was a crisis for the authorities of the new capital, even worse was the violence which erupted in the weeks before and after Independence. Muslims from the surrounding districts of Meerut, Rohtak and Gurgaon sought refuge in the city, in the hope it was more secure than their own neighbourhoods. Living (as they did) cheek by jowl with the huge numbers of Hindu and Sikh refugees in the capital, the situation was a tinderbox and became so tense that the district magistrate clamped curfew on the city from 28 August to 1 September as Muslims came increasingly under attack. The worst hit areas were Sadar Bazar, Sabzi Mandi, Paharganj and Karol Bagh, but violence was sporadic all over Delhi. Ishtiaq Husain Qureshi, dean of the arts faculty of Delhi University, recalled, 'The mohallas of the old city developed into arsenals. One could see that an unofficial war was in the offing.'[2] W.H. Morris Jones, then on the staff of the last viceroy, Mountbatten, described the mood of those hot August days: 'The lanes were eerily deserted, but not completely so; corpses lay uncollected, animals roamed and little gangs of running killers played grim hide-and-seek with the police.'[3]

Despite the curfew a bomb exploded in Karol Bagh on 1 September, leading to widespread riots and looting. A Delhi jeweller, Sithal Das Rakhyan, who owned a shop in F Block Connaught Place, has never forgotten the mobs rampaging through Connaught Circus, hurling stones at the plate-glass shop windows and carrying away as many goods as they could. One such shop belonged to his good friend 'Master' Mohammed, Jawaharlal Nehru's tailor. 'No one stopped them, they just burned and broke everything they saw.'[4] Manish Sahai, a chartered accountant, whose Lahore-based parents had bought a flat in Connaught Place in the '30s, remembers that several Muslim friends of his parents sought refuge there in the tense days of August 1947. At the same time, many friends and relatives, displaced from Lahore, were also staying with them. Tensions were palpable, but everyone kept their emotions in check. 'At one point there were sixty people living with us,' Sahai recalls. 'My mother would cook a huge pot of *alu sabzi* and line up everybody at mealtimes.'[5] His mother also hid their two Muslim servants in a godown at the back of the house for two of the worst months. Sahai, then a child, witnessed some appalling scenes. 'A group of Muslim families was on its way to the railway station when it was stopped by a mob. I saw at least twenty people hacked to death.' It was a terrible time, but there were redeeming strands. Sahai remembers seeing Pandit Nehru riding through Connaught Circus several times in an open jeep accompanied by armed troops. 'He would shout, "Stop it. Stop it" at the looters.' Sometimes they did stop.

Throughout August the situation was grim, so grim that the studiedly unemotional Delhi *Gazetteer* observed, appalled, that 'the *central government* employees did not attend offices' (emphasis mine).[6] Telephones worked fitfully and the mail was not delivered for two days. The airports were affected and fresh milk, meat and vegetables were scarce. Lord Mountbatten rushed back from Shimla to set up an Emergency Committee which divided the city into five zones headed by senior administrators who, with the help of prominent local people, were to restore control. When Gandhi came to Delhi in early September he was so appalled by the unravelling situation that he asked at a prayer meeting, 'Has Delhi suddenly become a city of the dead?'[7]

Religious places, too, became targets. Official estimates record that 137 Delhi mosques were damaged and the medieval marble *jali* screen surrounding the grave of the thirteenth-century saint Bhaktiar Kaki in Mehrauli had been wantonly smashed. But sectarian issues were not the only consideration: property had entered the calculations. Historians Tai Yong Tan and Gyanesh Kudaisya, citing unofficial estimates, say that '44,000 houses belonging to Muslim families in the old city had been abandoned or forcibly evacuated. A stage had come when more Muslims lived in refugees camps in Idgah, Nizamuddin and Purana Qila than in the safety of their own homes. Many frantically made arrangements for their departure to Pakistan while others wondered, if such could be the scale of violence that could rock the capital city of the new republic, what could they expect in the future as a minority?'[8] Ultimately, an estimated third of the city's population left for Pakistan.

Many Muslim families wanting to leave for Pakistan were placed for safety in the Red Fort. Special flights ferried them to their destination. One individual, Gulam Rasool, now a well-known Islamabad-based artist, remembers the day Mahatma Gandhi was assassinated.[9] His mother, fearing her children would wander out of the camp and be attacked by the grieving crowds, tied him and his four young brothers together with a clothesline and then fastened one end to her own leg. As many as 60,000 Muslim families took refuge in Purana Qila, the women donning *bindis* in order to reach there safely, in a city that had been their home for generations, suddenly hostile and dangerous. Over 30,000 Muslims sought shelter in the Jama Masjid.

It was the worst of times. The *Hindustan Times* of 14 April 1948 reported Acharya Vinoba Bhave's plea that Muslims who had 'temporarily abandoned their homes' should be allowed to return if they wished to. What was happening in Pakistan, said the Acharya, did not matter: 'We should do our utmost to make returning Muslims feel at home and do everything to make the two communities live in mutual trust.' The same paper reported on 22 April 1948 that 130 Muslims had returned to Delhi's villages. Forty of them went to Shahadra police station and were given a share of crops from their land. Returning Muslims were also, said the same report, welcomed by Hindus in Bhakiawarpur.

At the same time, Jathedhar Udham Sigh Nagoke, a veteran Sikh leader, exhorted that refugees who had lost everything in Pakistan should not be turned out to accommodate Muslims returning from Pakistan. They had, he said, 'gone off on their own accord and should not be given preference against Sikh and Hindus who had had to flee to India.'

The newspaper reports not only indicate that there was considerable crossing and re-crossing of borders by those unable to bear uprooting from their homes, but also, despite the flat, factual tone of the reports (feature writing had still not come into vogue), convey an atmosphere of uncertainty, a real fear of uncontrollable anarchy. There is a sense of the fledgling country struggling to cope with a million impossible situations, of a refugee population that had taken over the city and was in desperate straits.

The government set up the ministry of rehabilitation in September 1947 and its first task was to find accommodation for the vast numbers streaming into the capital; it was to be a monumental task. As late as in April 1948, Acharya Vinoba Bhave was expressing his concern at the still 'indescribable conditions' of refugees.[10] At this point, eight months to the day after Independence, some 16,000 refugees, mostly from East Punjab—the rest from Sind and NWFP— had arrived in Delhi. They were camped out in the open and, said the Acharya, government efforts towards their rehabilitation were woefully inadequate. He said everyone who could accommodate even one refugee should do so. Large numbers were still in tents and the papers of the day were full of suggestions, some quite ingenious, on ways to improve their conditions during that hot, endless summer. One suggestion was to dig the tent's floor some two feet down and use the excavated mud to build low walls round the tent which would, it was hoped, increase insulation against heat. Another advocated the use of fly-netting to be draped over the tent and even calculated that the cost would not be above Rs 3-12 per tent. Yet another suggested thatching the tents, and this was, in fact, carried out in the Purana Qila encampment.

What emerges from a reading of the records, formal and informal, of that time was the involvement of the whole community. Delhi residents clearly felt that the refugees' fate was their concern; there was a sense of community responsibility on the part of government and citizens alike for a specifically Delhi situation which had to be dealt with even while the new national project got underway. These details are significant as they show that while the aim of the government was certainly crisis management, there was a simultaneous awareness that systems needed to be set up to make refugees self-sufficient, and the state was willing to invest money and effort to bring this about. The authorities were seeking long-term solutions and this mind-set had a profound impact on the paths the refugees' lives took in subsequent decades.

It was not simply a matter of accommodation; the minister for relief and rehabilitation, K.C. Neogy, was speaking of the need to build an economic and professional infrastructure in Delhi which could support such unprecedented numbers. As early as April 1948, some 1,500 stalls were allotted to refugees in Lala Lajpat Rai Market opposite the Red Fort. People were so desperate for a livelihood that over 10,000 applied for 2,500 pavement stalls in Chandni Chowk. Meher Chand Khanna, himself a refugee and a Congress politician from North West Frontier Province (NWFP), was adviser to the rehabilitation ministry. In April 1948, he inaugurated several stalls in Tis Hazari Maidan and in the same month, several fruit and vegetable stalls were set up at Phoota Gate (near Mori Gate). The refugees, in effect, became an important constituency.

Among the earliest rehabilitation schemes was the accommodation of eighty families in Savitri Nagar; this was some ten miles from Delhi proper and the idea was to develop it as a village run on cooperative lines. To this end, centres of spinning, biscuit making (this accounts for the many bakeries in refugee markets like Kalkaji), carpentry, basket weaving, painting, oilseed crushing and gardening were established, and once the refugees were trained, they could earn incomes of up to Rs 300 a month. The figures are invariably modest. A 53-bigha garden attached to the village allowed an income of Rs 160 per cultivator.

Similarly, industrial training centres were set up in Purana Qila, Kingsway and Tis Hazari camps. It was assessed that there were some 2,312 families at Kingsway Camp alone who had no income whatsoever, therefore training programmes in skills as diverse as knitting, trunk-making and the manufacture of sports goods were initiated to give them a means of livelihood.

The same approach led to a serious investment in the education of refugee children. The ministry of rehabilitation set up some thirteen high schools, twelve middle schools and fifteen primary schools, as well as vocational centres. There were about 4,000 schoolchildren in Kingsway Camp and three schools were set up there; a middle school was functioning in Purana Qila—although in the open. The central relief committee opened schools at the Followers' Barracks in Anand Prabat and two others, in Bela Road Barracks and at Kalkaji. Women's organizations under Hannah Sen, a prominent social worker, and Achamma Mathai (wife of the transport minister) set up children's centres at camps including those at Sabzi Mandi, Karolbagh and Paharganj. Notices in the papers alerted students that 30 April 1948 was the last date for applications from students of the ninth and tenth standards whose parents were registered as refugees. The rehabilitation ministry also provided free grants towards tuition, books and stationery, and monthly stipends (called freeships) were given to students whose parents could not afford to pay for educational expenses. Today, the amounts seem unbelievably small: Rs 5 for primary, Rs 20 for Class 10 and Rs 40 for the intermediate class.

Delhi, being Delhi, still managed in the midst of this trauma, violence and chaos to function at another level as well. Alongside newspaper reports of continuing shortages and outbursts of tension, were others indicating that life was carrying on in its own pre-Partition fashion. *Neel Kamal* was in its 'fifth glorious week' at the Imperial Talkies, while *Hindustan Hamara* was—appropriately enough—drawing crowds at Regal. Alan Ladd and Dorothy Lamour were playing in the night show of *Wild Harvest* at the Ritz. Novelty was showing *Samrat Ashok*, while *Anthony Adverse* was playing at Odeon. There are no reports of cancelled shows, of advance ticket money being returned, and the very fact that people were willing to go out and drool over Alan Ladd at a night show reveals that the situation was safe enough for such non-essential outings. This is, even today, a situation that recurs in Delhi. Some parts of the city might be under curfew, in others Section 144 might be in place, but in the non-affected neighbourhoods life goes on in its relentless, if occasionally frivolous, fashion.

Equally there were, even then, in the midst of the surrounding chaos, many signs of people struggling to establish a sense of normality. An advertisement in a newspaper asks if anyone is willing to exchange a B-type quarter in Link Road for a B or an E-type quarter in Karolbagh. Similarly, there is a report advising people who wanted to go sightseeing at the Purana Qila to go on either Sunday or Wednesday since the fort was now a refugee camp and the authorities could not cope with daily visitors. Sikand and Co. were advertising Standard cars for the sums of Rs 10,500 and Rs 7,000. On 21 April 1948, prime minister Jawaharlal Nehru laid the foundation stone of the National Institute of Medical Sciences (later the All India Institute of Medical Sciences) thus expressing his faith not just in future medical infrastructures, but in the existence of a society where such aims would be possible. 'We must do our utmost to foster science,' he declared. There was a feeling that things would settle down, that—somehow—a life that made sense would be restored or rescued or reinvented in the capital of this new nation.

One of the most important prerequisites of a stable existence was the need to settle the refugees in permanent accommodation and to do so quickly. The authorities started looking around for suitable areas and fortunately, as New Delhi extended to Lodi Road on the south and Willingdon Crescent on the west, expansion was possible in the areas beyond. Jag Pravesh Chandra, a former municipal commissioner, was a member of the rehabilitation ministry's advisory committee along with Sucheta Kripalani and

Dharma Vira, who was the secretary to the ministry. Chandra recalls driving around in a ministry of rehabilitation car looking for open ground, any ground, suitable for refugee quarters.[11] C.S. Gupte, too, remembers the process of rehabilitation, which sometimes involved more than planning. 'In 1948 I was instrumental in selecting plots for refugee colonies with (Delhi's) Chief Commissioner M.S. Randhawa,' he explains. 'We drove to Lado Sarai where the road stopped. Then, on horseback, we toured (what was to become) Malviya Nagar and Kalkaji. I had never ridden before, though, of course, Randhawa had.'[12] The whole area was level agricultural land, he recalls, and rows and rows of vegetables grew there. 'We also looked at the land near Tihar in the west. All these sites became refugee colonies.'

Gupte says the district board purchased land from the agriculturalists at a pittance; so, later, did private developers such as the Delhi Land and Finance (DLF). Land was purchased against *khasras*—which outlined ownership of land according to the patwari's map—the basic land record. Areas were often irregular in shape, accounting for the often odd alignment of roads and the mysteriously non-sequential numbering of houses in many Delhi colonies. While most units were allotted at highly subsidized rates to refugees, some were auctioned. In some of the developer-built colonies the roads were narrow and the water supply came from borewells. But the refugees were so desperate for permanent homes that they moved in regardless.

Ultimately, the government allocated land for a total of thirty-six permanent rehabilitation colonies. In west Delhi, the colonies included Moti Nagar, Rajinder Nagar, Ramesh Nagar, Tilak Nagar, Tihar, Azadpur and Patel Nagar. In the north, some of the colonies established were Malkaganj, Kingsway, Shakti Nagar and Vijay Nagar. In the east (across the river), Krishna Nagar and Gandhi Nagar near Shahadra came up, while in the south, the enclaves included Nizamuddin, Jangpura, Lajpat Nagar, Kalkaji and Malaviya Nagar.

All the new neighbourhoods were, by and large, laid out in plots. The layouts were influenced by the town planners who were starting to formulate a new Masterplan for the expansion of the national capital. Most refugee colonies were provided with their own markets (the shops were allotted to refugees) and eventually, after trial and error, the U-shaped design with an open, green space in the middle, with the fourth side being the main road, became virtually universal. The colonies were also provided with schools, post offices and—usually—at least two parks. Santosh Auluck, who was then a member of the Town Planning Organization, observed that the 'CPWD and others did a tremendous job in those years. These colonies are very well laid out.'[13] The Delhi Improvement Trust handled the city extension schemes of Shakti Nagar and Kamala Nagar which came up on open land in the north around 1948, by first developing the infrastructure and then selling plots. While most refugee colonies were government projects, the sheer numbers made refugee accommodation an attractive financial proposition for private developers as well.

These colonies established a template for the future when Delhi's private colonies established by developers like the DLF, as well as cooperative group housing societies like, for instance, Vasant Vihar or Gulmohar Park, came up from the late '50s onwards. The largest plots were on the main roads. A typical refugee colony, Rajinder Nagar, for instance, had 5,000 plots, of which 1,500 were along narrow roads within the colony.[14] This pattern, devised when few people owned—or expected to own—cars, was to prove a liability.

Around four decades later, two-car families have become common in Delhi and many single plots are now multi-flat complexes. The lack of garages and the narrowness of the roads have made parking and navigating the congested lanes a nightmare.

Much of this massive infrastructural activity was achieved in an impressively short time. By 1950, 190,000 refugees had been accommodated in evacuee accommodation and an amazing 100,000 refugees were settled in new constructions. By the end of 1951, over 15,520 residential units had been constructed. Some 1,100 plots had also been allotted to refugees who built houses themselves. An additional 600 shops-cum-residences were built. A further 8,600 or so residential units were under construction. Altogether, 1.2 million homes and 4,752 shops were built for refugee rehabilitation.

The houses were of mainly of three types: a bungalow which consisted of three rooms, kitchen and a bathroom, with a small lawn in front; another was the single-, occasionally double-storey model, which had three rooms on each floor, along with a kitchen and a bathroom; the most common, however was the small single-storey house which consisted of two rooms and a kitchen and bathroom with a small courtyard at the back. At the other end of the refugee scale, Nizamuddin was constructed by the Land and Development Office in the '50s. Here, one-storey units built on separate plots were auctioned, although the original units are now unrecognizable; the internal courtyard was the first thing to go, reflecting the change in lifestyles. The colony has retained its green and open character, though the houses have, more often than not, changed hands, making Nizamuddin today the most upmarket of the erstwhile refugee colonies.

Yet in all refugee colonies in the early years, despite their differences in façade and their uniformly quiet, unremarkable appearance, was a churning; a silent struggle waged by men and women as they came to terms with the enormity of the changes they had had to absorb.

Ajeet Caur, writer and activist, grew up in a sprawling house in Lahore's Chamberlain Road. Her father was a doctor with a flourishing practice; her mother's father was a large landowner in Gujranwalla, famous for the red malta oranges that grew in his orchards. Theirs was a whole, settled, comfortable world; the reality of Partition for Ajeet Caur's family, like so many others, took them unawares. Violence had been spiralling and hundreds of departing Hindus had been in camps in Lahore's DAV school and college for months—Ajeet's Caur's mother had even donated some *razais* to the inmates—but the idea that their own family, too, would have to leave, seemed implausible. The possibility of Partition had been rumbling around on the distant political horizon for ages, but that entire lives would be permanently uprooted—this was a situation that even the most politically aware found impossible to grasp. Prakash Tandon, former chairman of the Punjab National Bank and chronicler of the post-Independence corporate-Punjabi experience, has written: 'The thought that this was a going away for ever, never crossed anyone's mind.'[15] Ajeet Caur's family was on holiday in Simla when her parents realized that they must leave Lahore. They rushed back, only to find their bank accounts had been frozen. The bank manager, an old family friend, helped them open their locker, and with just a few belongings, they arrived in Jullunder, where they lived for a year before moving to Delhi.

'We floated like leaves,'[16] she says of her family and many, many others during those early decades when it seemed nothing would be the same again. She recalls seeing her parents' friend Gulab Singh, one of Lahore's affluent men, the owner of the A.H. Wheeler railway bookshop chain, selling salwars made of parachute silk from a trolley on a Jullunder street. 'My mother waited at a distance and sent me to buy a salwar from him. Had she gone herself, he would have felt embarrassed by her seeing the change in his circumstances.'

In Delhi, Ajeet Caur's father refused a plot in Nizamuddin as her mother was disturbed by both the open scrub on one side of the colony and the smell of blood from the meat shops of the bustee on the other. They decided on West Patel Nagar, which was cleaner, more open and had, at that time, what she described as 'only some small yellow houses'. They built a house, they settled down, but they missed the life in Lahore. 'We Lahoris didn't think much of Delhi people; to us they were "grass cutters, *bhaiyon, mailli dhotiwallas*,"' she says wryly, having spent her whole adult life in Delhi. Today, over five decades since that uncertain arrival, Ajeet Caur is a critically acclaimed writer; her daughter, Arpana Caur, is one of the most successful painters of her generation. The Delhi they live in now is another world, but the journey made by Ajeet Caur, her parents and others of their generation to reach it was difficult, bewildering, even painful.

It is surprising, then, that so little has been expressed about the *post*-1947 journey. It took three decades for Partition memories to surface in the Delhi consciousness, Khushwant Singh's *Train to Pakistan* and the writings of Sadat Hasan Manto being notable exceptions. It was not till 1986 that *Buniyaad* appeared on Doordarshan—and met with a huge popular response—and today Partition studies is a flourishing industry. It is as if the blocking-out of those events in the early decades after Independence was necessary for the refugees' ability to cope with their new realities. Perhaps the post-Partition refugee experience, too, is waiting to cross some invisible Rubicon, before looking beyond the safe, upbeat rags-to-riches myths to explore the human costs in terms of suffering, fractured lives and personal loss.

Refugees changed the social profile of Delhi after 1947. While many upper-class Muslims left Delhi, the majority to leave were artisans and semi-skilled labour. Incoming refugees tended to be non-cultivating landlords, doctors, lawyers, teachers, traders and small shopkeepers. Many of them re-joined their old professions; others took up whatever they could find. Many with little previous experience of entrepreneurship went into transportation, services, manufacturing and commerce. Many sold whatever assets they had—including, in some cases, family jewellery—to provide start-up capital, but they also benefitted from substantial loans and subsidies from the government. In 1948 alone, a total of Rs 42, 640, 75-worth of government loans was sanctioned for rehabilitation.

One reason so many refugees made good was that they were not only forced to start from scratch, they were quite prepared to do so. Refugees were willing to become vendors, ready to accept the smallest of profit margins, try out new goods and, if necessary, undercut established shopkeepers, often standing in front of established shops while doing so. It was this—the historian V.N. Dutta calls it their 'drive, patience and competitive spirit'[17]—which informed subsequent refugee mythology. V.K.R.V. Rao, a former vice-chancellor of Delhi University, observes that while the many success stories were certainly due to substantial assistance from the government, their determination showed 'the crucial role of the human factor in economic development'.[18] It helped that most refugees were literate, often better educated than locals, yet they did not allow their pre-Partition status to rule out less socially acceptable occupations. Pragmatism and a refusal to cast themselves as victims, along with state help, changed their lives and Delhi.

Asok Mitra, former census commissioner, recalls in his book *Capital City* an encounter with a young Sikh orphan who was hawking newspapers in Connaught Circus just after Partition. Mitra offered the child some change but the boy refused to take it unless Mitra first accepted a newspaper. The boy's sense of pride and stubborn self-respect humbled Mitra. The refugee archive has a fund of such tales—less frequently told in recent years, but floating around somewhere in the collective memory at all times. A typical one, for example, is Mr Pritviraj's story. I met Mr Pritviraj when I was researching an article on Lodi Colony; he was then in his eighties but still erect. A man of few words, he sat in his shop in Khanna Market and conveyed the sense of being in full control of his universe and fully content with it. He had come to Delhi with his elderly parents, his wife and two small sons from Rawalpindi. They moved first into an unoccupied flat in Lodi Colony and he was later allotted a shop in Khanna Market through the good offices of Congress politician Mehr Chand Khanna. He lived in the back room of his shop for many years but was then allotted a plot in B. Dutt colony, a small enclave between Lodi Road and Jorbagh—which at today's real estate prices is worth an astronomical amount, but Mr Pritviraj had no plans to move out. He handled the shop alone. His wife raised the children in the shop, letting them run around between the back room and the front counter while she flapped a hand fan to prevent flies from settling on the foodstuff. The sons went into business and did well.

Today, Mr Pritiviraj's shop, unlike other provision stores, has not transformed itself into a pseudo supermarket, with shelving and wire baskets. Goods are still piled at random on the shelves behind the counter and dried chillies spill out of gunny sacks at the entrance. Mr Pritviraj is proud of his shop, though he is aware his grandsons will ultimately sell it. His eldest son's son is studying management in Ohio and his younger son lives in NOIDA with his own family who are pursuing careers far removed from shopkeeping. Mr Pritviraj is justly proud of having steered his family through adversity into the safe harbour of education and affluence, although he is reticent about the cost to himself, about all those years of struggle and uncertainty. All he says is, 'It was terrible (then) and I think my wife's early death was because of all that anxiety and then all that hard work. But it's over now and my sons live better than I did in 'Pindi.'[19]

There is a stoicism to all refugee sagas in Delhi and they differ considerably from the other Partition refugee experience, that of Bengal, where the stories are of anguish and desolation. It is the difference between the films of Yash Chopra and those of the Bengali director, Ritwik Ghatak. Chopra, himself a refugee from Lahore, made films like *Kabhie Kabhie*, for instance, or *Dilwale Dulaniya Le Jayenge*, with their technicolour emphasis on the virtues of hard work and self-confidence which lead to the trophies of the girl and the bungalow. This is a world far removed from Ritwik Ghatak's masterpiece *Meghe Dhaka Tara* with its shadowy black and white notes of mourning and lost identities. Delhi's real 'feel-good' refugee sagas are firmly in the Yash Chopra mould, and the ones that resonate in the public imagination are the ones which take the protagonist from the loss of absolutely everything in 1947 to a farmhouse in Mehrauli in 1997.

Prakash Krishna's story is well known. Arriving from Lahore with no other possessions except Rs 60,000 worth of books, he was worth several times as much in three decades—he became the proprietor of the Ram Krishna bookshop in Connaught Place. The shop, for decades one of Delhi best-known bookshops, closed down a few years ago. No less familiar is the story of Madan Lamba who left behind the successful Volga restaurant in Lahore, and set up the hugely popular (up to the mid-'70s, anyway) Volga and Kwality restaurants in Delhi.

One indicator of refugee energy is the rapidity with which they acquired shops from local owners in Chandni Chowk and Connaught Circus. By 1961, according to the census, the largest proportion of Delhi's income came from commerce and trade. Helped by substantial government loans and concessions, many erstwhile refugees set up small industries—the number of registered factories in Delhi doubled between 1945 and 1951, reaching a figure of over 400. The Okhla Industrial Estate was set up to accommodate refugee enterprises which included such well-known names today as Bharat Steel Tubes, Frick and Ranbaxy. 'This reservoir of energy,' observes V.N. Dutta, 'laid the foundation for the rapid urbanization of Delhi in recent decades'.

The post-Partition decades in Delhi witnessed the rise of the Punjabi Khatri and Arora communities with names that were to become very familiar in all spheres of Delhi life: the Kapoors, Khannas, Chopras, Malhotras, Seths, Puris and Tandons. Most settled first in refugee colonies, but later, as their fortunes improved, many moved into the new south Delhi colonies that were coming up—Golf Links, Vasant Vihar, Greater Kailash, and Maharani Bagh. This dispersal reflected the growing diversities in the refugee profile: they were not a single monolith of displaced persons, but a varied and many-shaded category, internally different, but together changing Delhi's landscape irrevocably.

Politically, they were also more diverse than they have been given credit for. The established belief is that the refugees were the backbone of the Jan Sangh, staunchly supporting it against what was perceived as the Congress' appeasement of Pakistan. In fact, as Christophe Jaffrelot in a study of post-Partition Delhi politics points out, refugees and those native to Delhi were divided equally in their support to the Jan Sangh and the Congress. He argues that Hindu organizations were well established in Delhi long before Partition and had enjoyed considerable local support. Both the Arya Samaj and the Hindu Mahasabha had substantial numbers of adherents in Delhi from the end of the nineteenth century.

The Samaj established its headquarters in Delhi in 1909, while the Hindu Mahasabha did so in 1918. The Rashtriya Swayamsevak Sangh (RSS) started with six *shakhas* in 1936 which had increased to a hundred by 1947. The latter two bodies were extremely active in refugee rehabilitation, recognizing early the potential of the refugee support vote base. Several leaders of the post-Independence Delhi Jan Sangh were indeed refugees from west Punjab. Balraj Madhok, Vijay Kumar Malhotra, Bhai Mahavir, among other subsequently well-known leaders, had joined the RSS in Lahore, while Madan Lal Khurana was a *sanghchalak* from Lyallpur in west Punjab. Support for the Jan Sangh was widespread among the Hindu middle class as a whole. While the party was active in championing refugee causes as, for instance, the deferment of refugee loan payback over thirty years as opposed to the government's proposal of three years, other parts of its agenda—concessions for traders, for example—appealed to refugee and non-refugee alike.

At the same time, the All India Refugee Conference and the Central Refugee Front certainly were two influential Jan Sangh-based organizations, and in 1954 no less than four refugee members of Parliament were elected from constituencies with a refugee majority. Writes Jaffrelot: 'Many of the Punjabis who settled in Delhi may well have voted for the Jan Sangh because they lost everything after Partition, a catastrophe they attributed to the Congress. But others, especially from the NWFP, still preferred the ruling Congress party because they perceived it as a Hindu party anyway and depended on it for rehabilitation.'[20]

Mehr Chand Khanna, though originally in the Hindu Mahasabha, came from the NWFP and became a prominent figure in post-Partition Congress circles in Delhi. He was a staunch advocate of all refugee causes through his organization, the United Refugee Front. His tireless work for this constituency is memorialized by two markets in Lodi Colony named after him—namely, Khanna Market and Mehr Chand Market.

While the refugees always formed a powerful constituency, their increasing influence became manifest in the '70s. The worst of their struggles was over and they were beginning to emerge as a self-confident, financially secure and articulate force. At the time Delhi was still overtly a government city. Power resided with the bureaucracy and politicians; economic power belonged to a handful of industrialists and—increasingly—the successful sections of the refugee community. The transformation of Delhi with the Asian Games of 1982 accorded well with the notions of what the increasingly prosperous refugee community felt a city should be. Through this decade and the next, what has been regarded as the growing 'Punjabification' of Delhi, could in part be attributed to the refugees' increased confidence in asserting their own tastes and inclinations.

Increasingly, their substantial economic clout made itself felt in their influence over the political and social spheres of Delhi. The losers were the bureaucracy who lost their pervasive political influence, but settled for trading their old absolute power for a continued share in the spoils. Delhi thus saw a tectonic shift in its centres of influence. The coming of multiplexes and malls, the proliferation of brand name outlets, coffee shops, the gentrification of Karol Bagh and West Patel Nagar, the rise of local markets, South Extension for instance, and the growth of exotically named developer enclaves were, if not wholly refugee-triggered, related to the steep rise in their disposable incomes in the city they wished to reinvent and the people—new and newer Delhi residents—who bought into the vision. Delhi, without the refugee influx, would have been an entirely different city—not better, not worse, just very different. The refugees have shaped and formed the dynamic, complex, prosperous city we see today. Think of the old black-and-white photographs of refugee camps with their rows and rows of tents. Remember the pitiless elegance of Cartier-Bresson's shots of the seemingly endless lines of dispirited, weary, wary people, less concerned with where they were going than the need to keep going. Then think of the futuristic shapes of the Hafeez Contractor buildings in Gurgaon, the baggy-trousered teenagers at Barista, the event-managed weddings at large hotels—because there is an invisible line connecting them all.

Those who still crave the nankhatais, buns and pastry twists, so greasy that the oil seeps immediately onto the paper bag they are packed in, must now buy these treats from proper cake shops where they are served in cardboard boxes by white-gloved attendants. They do not taste the same, although they cost six times as much and are six times less oily. The Kalkaji bakery was amongst the last of its kind and its passing exemplifies the changes in the refugee identity, in refugee colonies, in the refugee idea itself. Kalkaji itself is in transition. The small plots once contained long narrow houses with a courtyard at the back. In the front was a small, paved area where, on winter afternoons, the women of the house would sit on charpoys and knit brightly-hued, unidentifiable garments, exchanging gossip with their neighbours, engaged in similar pursuits, across the wall. Today, many of the plots have been bought by developers who have managed to cram three flats into the narrow space, the frontages smartened by a pillared pediment and pink sandstone cladding. The narrow road in front, where the first generation of refugee children played, preferring it to the dusty parks with their broken swings and cracked plaster Sanchi replica gateways, now has cars parked nose to tail on both sides. Some families have retained a flat in their old plot, others have moved to other south Delhi locations, or to NOIDA or Gurgaon. The identity of a 'refugee' colony is now redundant. Refugees do not live here anymore.

# 5

## GOVERNMENT DELHI

ON SUNDAY EVENINGS IN LODI COLONY, RESIDENTS
gather in the park in front of the market. They stroll gently
round the perimeter; a few do yoga asanas; most just sit and
engage in desultory chat. A few years ago this park, nameless
for five decades, was designated, with some fuss, as 'Veer
Sarvarkar Park', eliciting strong reactions both for and against
the appellation. But on this late spring evening, the currents
of national politics seem distant, as women in voluminous
Lajpat Nagar nighties sit together on their doorsteps and
watch their children play cricket. Some small boys play—
not very seriously—with their distinctly out-of-condition
dads; others are engaged in more serious games, using a
dining chair as a wicket, accompanied by rather acrimonious
discussion on the fairness of the batting line-up. Teenage
girls sit in a row on a low wall, while the local male talent,
sporting identical tight black jeans and centre-parted hair,
make their slow progress towards the park. When they pass
the girls, the boys' heads do not turn, their animated

discussion does not slacken. Nor do the girls pause in their low-voiced chat, but the boys' pace slows infinitesimally and there is a barely perceptible swish in the girls' shining curtains of hair . . . and then the moment passes.

But everyone has noticed and even the matrons on their steps allow themselves a dour smile, a mere twitching of the mouth, as they take note of this slight but cosmic ripple in the universe; a timeless obeisance to youth's brief but shining moment. Only the children continue their games unregarding, and the *chaat*-seller sets up his wicker stand for a family on its way to the bus stop, but hijacked by the thought of some *bhelpuri*.

This is government colony life in a form unchanged for decades. The nitty-gritty as well as the magic of the everyday, the internal rhythm of lives less ordinary . . . here is the irreplaceable moment in time when the woman watering her unbelievably giant cannas talks to the woman in the balcony above, who is picking out the stones from a portion of dal. Lodi Colony is a good colony, the residents all say; some have lived there for fifteen years, refusing better accommodation to which their seniority would entitle them. Yet this apparent community satisfaction cannot disguise the tectonic shifts that are taking place today over the whole of government Delhi. Behind the contentment (complacency, the uncharitable would say), Lodi Colony, just like the rest of government Delhi, has changed.

Today, when government is not as central to Delhi as it once was, it is still both an address and a state of mind; a physical space and an attitude. It is a recognizable way of life. Government Delhi's golden years were arguably the '50s, '60s and early '70; it was, in the recollections of people who lived in it, a gentle, kindly place, evoking a sense of unruffled, unquestioning security. In those decades, there was a dutiful, if boring, earnestness to the government project. Government officials were not affluent; on the contrary, the world view of the time held that the only people who had lots of money were smugglers or tax-evaders, or corrupt politicians or other bad guys; the type of villains routinely trounced by a uniformed Amitabh Bachchan in the major movies of the time. The redeeming innocence of those decades was that few seriously considered the possibility that the bad guys could win. Recalling those early decades, Shaila Sathe, whose husband was an undersecretary in 1948, speaks of a sense, just after Independence, 'of excitement and hope. We felt India was going to change completely and we were at the heart of that change.'[1]

The inhabitants of government colonies believed they were the natural successors to the British, whom, by and large, they held in respect rather than abhorrence. A retired official describing the common mindset of civil servants of that time, remembers 'The carnage of Partition was still so recent, vivid, and so horrifying—you heard so many tragic stories (about Partition) all the time—that it overshadowed anti-British feelings.'

Jawaharlal Nehru's mantras of planning, public sector building and a strongly centralized polity—if not his socialist vocabulary—dovetailed very nicely with the babus' own conviction that power and influence in the new nation should be vested in government officials. This was expressed in terms of 'service', of being 'dedicated to building a new India'. The people they were serving were expected to be grateful and hard-working. In due course they would be uplifted, but no one was giving any deadlines.

This feeling of privilege combined with righteousness lasted till June 1976—till the state of Emergency was imposed on the country by the prime minister, Mrs Indira Gandhi. The Emergency was a defining moment in the life of government Delhi, though its real legacies were overlooked in the euphoria of the 1977 election results when the Congress Party was decisively defeated and Mrs Gandhi lost her parliamentary seat. A senior official offers the argument that the Emergency was a last-ditch attempt by the post Independence governing elite to hold on to their absolute authority in the face of the new—and competing—centres of power that three decades of democracy had generated. But, whatever the causes, one of the Emergency's most damaging effects on government Delhi was to reveal the fragility of the veneer of 'service'.

With their security at stake, few spoke out when the institutions they were supposed to be upholding were being systematically undermined. If in 1976 it became clear that the official class—with a few honourable exceptions—prized their security over any abstract sense of social responsibility, their timidity paved the way for their inaction during the anti-Sikh 'riots' in the aftermath of the re-elected prime minister Indira Gandhi's assassination at the hands of her Sikh bodyguards in 1984. The official class had learnt that averting their gaze from state-sponsored injustice did no harm; if anything it would count in their favour during the next round of empanelments. In such a situation, few would risk promotions and full pensions to speak out. If the official class were content to trade moral authority for security, official Delhi was also ready to cede its absolute authority for a continued share in the spoils. It was to reinvent itself: but keeping its outer visage intact. The rhetoric of 'service' is heard less, though it has not completely disappeared.

This Delhi might be in retreat; but it is not in decline— yet. Nearly 200,000 candidates sit for the Civil Services examination, indicating that government jobs are still coveted. It is the profile of those who covet them that has changed. Today, behind the tidy hedges of the government colonies it is not, significantly, government that is the chosen career path of the officials' offspring. Instead, law, banking, management, engineering, medicine and increasingly, IT, are the preferred options. Few government progeny in Delhi attempt the Civil Services exam. For one thing, they have lost their competitive edge—the exam no longer privileges English and a liberal arts education. The scrapping of the essay question and the rule allowing the exam to be given in any Indian language has opened up the recruitment pool enormously. Most importantly, Reservations have cut down the number of seats in open competition.

It was not a coincidence that a government colony, Sarojini Nagar, was one of the main centres of opposition to the Mandal Commission report in 1990 which advocated a reserved quota in the civil services for candidates from the Other Backward Classes. The children living in these government quarters saw their grasp on the civil services— and with it a well-charted, stable future—slipping. Today, other professions offer more openings, larger incomes, better cars and accommodation, and it is an indication of the loss of confidence in—among other factors—the national project, that so many children of government officials live abroad. Whereas their parents were willing to trade affluence for security, this security is no longer certain, a casualty of liberalization, globalization and the inescapable certainty that one day the State will simply have no option but to jettison huge bureaucracies and public sector enterprises, and then the whole edifice of a comfortable job for life will vanish. Since the Mandal Report was implemented, the number of Delhi candidates for the Civil Services exam has dropped. The actual numbers are lower than the published figures suggest, as candidates from regional capitals flock to Delhi because the coaching classes are thought to be superior there and because Delhi University's syllabi are still more attuned to the exam's requirements, survivals of the time when for all government progeny the Civil Services exam was as much part of life's and education's natural progression as kindergarten, school and marriage.

Till the early '70s, it was all very different. Then the senior government colonies of Shan Nagar and Man Nagar, of Chanakyapuri and Pandara Park, exuded patent self-satisfaction. Within, every available balcony and porch was enclosed to accommodate the three children and the elderly parents; the furniture was a simple three-piece 'suite', with a divan made by covering the many trunks that were an inevitable part of such transferable jobs. The glass-fronted cupboard held souvenirs of coveted foreign trips, especially the Air-India mascot, the bowing maharaja, partly because it advertised that the owner had been abroad, and partly because it was considered quite grand.

People slept outside in summer; air-conditioning was unknown in private houses and desert coolers only arrived on the scene in the late '60s. Flaunting consumer goods—then rare and expensive—was called a 'vulgar display of wealth'. Salaries were meagre, though it was then fairly widely felt that the access to power, and the sense of status that it conferred, compensated for it. Almost no government wives worked; they would ensure that their husband's lunches were ready by 12.30, when the ubiquitous office peon would come to pick up the tiffin carrier. Shaila Sathe recalls that her husband, as an undersecretary in 1948, received a salary of Rs 300, which was enough to live on, but required economizing with some ingenuity. She remembers buying curtains for her government quarters and deliberately selecting a pattern which could be later cut up into a dressing gown when the inevitable transfer took place. Yet, no matter how straitened the circumstances, the pay scales were still high in comparison to others. In 1963-4, for example, a secretary to the Government of India received Rs 3,500; his peon got Rs 55.[2]

Despite the occasionally hand-to-mouth existence for senior officials, particularly at the end of the month, government life was pleasant. Officials socialized with others of similar rank. Senior officials followed pre-Independence patterns and went to dinners and dances at the Gymkhana Club which was, until the late '60s, still insisting on black ties and cummerbunds. Shaila Sathe remembered there was little contact with businessmen, and there were almost no industrialists in Delhi. You met your own kind. 'There was a real sense of camaraderie among people of the same service,' she says.

The government was, till the late '60s, still quite small; people knew not only their contemporaries, but also their seniors and juniors personally. The mix of castes and regional origins served to bring about a sense—not very deep perhaps, but novel nonetheless—of a national identity, a mutual participation in the most important project in the country: that of governing. While regional identities were still very important, lifestyles among senior officials paid at least lip service to the Nehruvian ideal, current at the time, of 'unity in diversity' a secular, pan-Indian idea that sometimes splintered in later decades when put to the test. Government colonies in Delhi were among the earliest spaces where people from all parts of the country came together: inter-regional, inter-caste interactions took place as the residents were connected by profession as well as by being neighbours.

The children all played together in the park; the wives were often friends; the men had joint car pools; for many it was the first time that they interacted frequently with people outside their communities.

Corruption had a different face in those early decades. Those who were junior officers then aver it was rarer. They say the emphasis on frugality, on Gandhian ideals, however superficially enforced, led to less pressure on having expensive lifestyles; moreover, the relative unavailability of expensive, imported goods limited greed. The word often used is 'innocent', evoking a prelapsarian time, before malls, television and expensive holidays made their appearance and corrupted everyone. Shaila Sathe, speaking of the first two post-Independence decades, admits there were a 'few known corrupt officials, but their colleagues avoided them'.

This is hard to establish, but the changes in the idea of corruption—its definition—can be looked at through the nature of Diwali gifts to government officials. In the '60s Diwali offerings consisted of *barfis*, fruit, or assorted biscuits in virulently coloured tins. Today blankets, sets of glassware, flasks, hotcases, crystal vases and cakes from very upmarket hotel patisseries are among the more modest presents on offer. *Barfis* will come arranged on silver *thalis*, dry fruits in cut glass baskets. Music systems, microwave ovens, Mont Blanc pens and, of course scotch whisky, are far from unknown despite government rules that proscribe the giving and taking of gifts above a certain value.

Other ingenious ways of influencing officials in key positions include free theatre and concert tickets, invitations to food festivals at restaurants, and free or hugely subsidized stays at expensive hotels in resorts such as Goa and Kovalam. Bribery is not just handing out wads of bank notes to influence the decisions on particular files—it can also be the establishing of an atmosphere of 'goodwill' until specific

IOUs are called in. The wining and dining of officials at upmarket restaurants is par for the course today and is a standard head in the accounts sheets of PR departments of multinational firms. Businessmen lend their farmhouses to officials for their daughters' weddings or for other social events. These practices are now so routine that they are not considered corruption—corruption is a politician stretching out his hand to take cash on camera. It is not candidates for the Civil Services exam indicating the Customs, Income Tax or Revenue services as their first preferences and using every possible method to ensure they get their preferred state so as to further the interests of their families or friends. The dowry rates for IAS officers are said to be lower than those for Revenue or Customs or Income Tax officials in certain states. This, inescapably, gives rise to the conclusion that in some quarters government positions can now have quoted values like commodities on the stock market.

Yet, while government Delhi has changed fundamentally in the decades since Independence, there has been almost no alteration in its appearance; the look has barely changed since government colonies first came up. Before that, house size and location were a function of official rank: secretaries, members of the executive council, and judges lived in bungalows which had compounds fifteen times the size of the house; a junior British clerk had a garden the same size as his *kothi*, Indian clerks and the lower ranks of railway employees were parked in houses built round a common garden, for instance in Havelock Square or Dalhousie Square (many of these houses have since been demolished). Proximity to the Raisina complex indicated seniority.

Post-Independence housing followed these formats, but as government Delhi had to expand exponentially to accommodate the huge increase in the numbers of officials, the factor of proximity to Raisina had to be abandoned. The colonies of Bapa, Rabindra and Bharti (formerly Man and Shan) Nagars, Pandara Road, Pandara Park and Shahjahan Road were fitted in—and these continue to be the colonies in greatest demand. Moreover, the garden-to-house ratio was reduced drastically. But the basic idea that the house was a marker of rank, remained. Most post-Independence government housing in Delhi was constructed by the CPWD, a pre-Independence entity with a long history.

In the mid-eighteenth century, military boards staffed by British military engineers were set up in the Presidency towns to provide the East India Company with suitable buildings, mainly for commercial purposes. In time, this expanded to include irrigation works and roads, and the PWDs formally came into being in 1855. 'The buildings produced were standard and strictly utilitarian,' say architectural historians Lang, Desai and Desai, who add that these agencies had, by the 1870s, 'developed a standardized form for almost all the military structures and civil buildings of the British Indian administration . . .'[3] The standardization of the structures and procedures are still all too familiar features of PWD construction more than 140 years later. The monotonous, identical, assembly-line buildings which look old almost immediately, but never wholly vanish, have a long history. Lockwood Kipling (father of the writer Rudyard), principal of the College of Fine Arts in Lahore, observed caustically in the late nineteenth century that the PWD's buildings were entirely 'without architectural sense of mass (with) no distinguishing features and no detail to speak of . . .' It seems nothing has changed. The

PWD has always been notoriously conservative and resistant to change. Yet the Indo-Saracenic style of architecture it established still makes up the familiar skyline of Indian provincial towns in every corner of the country. Many believe that this was the PWD's greatest achievement—though Lutyens was famously unimpressed. In fact, today a school of thought holds that the Modernist design of PWD housing is both architecturally sound and—for their time—innovative; some even hold that they are the genuine face of uniquely modern Indian architecture.

While this idea is bound to be greeted with derision by many, the fact is that government Delhi boasts some 65,000 residential units today which are administered by the directorate of estates under the ministry of works and housing. Residential accommodation is divided into nine different types, from Type 1 to Type 8 (Type 4 has a second 'special' category—why this is not called Type 5 is one of those administrative questions that will drive even the most earnest researcher to insanity). About 56,000 such units are of Types 1 to 3, which are for the lowest ranks of government employees—but despite these large numbers, there are over 33,000 people in the queue.

At the upper end, Type 8 housing (mainly bungalows in the heart of the Imperial zone) is reserved for judges, generals, ministers and other luminaries. Despite there being 300 such units, demand is double that. Bungalows are rarely allotted to civil servants; many are central offices of political parties, one a club for women journalists, one a tribal museum and four are dedicated to former prime ministers: Indira Gandhi (two), Lal Bahadur Shastri (one) and Charan Singh (one). This trend started when Teen Murti House (once the residence of the pre-Independence Commander-in-Chief) was turned into a museum on the life of Jawaharlal Nehru. The principle behind government housing allotments is that the overflow is then allotted the category below, and the reality today is that the majority of people in government accommodation are in houses one or two categories below what is known as their 'entitlement'. It is an indication of the declining power of the bureaucracy that officials of the rank of secretary have been firmly excluded from the stately graces of so called 'Lutyens's bungalows' (bungalows that were, in fact, designed by Herbert Baker and Robert T. Russell; Lutyens designed only two in the President's estate) and today are fortunate if they retire from 'C1s'.

In the matter of housing, too, the political class has learnt to capitalize on its subsidized accommodation for personal gain. Newspaper reports indicate that some 5,000 out of the 65,000 government houses sported unauthorized constructions and these range from the senior officials' enclaves of Pandara Park and Rabindra Nagar to the junior level officials' colonies of Nanakpura and Pushp Vihar; at least 5,000 government officials have resorted to the lucrative pastime of subletting their accommodation.

Government Delhi is undoubtedly a pleasant place to live in. It is spared the worst of the power cuts and water crises. It is central. It is well laid out. Only 24 per cent of the area is covered by buildings, its wide roads constitute 25 per cent of the area, its public facilities make up 12 per cent, parks cover 23 per cent of the space and what are termed as incidental open spaces are a good 16 per cent of the area. Consider this statistic: the NDMC areas use fifty-five gallons of water per head per day, while the rest of the Union Territory uses five gallons per head per day. The NDMC's budget is four times as much as the MCD's for a quarter of the area.

If anything, Lutyens's Delhi is even more protected now than it once was. While many monuments dating back several hundred years are in a state of disrepair (the fifteenth-century tomb of Bahlol Lodi in Chiragh Delhi is one example), these twentieth-century bungalows are well protected in the name of 'heritage' despite the fact that many occupants have added or removed porches, doors and windows—thus defiling the classical facades—for the sake of vaastu or feng shui. The low-density building regulations and the lowrise structure rules are largely observed—this despite the chronic housing shortage. For official Delhi, VIP security is also used as a mantra to keep encroachments at bay.

Government Delhi was born in 1931 with the inauguration of the new capital, but it has repeatedly proved its ability to mutate, accommodate and adjust to changes in power equations. The government way of life did not change substantially after August 15, 1947 despite all the rhetoric of nationalism and freedom at midnight that accompanied it. Today the acres of government colonies, spread over some of the most valuable real estate in the city, still share a common ethos, but the ethos has changed. In the three decades after Independence, it seemed as if this world would last forever: in those decades, government Delhi was small, it was privileged; above all, it had self-belief. Today in Lodi Colony, the present is pleasant, but none of the teenagers in the park would want to live there as adults.

# 6

## COLONIES: THE SHAPING OF
## MIDDLE-CLASS LIFE

DELHI BEFORE 1947 WAS ANOTHER COUNTRY. OPEN fields, mango groves and graveyards existed where south Delhi stands today. Across the river in east Delhi, Shahdara was a small settlement in the middle of fields and scattered villages. New Delhi was occupied, but had great swathes of empty spaces; it was bare and dusty, today's stately spreading trees were still frail, young saplings. To the north, the old city was a significant centre of gravity, and the neighbourhoods of Civil Lines, Alipur and what is now the university area, were hubs of middle-class activity. Among the first stirrings of the form that urban Indian middle-class living was to take began to the north and west of the old city.

The first modern 'suburb' in Delhi was Trevelyanpur or Trevelyangunj, north of Paharganj, one of four estates belonging to Englishmen in the early decades of the nineteenth century, all situated in the area between the

Ridge, Lahore Gate and the river; the other three belonged to David Ochterlony, William Fraser and Charles Metcalfe, who all held the post of British Resident in Delhi. Charles Trevelyan was an assistant commissioner in 1830 and, writes urban historian Narayani Gupta, 'prepared a ground plan for Trevelanpur, a suburb . . . on a grid pattern, with streets ninety feet wide and with names such as Blake Street and Babar Street (shades of New Delhi!). There was a public garden and a central colonnaded market called Bentinckganj.'[1]

Settlements exclusively for Indians were started a hundred years later in Karol Bagh, Western Extension Area (WEA) and Paharganj. These areas were originally orchards (hence the 'bagh' in Karol Bagh which was, along with Jorbagh, possibly planted during the reign of Ferozeshah Tughlaq in the mid-fourteenth century. Karol Bagh, the colony, was set up in 1937 as a Delhi Improvement Trust scheme to accommodate the spillovers from what was regarded by British administrators as the increasingly congested city. Dev Nagar, too, had come up a little earlier, home to junior-ranking Indian officials who had not found space in New Delhi. These new areas also accommodated professionals from other parts of India, who were coming with their families to settle in New Delhi—the early beginnings of the movement that brings 1,300 migrants *a day* to Delhi now.

Daryaganj had been occupied by the army as part of the brutal reorganization of the old city after 1857 when swathes of Shahjahanabad were razed to the ground. The army moved into the Red Fort and nearby areas to ensure its unhampered access to any nascent rebellious tendencies in the old city. In the '20s, the army moved out to Jhandewalan, and the Daryaganj area was made available for middle-class dwellers.

Bungalow-living for Indians in Delhi had begun when the families—or parts of families—moved into Civil Lines, a movement that began very gradually in the early years of the twentieth century, partly because an epidemic of the plague was then feared to be imminent but mainly because some members of the rich merchant families of the walled city wanted to change their lifestyle. So it was a movement not just of residence but also in the idea of family. Usually a single branch moved out of the family haveli, and while two or three generations lived together in the new dwelling, a re-designation of spaces and relationships ensued. Bungalows had specific spaces for sleeping, eating and recreation, unlike havelis, and with this change came a new tilt in family relationships—the nuclear family unit gained importance as did the conjugal unit, though this did not mean any accompanying reduction in the importance of patriarchy. For instance, one way of expressing social mobility was to participate as a couple in the anglicized rituals of making social calls, going to the club or to dinner parties, thus taking the couple into worlds which the rest of the family could not penetrate.

Colonial cities allowed a choice of lifestyles because of their more heterogeneous population—as well as their concentration of wealth. The middle class—traders, lawyers and civil servants—had hitherto lived in the *gallis* of the old city. Delhi's Baniya and Kayasth communities were the Delhi bourgeoisie. Kayasths (Mathurs, Narains, Bahadurs and others) had long served the Mughals as *munshis*, and many had availed of the opportunities of education in English to join the ranks of the Raj's administrators or become lawyers, professors or doctors. Some of the basic strands of middle-class life that we see today evolved within those Kayasth families. They invented their own style of

Indian-English behaviour, selecting certain Anglicized practices, rejecting others.

The late Sheila Dhar came from one such Kayasth family. She lived in the Civil Lines for much of her life, and looking back on the reasons for the family's move out of the old city, she reflected, 'My grandfather and his three brothers and all their families lived in the large family house in Chelpuri mohallah. But then my grandfather was sent by his father to England to study at the bar. When he came back, he was sufficiently anglicized to want to live in a kothi, or bungalow—this was common among those who had higher education and (therefore) anglicized aspirations. That was when my part of the family moved out of the old city to Civil Lines.'[2] Not all Kayasth families shifted out of the city to Civil Lines; many families of Narains, for instance, had moved to the newly opened up areas of Bengali Market. After 1947, however, the trend southwards accelerated. Sheila Dhar remembered, 'We never really related to the newer colonies while we still lived in the old city. We used to say, "Oh they live *there*"—there was always that slight air of dismissal.'

The sense of belonging to a wider community—the extended family, the caste group, the closely-knit neighbourhood where relatives lived just a few doors away—was an integral part of middle-class life in the old city. 'Today, that particular spirit doesn't exist any more,' Sheila Dhar said, not altogether regretfully. She spent her final years in the same place she grew up in, but the old house had been demolished and the plot parcelled into flats; and though her cousins lived in the neighbouring flats, they met but rarely. Commenting on the seismic shifts in family relationships she had seen in her lifetime, she said: 'My cousins and I grew up bathing from the same bucket . . . but just keeping the nuclear family going [today] is such a full-time effort. Things like fridge repairs take over your life. There is still attachment, of course, and though we have such different lives, I know I can call up any time and ask for anything.'

∼   ∼

The city's Indian bourgeoisie had built themselves large mansions in New Delhi before Independence. Barakhamba Road, Sikandra Road, Bhagwandas Road and later, Prithviraj Road, Ferozeshah Road, Curzon Road and part of Aurangzeb Road had houses belonging to affluent Indian industrialists and contractors who were on genial social terms with the British and who could, moreover, afford the prices. Lala Shri Ram, for instance, had a large house with a swimming pool on Curzon Road (now Kasturba Gandhi Marg). Not all settlers had been initially enthusiastic about the new areas, unconvinced that the jackal-infested jungle around Connaught Place would ever be habitable. Some even had to be 'persuaded' to buy the plots. As it happened, they were undeniably good investments.

One family that moved willingly to New Delhi was that of Sir Abdur Rehman, an eminent lawyer who became vice-chancellor of Delhi University. The Rehmans left their house in the old city and moved to Ferozeshah Road in the late '20s. Sir Abdur's new house had a Lutyenesque façade, with deep verandahs, Corinthian columns and a small dome. The family left for Pakistan in 1947 and the house became the headquarters of a missionary society. The society sold it to a private individual, and the original façade was refurbished with the 'contemporary' Lutyens look of pink sandstone and arches. In today's terms the sums paid in the '20s sound trifling, but it was beyond the reach of most of the middle class. To accommodate the demand for private homes, the earliest 'colonies', that is, plotted, residentially demarcated neighbourhoods, came up after 1947 on the outskirts of New Delhi, and the plots were auctioned. These were the colonies of Jorbagh, Sundarnagar and Golf Links.

The use of the term 'colony' to describe a discrete residential neighbourhood in Delhi is an odd phenomenon of nomenclature, a surprising label for a newly independent capital to choose.[3] But whatever its origins, New Delhi has stuck with it and evolved a way of life, a set of rituals and behaviour which involve living in a certain demarcated space within the larger, heterogeneous universe of Delhi. The earliest post-independence colonies had streets with rows of same-sized plots and, typically, several parks, possibly a school, a small market selling basic provisions, and usually a religious or civic institution—a mandir, gurdwara or post office. The inspirations behind such residential neighbourhoods included American surburbia with their air of calm affluence, British cantonments with their parks and symmetrical plots and, most recently, from the layout and planning of New Delhi, with their bungalows and tree-lined streets.

While these are the well known impulses behind the evolution of colony life in Delhi, equally significant is the influence of Model Town, Lahore, a colony which was established in the 1930s by Diwan Khem Chand, a lawyer. He was influenced, while studying for the Bar at Gray's Inn, by the ideas of the nineteenth century town planner, Ebenezer Howard (1850-1928), who proposed the concept of a 'Garden City' when it was a widely-held feeling among the progressive middle classes in Britain that cities were growing too congested and unhealthy for a sufficiently fulfilling existence. Fired by these ideas, Diwan Khem Chand and the renowned philanthropist Sir Ganga Ram (of Ganga Ram Hospital fame) persuaded the city authorities in Lahore to allocate some 2,000 acres for the project.

The new settlement met with an enthusiastic response from the city's sizeable Indian middle class who, as Chand put it in one of his writings, 'by their better training, education and social position desire to live a better life'. The shape that this 'better life' took was bungalows in gardens along broad, tree-lined streets. Model Town was planned with schools, markets and civic buildings located in the centre, surrounded by eight identical residential sectors, all connected with each other by a series of concentric circular roads. Some 400 enthusiastic, doctors, lawyers, civil servants and engineers bought plots and constructed houses which were, according to a contemporary account, 'curiously alike, having been patterned on the government bungalows which had been their homes, and the dak bungalows which had been the scene of so much of their activity'.

Yet, they adapted (perhaps they were the first to do so) the features according to their personal lifestyles: the front of the house followed the British pattern of a flowerbed-bordered garden, verandah, drawing and dining rooms, and the back had the local features of courtyard, kitchen and multipurpose rooms for sitting and sleeping in. Model Town had many parks and open spaces, it had its own electricity and water supply and efficient sewage disposal scheme as well as a security system devised by Diwan Khem Chand himself, which included bicycle-borne chowkidars who could more effectively chase thieves. Today, Lahore's Model Town has, despite skyrocketing real estate prices, retained its open, spacious character and holds some of the most expensive properties in the city. The colony was well run due to—or despite—the forceful personalities of its residents. Prakash Tandon, whose father owned a house there in the late 1930s, observes the politics of the Model Town Cooperative Society: 'Having spent all their lives as officials, they now all tried to run the Society office and its poor secretary, who usually never stayed long in the job. The retired conservator of forests took him and the *malis* to task about the trees and hedges; the engineers . . . forced their advice about the roads, buildings and canal water ditches, while the retired ICS just laid the law down about everything.'[4]

Many of the elements of Model Town, Lahore, were followed in the colonies that came up in post-1947 Delhi, including one also named Model Town. As Delhi's economy expanded, it became a magnet for migrants from all walks of life, from all over the country. Then, as now, the poorest lived wherever they could find space and the luckier ones managed to build rudimentary shelters—mere structures of asbestos or corrugated iron sheets and tarpaulin. Groups of these were, in time, officially recognized as *jhuggi jhonpris* ('JJ clusters' in governmentspeak) and, in due course, with political support, many became 'regularized' as colonies, triggering more and more jhuggi settlements. With political support again, such clusters become colonies. Residents of regularized colonies are eligible for ration cards, have access to regular sources of power and water, medical care and—most important—a claim to the land they live on. Attempts by slum-dwellers to become a regularized colony are, therefore, very strong; equally strong is the opposition to such moves by middle-class colonies adjacent to them.

In the '50s Delhi as we know it had not come into being. While the refugee colonies of Kalkaji, Malviya Nagar and Lajpat Nagar were under construction, there were still no proper roads linking them. In fact, south of Lodi Road, the road network was almost non-existent: Defence Colony had no road linking it with Safdarjang Hospital. P.N. Tandon, neurosurgeon and former chief of the All India Medical Institute, recalls going in a tonga in the very early '60s to look at the stretch of scrub and fields that was earmarked to be, one day, Greater Kailash. After a point even the rudimentary dirt track petered out and Tandon had to abandon the tonga and walk the rest of the way.

All this changed in the space of a few years. By the late '60s, South Extension—deemed in those innocent days to be the southern-most point that Delhi would expand to—was established. Today, when South Extension is considered central, it is hard to believe that just four decades ago people thought the way they once did. Similar apprehensions arose when Vasant Vihar, the housing society started by government officials, was first mooted. Potential buyers surveyed the rocks and *keekar* trees interspersed by crumbling gravestones with disbelief. This is hard to credit when you consider the hub of bars, movie theatres and fast food outlets in today's Basant Lok, the market complex abutting Vasant Vihar. Just four decades ago, the area between Safdarjang Hospital and Palam was a jigsaw of villages, fields, rock and scrub. It is not only that the Delhi we know is changing; the Delhi we know did not exist till recently. It was always changing.

Middle-class colonies proliferated over the decades: government colonies, refugee colonies, group housing society colonies and colonies built by private developers. The last category included Haus Khas, Green Park and South Extension, developed by the DLF group in the '60s. In the '70s, came all the Kailashes—Kailash, East of Kailash, Greater Kailash I and II. Group housing societies organized on professional or regional lines came into being. Two of the earliest were Tagore Gardens and Safdarjang Enclave. Almost all colonies that subsequently developed in this category, Vasant Vihar, for instance, or West End, Santiniketan and Anand Niketan, were formed on the basis of certain commonalities, whether common offices, professions, or regions. For instance, a group of Income Tax officers originally formed Panchsheel Park in south Delhi, Kashmiri Pandits established Pamposh, and Bengalis from the former East Pakistan were allotted land by the ministry of rehabilitation and established Chittaranjan Park.

Meanwhile, in the '70s, the DDA began its foray into house-building, the first attempt being the flats along Press Enclave Road in Saket. This was the first of many DDA colonies, which would encompass three basic types: middle-income and lower-income group housing schemes and the more upmarket self-financing scheme. In the '70s, apartment living was still relatively new in Delhi. Among Delhi's earliest apartment buildings was Sujan Singh Park, designed by Walter Sykes George for Sir Shobha Singh in 1945. These were lowrise blocks of buildings, constructed round a park, and the pattern adopted by the DDA's planners was not dissimilar, the difference being there were several such units within a larger colony. Thus the single building was not the significant neighbourhood unit—as it is in Mumbai, for instance—but the blocks round a park were. This is recognized by today's Residents' Welfare Associations (RWAs) in DDA colonies, from the small Munirka Enclave to the megacolonies of Vasant Kunj, Dwarka and Rohini, which are nearly all organized blockwise.

As south Delhi filled up, group housing societies applying for plots were, from the mid-'70s, encouraged to build blocks of flats rather than individual houses. Across the river, Shahdara was, during the early '50s and '60s, home to mill-workers and other skilled labour because of its very low rents. By the '80s, this side of the river had begun to catch the attention of the middle classes. It was then that the name of Patparganj became familiar to middle-class circles. Professional couples entering their mid-thirties, usually with two small children, had begun to think of the future when the rents they could even then barely afford for their DDA flat or south Delhi extended-by-kitchenette *barsati*, would rise beyond their reach. Their solution was group housing societies, and with space at a premium and construction costs escalating, most societies opted for apartment buildings. Mayur Vihar, Gurgaon, and NOIDA, the last just across the river in Uttar Pradesh, developed through the '80s and '90s. Some sectors in NOIDA had plotted developments, but the number of apartment buildings was substantial. Interestingly, unlike many older Delhi colonies, a club and a golf course were developed simultaneously, indicating the development of a consciousness that was suburban rather than metropolitan.

By the '70s, a way of 'colony living' evolved; it was not a conscious development and did not follow absolutely identical patterns; but it was the process though which a post-Independence middle-class way of life was invented. In the spaces between the houses—the parks, the markets, the tree-shaded street corner—developed relationships, modes of interactions and mutual dependencies which were usually harmonious, only occasionally spilling into acrimony. It was through such connections that a relationship with Delhi was expressed. It is with immediate neighbours that the first and most immediate sense of a link with the non-family outer world of a city is articulated.

Defence Colony was among the earliest south Delhi

colonies and was established through the efforts of Mehr Chand Khanna, a Congress politician from NWFP, who was a leading advocate of the refugee constituency. The colony was set up primarily to relocate officers from the armed forces displaced from Pakistan. The land earmarked for the colony was then on the outskirts of New Delhi, but is now one of the most centrally located Delhi colonies.

Sharda Malik, now in her seventies, is one of Defence Colony's original plot-owners. She sits in her neatly paved front yard, surrounded by flourishing pot plants and creepers. A row of Ashok trees screens off the busy Defence Colony flyover just metres away. Her husband was allotted this plot fifty years ago. The Malik family originally came from Jhang in Pakistan. In 1947, Sharda's husband was an army officer posted in Karachi. The rest of the family had to leave Jhang hurriedly, having believed, like so many others, that Partition would never actually affect them. 'There was no time to take anything. My youngest brother-in-law was a baby then, so my mother-in-law just snatched up his feeding bottle. That was all she took with her,' Sharda recalls.

After Independence, her husband was posted to the Andamans so they did not come to Delhi till 1950 when they heard through the forces' grapevine about a colony for displaced army officers from west Punjab. Her husband paid Rs 150 for the form which established his 'west Punjab displaced officer' status. His only request was that the plot should face east and the plot was duly allotted in the late '50s. It is Mrs Malik's recollection that the original allotment pattern in Defence Colony was according to army rank. For instance, Blocks B, C and D were given to captains and majors. Junior commissioned officers were allotted plots in A Block, while E Block was reserved for generals. F Block

was originally earmarked for war widows—but few took up
the offer. There were also several 1,000-sq.-yard plots which
were allotted to armed forces personnel who were able to
pay the whole amount at once.

The Maliks did not build the house till the '60s after
they received a notice warning them that the plot would be
revoked unless built upon. 'Serving officers had very little
spare money—we had to think of the children's education,
our daughters' marriages and so on. So we sold our car and
borrowed some money to build the house,' Mrs Malik
explains. At that time, today's neat, manicured Defence
Colony was a churning, dusty construction site. Most houses
that came up then were single-storeyed units. In those pre-
architect, pre-'Bania Gothic' days, these were designed by
the owners themselves, though, as Mrs Malik acknowledges
ruefully, this led to a lot of 'mistakes and wasted space'. The
house was a roof, a safety net and an asset. It had to look
decent enough for potential tenants, but that was as far as
interest in the look went. The construction was often overseen
mostly by the wives of the allottees; their husbands were,
more often than not, posted outside Delhi. Once the houses
were built, most were let. It was only in 1969 that the Maliks
moved in and built a first floor as the family was growing
and needed more space.

The colony club, established in 1973, became a major
hub of colony activities, a pattern common in other south
Delhi locations. 'We went sometimes; not for cards—you
know army officers never have much money,' remembers
Sharda. Socialising in the '60s and '70s was still family-
centric: 'All our relatives were in Delhi, in Lajpat Nagar and
in Chiragh, and we got together for all the important
occasions.' Sharda's main recreation then was meditation: 'I
used to go to the Ram Sarnam ashram across the *nalla* (a

broad drain that cuts through the middle of the colony)'. An RWA was started in the '80s and was, initially, concerned with day-to-day practicalities—the provision of plumbers, electricians and engineers. It was only towards the end of that decade that the body began to have elections and, with the coming of the *bhagirdari* scheme—a partnership established between residents' organizations and the civic authorities, became an influential force in the residents' lives.

In those early years Defence Colony was a closely-knit community. 'All of us ladies knew each other, and we would meet all the time to discuss our problems,' says Sharda. Her daughter-in-law, Sudha, came as a bride to the colony over twenty-five years ago. Sudha has many friends in the colony whose lives have followed similar routes: they met as young brides, their children were born in the nearby Moolchand Hospital, they took their toddlers to the park together, progressing to the school bus stop as the children grew older. The children became friends too, going for cokes to the then small, sleepy market and ordering lurid pink and yellow birthday cakes in the shape of trains and planes from Auto Bakeries; they played cricket together in their driveways and then badminton in the court which came up at the club, and when they reached college-going age, met at the Andrewsganj U special stop. Even today, the connections remain strong.

The real estate value of Defence Colony has appreciated enormously since the '60s. With the death of many of the original allottees, plots have been sold to builders, and most families have retained one or more flats in the new building. Sharda views this development pragmatically: 'After all, many people sold their houses within five years of building them, even though there was a 'no sale' clause. We didn't;

we couldn't afford to sell—we only got Rs 7,500 for our house in Jhang.' Looking back, Sharda Malik says, 'I've enjoyed living here. It's well located. I have friends here. We meet often; we have *satsang* gatherings and Gita classes.' Only some things have changed: 'Today, from numbers 44 to 70 of D block—we are, all of us, widows; our husbands have all died.' Pointing to a row of Ashoka trees, she says, 'I planted those when we first came here. My neighbour planted that Shahtoot. Look how tall they are now.'

≈　≈

Each area of Delhi has its separate ambience. Much of it came up piecemeal; contiguous stretches of land were acquired by different buyers: the government, private developers and housing societies. Residents of neighbouring areas, therefore, could differ appreciably, though the colonies were developed along basically common patterns. The DDA specified the maximum plot area, the density, the extent and distribution of open spaces, the land for utilities and so on. Within colonies, people from roughly comparable income groups resided, their social attitudes and aspirations not, in most cases, too dissimilar. Government colonies were in their own way fairly homogeneous, their differences in regional origins balanced by the commonalities of rank and profession. Internally, then, most colonies had residents who could find some things in common.

The evolution of Delhi as a set of separate, —even if the lines of demarcation were invisible—universes began sometime in the '60s. These worlds were sometimes linked; sometimes not at all apart. Physical proximity does not necessarily lead to familiarity. Take, for instance, Lodi Colony, in south Delhi, where middle-level government officials reside. It is adjacent to Jorbagh, one of the most expensive pieces of private real estate in Delhi, but few residents of Lodi Colony claim friends or acquaintances in Jorbagh. Lodi Colony's residents are similarly unacquainted with any of the residents of the Class IV colony of Aliganj which borders Lodi Colony on the west; but many had close friends in Netaji Nagar and Sarojini Nagar, about two miles away, and routinely travelled considerable distances to see them there and in far-flung areas of Delhi. The social and emotional universe of each Delhi person, then, is non-spatial and unique. Invisible threads bind disconnected territories to each other. All metropolises have similar sets of cat's-cradle linkages, looping like humming telephone wires across cities, invisible to the naked eye, known only to each individual or family group, but Delhi more so, because the majority of the residents have lived here for less than two generations.

Cities in general, and New Delhi in particular, are worlds of strangers who manage to forge linkages with each other. Yet, people recreate what they know; in time neighbourhoods develop their own patterns of interaction, even if they are sparser and more perfunctory than what has been left behind. The urban middle-class behaviour that has evolved gradually in Delhi has led to a sense of community—sometimes fragile, sometimes strong—in most neighbourhoods. Often, the residents are drawn together by mundane issues: common grievances against power cuts or water shortages or the need for another gate near the school bus stop. Small matters, perhaps, but leading to a forging of interdependence between individuals whose grandfathers—perhaps even fathers—would have regarded each other with incomprehension.

Walking through a colony and noting the faded *alpana*

(of rice flour patterns) on one doorstep and the auspicious string of dried leaves hanging from the lintel of the house next door, we see indications of the shaking up and mix of identities that is common to all urbanization, but more profound in post-Independence New Delhi because of the greater number and variety of its migrants.

Sometimes, however, the trend can reverse. The horrors of the anti-Sikh attacks in 1984 led many Sikh families to move to neighbourhoods where their community was in a majority. Nonetheless, there is in the city a faint but perceptible beginning of a 'Delhi' identity—particularly among the second generation of middle-class migrants who harbour an affection—even if it is rarely articulated—to the city of their birth.

Homogeneity comes at a price. Twenty years ago, the difference of ambience between Chittaranjan Park and Kalkaji was like that between two planets. Chittaranjan Park had a very consciously Bengali flavour —women with their partings prominent with sindoor, cluttered, noisy markets and the inescapable Rabindra Sangeet on loudspeakers during seemingly endless festivals. Neighbouring Kalkaji, on the other hand, was robustly Punjabi refugee—the jars of preserve atop the garden walls, the salwar-kameezed women, the portraits of Guru Nanak in the markets. It was a difference so tangible that, by crossing just a street, you would be in a different world. This has changed in the last decade with the builder boom which resulted in old single-unit houses being replaced by multi-storey flats, which led in turn to an influx of new residents, most of them from different parts of the country. Chittaranjan Park now is visibly less Bengali as well as visibly more prosperous; its once ramshackle markets, with their rows of fish displayed on naked slabs of dubious ice, its shops selling *alta* and vermilion, the long hours of afternoon when shopkeepers disappeared for their siesta, are rehoused in a spanking new DDA market complex in which the shops have been sold by auction. While Bengali festivals are still celebrated with huge and commercialized enthusiasm, the songs on the loudspeakers are often the newest Bollywood soundtracks.

Meanwhile, Kalkaji too has lost its refugee character. Honda Civics and Santros line the lanes instead of two-wheelers and no one makes achaar at home anymore. Perhaps these are inevitable accompaniments of urbanization and prosperity, perhaps they are for the good, but the distinct flavours and smells have all but vanished. What is lost is the feeling that existed till the '70s: that if you shut your eyes and breathed deeply, you would know which part of Delhi you were in.

Inevitably, the ideas of Delhi clash. The middle classes want a city which looks like a Hollywood version of American suburbia. They want service personnel, somehow accessible, but out of sight. Others see the presence of large, disempowered sections in the capital as potential vote banks. The battlegrounds of these conflicting visions are expressed through issues such as the relocation of polluting industries, the regularization of unauthorized colonies, the rules regarding illegal construction and so on. Delhi chief minister Sheila Dixit's decision to regularize some 1,700 unauthorized colonies in October 2004 was described as 'populist' by sections of the English language media, but the reality is that politicians cannot afford to alienate so large a section of potential voters. These conflicting urban ideals inform the most mundane of issues; the positions taken reflect differing—and shifting—notions of the urban ideal.

Take the case of fish markets. Chittaranjan Park had not one, but two. They began as small stalls, and over time, grew into an entire township of shacks. One section of the residents felt the market was unhygienic and unaesthetic and adversely affected their house prices; they alleged that the inhabitants were illegal Bangladeshi refugees and suggested the whole place be demolished. This was fiercely opposed by another group that felt the availability of fish was integral to their identities as Bengalis and an anodyne DDA market would diminish the special character of the colony.

In neighbouring Kalkaji, an entirely different set of issues was raised when a proposal to establish a fish market within the colony was mooted. The Kalkaji RWA successfully resisted the plan by asserting such a move would offend the sentiments of the residents, many of whom were vegetarians. While this may well have been true, it also exemplified the tangle of identities (regional, dietary, class-based, financial) that are raised when urban development issues arise.

Civic amenities and environmental factors trigger increasingly assertive responses from Delhi's residents. Water and electricity are increasingly contentious issues and top the grievances of nearly all colonies in Delhi; the newer DDA colonies of Siddharth Enclave, Sarita Vihar and the sprawling 10,000-flat Vasant Kunj complex—all of which came up less than twenty years ago—suffer even greater water scarcity and the fear is that the problem will worsen unless immediate action is taken. Power shortages are endemic and the privatization of the electricity supply has not resolved the problem. Thieving of electricity is still rampant (though, according to some reports, somewhat reduced) in unauthorized settlements, office complexes, markets (authorized and unauthorized), and even private homes. These are not infrastructural issues alone: in Delhi, government colonies experience lower levels of power shortage and many unauthorized electricity connections continue with the connivance of the authorities.

Similarly, despite well-publicized drives, illegal constructions within residential colonies are the rule rather than the exception. Delhi's residents add balconies, floors, ignore set-back regulations—all quite visibly. Often, entire buildings come up in contravention of existing by-laws. The perpetrators come to 'arrangements' with the authorities, arrangements which become as institutionalized as the regulations themselves.

Meanwhile, changes in the Masterplan have allowed for some mixed use of land in residential areas. The MCD's drive in March 2006 to target commercial establishments operating in residential areas led to angry exchanges between traders and the municipal authorities, with sections of the public taking predictable positions on the issue. The BJP came out in support of the traders, while the RWAs claimed that commercial establishments increased the strains on already groaning infrastructures, added to traffic congestion and resulted in a lack of security for the residents. Certain south Delhi markets, for instance, M Block market in Greater Kailash I, Parts I and II of South Extension market, Green Park market and Defence Colony market, and Rajouri Garden market and Ajmal Khan market in west Delhi, among others, are places where the allocated space is wholly insufficient to contain the crowds and congestion.

Security issues and pollution aggravate the problem. Erratic power supply leads to the rampant use of generators—and in markets these tend to be large, powerful ones emitting noise and fumes and often taking up a large part of the pavement. In South Extension, the unstoppable expansion of the market has triggered a mushrooming of guest houses, restaurants and training institutes, mostly along the Ring Road, but some within the colony itself. This leads to fears about security; the high degree of publicity given to robberies and murders in middle-class colonies has added to people's anxieties. Security guards, entry and exit registers and gates which turn colonies into virtual fortresses are therefore becoming increasingly common in middle-class colonies.

The individual's interface with the authorities is one of constant negotiation; the regulation is just one element in the larger discourse. The area, the paying capacity or political connections of the person concerned, the personality and needs of the enforcer and other factors come together when an issue has to be resolved. Commentators on urbanism in developing countries often speak of chaos and anarchy; in fact, there are elaborate rules and courtesies, agreements are honoured, the system—call it corruption, call it a parallel polity—'works' in its own fashion and Delhi's residents have largely learnt to work it.

Today, there are an estimated 3.25 million slum-dwellers in Delhi, and the residents of middle-class colonies widely regard the proximity of slums as being responsible for the increasing incidence of crime, even though slum-dwellers provide the domestic services that middle-class colonies need. The residents of the DDA colony of Siddharth Enclave, for instance, cite security concerns to justify their opposition to the proposed location of a resettlement colony in an adjacent area. Another DDA colony, Mandakini Enclave, has successfully lobbied the Lieutenant-Governor (LG) of Delhi to have the slum on its doorstep removed.

While there is much discussion on improving conditions in slum settlements, those providing the facilities often have unrealistic assumptions. Jagadamba Camp is a twenty-year-old slum on the outskirts of Sheikh Sarai in south Delhi. Within its maze of open drains and precarious shanties, a non-governmental organization (NGO) constructed a row of toilets. But the slum-dwellers could not afford the Rs 1 charge each time they used them, so the toilets now lie abandoned. Residents of middle-class colonies apparently cannot understand these basic economic compulsions. 'Slums must be relocated to designated places and made to pay for the infrastructure and civic services,' writes a resident of a south Delhi colony on a website dedicated to civic issues. The writer adds, 'Most slums have mobile toilets, but the children defecate in the open—*more from habit than for any other reason*. Similarly, they know their surroundings must be kept clean, *but habit forces them to do the opposite . . .'* [emphases mine]

This complete disjunction between the clean, affluent city that middle-class residents want, the services they need, the opportunities that Delhi represents to the poor of the surrounding regions, and the potential support base that these sections represent to local political bosses, all function autonomously, each group pushing its interests, but rarely boiling over into open confrontations. This is ultimately how Delhi operates, its separate universes often seeming about to collide, but swerving at the last moment, achieving unspoken accommodations and arriving at strange and seething equilibriums.

If slums are a troublesome issue for the middle classes, greenery and open spaces generate a different set of controversies. These are today recognized real estate assets, as is evident from their frequent mention by developers to promote residential developments in Gurgaon and NOIDA. They are an accepted part of the middle-class home-ownership dream—this is what a city's surroundings *should* look like. A park's well-tended prettiness will add several thousands to the value of adjacent housing; yet, paradoxically, a glance at middle-class use of parks will reveal a complicated relationship to the use of green spaces. While the paved outer perimeters of some private colony's parks are used routinely for brisk early morning walks and by well-dressed children and their mothers in the evenings, parks in senior government colonies are deserted. Somehow, officials are too self-conscious to sit and enjoy the air—it seems to indicate the lack of something important to do.

In affluent private colonies, parks are used purposefully: for exercise or juvenile recreation. Middle-class adolescents have largely abandoned parks, too busy perhaps with tuitions, or perhaps their social scene has shifted to Barista or markets where they can 'hang out'. Contrast this with the casual, relaxed, crowded gathering in the park of the middle-ranking government Lodi Colony, where residents—old and young alike—often simply sit and talk. So while greenery is universally regarded as desirable, the actual way green spaces are used is a function of class identity.

Similarly, class affiliations also impact on issues that activate a colony's residents. For instance, Nizamuddin East is a former refugee colony—which in 1947 was open fields, and land sold for 16 annas a square yard—but is today one of the most sought-after areas in Delhi because of it central location, its wide roads and big plots, many of which still have single houses. The demographic profile of the residents is such that they are exercised by concerns that would not, perhaps, find echoes elsewhere—for instance, the campaign against the felling of an ancient banyan which galvanized its residents into organized protests. Similarly, interest in conservation—when translated into an interest in the protection of local heritage—is also the purview of social groups that have a sense of their own history, and which therefore see the knowledge or appreciation of history as part of their class identity Therefore, in some colonies, local heritage sites are regarded as an asset—Humayun's Tomb in Nizamuddin, for instance—in others as wasted valuable real estate.

Differing self-vision also impinges on activities as

unlikely as garbage disposal and environmental issues. One way of assessing the type of urbanization desired by different colonies is to look at the activities of the RWAs. The RWAs have gained importance through the establishment of the Delhi government's bhagirdari scheme, which—on paper anyway —empowers the RWAs to manage the interface between Delhi's residents and the civic authorities. This has been both a help and a hindrance. It has given a platform to the increasingly assertive middle-class citizenry of the capital to press their visions of how they wish to live. It has also, inevitably, led to an increasing politicization of the RWAs— not necessarily an adverse consequence, but one which has increased levels of conflict within colonies.

Water, electricity, sewage and the maintenance of green areas are the basic infrastructural issues that dominate RWA agendas, but other issues include cable operator charges, Holi and Diwali celebrations, the colony club, encroachments, illegal constructions and so on. RWA intentions are generally laudable, but not all their projects meet with success. The Defence Colony RWA experimented with a series of garbage separation schemes whereby waste material was sorted into glass, organic, plastic, etc., then sent for recycling. All very eco-friendly, but these failed because the majority of the residents (or their domestic help) were unable or unwilling to make the effort to separate their garbage.

Rainwater harvesting, however, is an ecologically conscious scheme which has appealed to many RWAs in south Delhi colonies, in particular, and has been a successful venture. Recycling waste water too, is a popular scheme. Vasant Vihar, a colony with some of the best amenities in south Delhi (home to no less than six former LGs of Delhi) has had one for a few years; so has Defence Colony; Tara Apartments and Yamuna Apartments depend entirely on waste water to keep their common green areas watered in summer. Similarly, Vasant Vihar's RWA, a very active association, has a newsletter, hires its own security guards to deal with the traffic snarls at Priya cinema, and organizes regular cultural programmes and tombola sessions, while the Vasant Kunj RWA successfully forced the colony's cable operators (themselves residents of the colony) to rescind a steep and arbitrary hike in the monthly charges.

The ambivalence that many inhabitants of Delhi nurture about their city is expressed through dissatisfaction at the recurrent civic problems in their basic neighbourhood unit, the colony. To some extent, the insistence on zoning is responsible for some of the anomalies, together with the unequal enforcement of regulations, municipal corruption and the multitude of urban issues that bedevil developing cities. It is one of the interesting aspects of Indian urbanization that despite the articulated commitment to a version of the American suburban dream, there is also a current that stays resolutely 'Indian'. Many city-dwellers want restaurants and shops at their doorsteps and are willing to endure considerable degrees of congestion and chaos to get them. Those that are absolutely determined to be suburban, head out to Gurgaon. The middle classes are reluctant to live adjacent to large sections of what the government euphemistically calls Economically Weaker Sections—most often this is expressed in terms of security concerns, but it is also an aesthetic judgement and a concern that their real estate value will diminish.

Many conflicts, ostensibly over civic issues, also demonstrate the range of attitudes to public space. In traditional Indian cities, public spaces were not regarded as the responsibility of individuals who would unconcernedly toss their rubbish onto the street. This mindset contrasts sharply with those who want beautifully maintained public spaces around them (whether or not they use them is another matter). These issues dealing with the *kind* of urbanization different groups of Delhi-dwellers want lie behind many of the conflicts that we see today.

Yet the distance travelled by Dilliwallahs in the last sixty-odd years is considerable. A new world, a new way of life has been created in the lanes of colonies, in apartment blocks and within sectors; new forms of social interaction have been invented. Some strands are taken from older lives in older settlements, others borrowed from other cultures— either visited, or seen on television or heard of. Differing visions of urbanization and disparities in its pace across Delhi generate conflict. Basic infrastructure is totally lacking in some areas, while others want more sophisticated facilities. Even in the latter group, there are differences between those who want Manhattan and those who want an updated version of Hampstead Garden Suburb. Yet the first stirrings of Delhi's post-Independence middle-class life that Sharda Malik witnessed as she watched her house come up in the churning construction site of Defence Colony all those decades ago, have evolved, coalesced into a whole way of life. It is often unsatisfactory, it is occasionally unbearable, but it is uniquely Delhi.

# 7

## REMEMBERED VILLAGES

I BECAME AWARE OF DELHI'S URBAN VILLAGES when I took the 541 bus from Chittaranjan Park to Connaught Place in the 1980s. The bus, on its circuitous journey to Regal cinema, did a sudden meander into Chiragh Delhi. It just about skirted the boundaries of the village, but the abrupt change of atmosphere—sandwiched as it was between the sedate south Delhi enclaves of Malviya Nagar and Panchsheel Park—was quite extreme. Through the bus windows were seen glimpses of a medieval wall, huge gateways and crumbling bastions advertising the telephone numbers of plumbers and tutorial services. The winding lanes looked shadowy and mysterious; the way of life inside the narrow houses seemed from another age, conducted to a different rhythm. I nursed this vision for years; Chiragh Delhi was always my unspoken exception to the inevitable homogenization of the city.

Years, decades, later, researching a guidebook, I entered the precincts of the village proper for the first time. It was

Diwali; early evening, just as dusk started to fall. This is probably the single most magic moment annually anywhere in India. Diyas were lit in small walled niches on either side of old arched entrances; they were lined up along low walls that were at least a century old. Strings of light bulbs were fixed to painted jharoka windows. Through lighted doorways, I could see women arranging sweets on stainless steel thalis. The children bursting bombs in the narrow gallis had shiny new clothes on—the little girls in satin sequined *lehengas* with butterfly clips in their hair; the boys, their hair slicked back, in pristine shirts and trousers.

I had come to visit the dargah of Roshan-i-Chiragh Dilli—for whom the village was named. I had been told that on Diwali, people from all communities came to light lamps at the mausoleum of the Sufi saint, Nasiruddin Mahmud, whose learning and wisdom were so renowned that he was given the title of 'Illuminated Light of Delhi'. Whole families had come from Madangir and Sheikh Sarai; they said it was their annual custom and spoke of the saint's miraculous cure of a father's diabetes, a daughter's asthma, a host of ailments that vanished at the intercession of Roshan Chiragh-i-Dilli. The dargah itself—white, spacious, with the saint's grave covered by a simple pavilion, was as unlike crowded, noisy, commercial Nizammudin as a dargah could be. It exuded the certainty that such miracles were possible, such faith was plausible; together with a secularism that was completely unconscious and spontaneous.

In the clear light of day, of course, such misty-eyed beliefs tend to wilt. Four gateways, in rather bad shape, lead into this compact village. The *burjis*—circular bastions—are used as shops and as storage space for sacks of unidentifiable contents, iron grilles and ramshackle rickshaws. The surrounding wall exists only in patches, but the village has kept within its original boundaries. The lanes leading off the four gateways are reasonably broad and straight, with smaller, more meandering offshoots branching off at irregular intervals that end in sudden cul-de-sacs, or unexpectedly return to the main road. The broader lanes open out into chowks, still typically with an old, gnarled peepul tree in the centre, surrounded by a paved platform on which village elders sit. The topography of Chiragh Delhi remains satisfyingly village-like.

Urban villages are so ubiquitous to Delhi's cityscape that their uniqueness rarely surfaces in our consciousness. We see them and we do not see them. They are part of Delhi's complex, jumbled skyline and are useful when we need emulsion paint, desert coolers or iron grilles. But the fact is the topography of most of these villages has not changed over some 200 years. Think of it, the lanes followed the same pattern when the 1857 revolt rocked the surrounding countryside, when George V was crowned King-Emperor at the spectacular, tented durbar in north Delhi in 1911, when Nehru spoke of his tryst with destiny on that hot, August evening in 1947. Most of the buildings in the villages have been rebuilt, some of them totally; some entire villages were relocated when New Delhi came up, and some have today virtually merged with the residential colonies that surround them. But the core characteristics of these settlements are unchanged.

One reason I wanted to explore urban villages was to discover the vocabularies of urbanization as it actually happens; to catch, for instance, the exact nanosecond when a person switches from toothpowder to toothpaste. Urban villages have had a stable population, changing from generations of agricultural activities to different professions. Because they tend to be old settlements, some villages contain monuments of great antiquity. Learning the inherited narratives about such monuments, understanding the way they fit into the village's world, is one way of unravelling attitudes to history.

The villages' names are evocative of their history. Thus the *pur* suffix (in Badarpur, Shahapur, Begumpur, Azadpur, for instance) indicates settlements that are largely urbanized ('pur' meaning settlement). 'Hauz' means reservoir, 'khas' denotes large, or special, thus Hauz Khas and Hauz Rani. Villages that are close to highways and thus have had resthouses for travellers, have a *sarai* affix , thus Sarai Kalekhan, Ber Sarai and Lado Sarai.

New Delhi's territory enfolded some twenty-two villages; these were uprooted and resettled, including, for example, Khairpur, the site of today's Lodi Gardens, whose villagers were relocated to Bhogal. The first Masterplan in 1962 cited 100 villages that the spread of Delhi would cover and a total of 357 villages have since been swallowed by Delhi's unceasing spread. After Independence, while the agricultural land was acquired, the actual villages were left intact. The village boundaries were called *laldora* (literally, 'red line') and the area within those boundaries was called *abadi* land (meaning the settlement) and given a different status from the rest of Delhi. In these, construction, for instance, was exempt from municipal control.

'Urban villages' were defined in the Masterplan in typical governmentspeak as 'villages on the urban fringe where rural type of activities existed and the population was engaged in such'. Initially, the villages were managed by the Gaon Sabha (village councils) and the Delhi Administration. Today, the Sabha no longer has any statutory authority, though each village still has a representative— usually someone influential in village affairs. These villages are still outside the purview of the Land Reforms Act and are currently engaged in a fierce battle to resist the imposition of house tax. The bulk of Delhi's villages are under the MCD, ten are with the Slum Wing and two are with the Cantonment Board.

In recent decades, as pressure on existing land in Delhi grew, the villages, particularly those in the heart of south Delhi, became a source of relatively cheap, regulation-free land and began to be used as centres for small-scale industries and the retail trade. Yet, despite their relatively recent makeovers, some of them fairly substantial—such as the transformation of Haus Khas village into an ethnic shopping mall—the basic topography of almost all villages is unchanged. Caste groups continue, by and large, to live within mohallahs which are linked to open areas—such as the chowk or the chaupal, or the bazaar—which serve the whole community. There is usually a temple or mosque attached to the village as well. In the past, the so-called 'unclean' activities were traditionally confined to the low-lying areas to the west. The village's dominant caste traditionally occupied the highest land in the centre or to the north.

Today, the peripheries of most villages usually have rows of shops. This is a change, because the old bazaar was usually deep inside the settlement. Nowadays, villages specialize in particular aspects of retail, usually linked to the construction or automobile trade. Thus Kotla is a centre for hardware, Chiragh Delhi for metal grilles and Mubarakpur for car parts.

But what is life actually like in these villages? Does the fact that the houses are on narrower roads, and do not have the 'colony' look of rectangular plots set on straight roads— the south Delhi colony imprint of shops, park and police station—have an impact on the nature of a community? Or are the villagers, like the rest of Delhi's population, coming to terms with the rapid changes in the urban world, with varying degrees of acceptance?

Shri Jutera is an important man in Munirka village, a member of the Gaon Sabha and the owner of several buildings on the southern periphery—the more expensive part. He is eighty-eight years old and has studied till class two. Gaunt and grizzled, he is dressed in a dhoti, kurta and a turban. We meet on the ground floor of one of his buildings in Munirka village. It appears to be a godown: sacks are stacked in one corner, bedding in another and taking up a lot of space in the middle is a large steel silo for storing grain. The low ceiling has wooden beams and the place smells pleasantly musty. The front wall of the room is open to the street and Juteraji spends his afternoons here—not in his adjacent residence—keeping a sharp eye on events in the street. It is surprisingly cool in the godown. He says that it is cooler than his residence next door where the desert cooler runs all day. Mr Jutera's family has lived in the village for five generations.

Today he lives with his sons and grandchildren. He is a wealthy man. His house, a new four-storey building, has been attached to the older structure. The old arched niches are plastered—nearly concealed—under a coat of pista-green emulsion, and the *angan* (the courtyard) is paved with a mosaic of green and white marble chips. His sons—his five daughters are all married and live outside the village—live in the modern part. His grandson and granddaughter, dressed in the uniform jeans and T-shirt of the urban young, are playing a computer game. One of his sons is a bank manager; the other is a *thekedar* (contractor). One of his grandchildren is studying IT at Acharya Narayan Dev

College, another engineering and yet another is doing an MBBS. 'Everyone is being educated now,'[1] he says (and one is left in some doubt if he entirely approves).

He approves, however, of research into 'the old ways'. The Jutera household follows well-established traditional patterns. 'We don't keep servants. The ladies do the work. Servants will steal from you or try and spoil your *izzat*— they might get the girls to run away,' he says by way of explanation. Nor does he believe in soft living. When the DDA acquired the lands of Munirka village, he used the compensation to buy some land in Qutubgarh and cultivated it himself, continuing to drive his own tractor. When that land, too, was acquired, he bought land in Barwala. He has leased it out now and gets paid in cash and kind, and the silo in the godown was full of grain. 'Our atta for a whole year comes from that,' he said with satisfaction. 'Barwala is a very nice piece of land, full of neem trees and sheeshum.' He says this rather sadly. Because his sons feel he is too old to work the land now, he has had to acquire new occupations. One of these is viewing TV. He watches the *Ramayana* serial regularly. He sticks to mythologicals; other programmes, he confides, are too embarrassing to watch in his daughter-in-law's presence (he implies she watches a lot of TV).

He's never really been ill, but once he broke his leg when a buffalo kicked him. His daughters-in-law have to force him to have iron capsules. Just as he is slightly suspicious of modern medicine, he is also fairly conservative about social mores. His sons and daughters all had arranged marriages with families from Nagloi (following a village tradition. The marriages observe well-established procedures to the letter. First, the girl's father and *chacha* go and see the boy. They look at how much land his family owns, how many flats, their rental income, whether the boy is educated and what his job is like. 'Yes, yes,' Mr Jutera says, impatient with my prodding, 'we also look at his character'.

With things growing so expensive, people actually look for a daughter-in-law who is employed—or has the potential to be so. But this has not led to a corresponding decrease in dowries, Mr Jutera tells me. 'Now people often have to give cars. When I was looking for a *bahu* (a daughter-in-law), I felt she should have height, be *saf-sutra* (clean and well-groomed) and educated.' (This was his order of importance.) With obvious pride in his own liberalness, he says that his daughters-in-law can 'talk directly to their *jaits* and *dewars* (brothers-in-law). Of course, my bahu doesn't address me directly. She calls me "So-and-so's grandfather".' He adds, 'Relations between *saas* (mother-in-law) and bahu are good in the good *khandaans* (families) but bad in the bad ones— even *gali galuch* (abusive language) can happen.' The Jutera khandaan, he indicates, is unquestionably in the former category.

Shri Jutera is a colourful character and enjoys being so. He is an articulate man and completely comfortable with himself. Underlying his conversation is an astute understanding of what you are looking for. He plays the role of salty village elder to perfection and with huge, infectious enthusiasm. His rusticity, however, is confined to his clothes, his obvious love of farming and his contempt for desert coolers. His views are not unlike those of any conservative octogenarian in Vasant Vihar, Karol Bagh or Narela. In significant ways he is 'urban'—and this is the crux of life in Delhi's urban villages. The term 'urban village' is not as much of an oxymoron as it seems at first sight. Munirka village's fields covered what is now Vasant Vihar, and stretched to Dhaula Kuan, R.K. Puram and Sarojini Nagar. The villagers raised buffaloes for milk and also sold calves. They grew jowar, bajra and vegetables. Water came from a bund in today's R.K. Puram. 'It was very hard work but we're very strong,' observes Mr Jutera. 'The Olympic swimmer Khazan Singh is from our village. We also have a lot of people in the army—majors and captains.'

This rural way of life changed irrevocably in 1959.

The acquisition of land from south Delhi villages had an enormous impact on the lives of all the inhabitants of Delhi's urban villages. Chiragh Delhi was engulfed in the urban sprawl of Delhi in the 1950s. It is surrounded by Masjid Moth, Soami Nagar, Panchsheel Park and Malviya Nagar to the south, east and north, and skirted on the west side by a nalla. Its walls, built by the Mughul ruler, Mohammed Shah Rangila (the Emperor Aurangzeb's grandson) in 1729, have kept Chirag Delhi a compact entity— even though, for largish stretches, the wall has disappeared. The Census of 1991 recorded the village's population as 12, 97,000. The presence of its renowned dargah too, has added a single overriding identity, which is definitely alive in the minds of the villagers. Chiragh Delhi is one of the oldest, continuously inhabited settlements in Delhi.

The village looks like an old settlement, with no vestige of suburbia. Houses jut out into the street, making the lanes even narrower and darker. As the site is still categorized as 'abadi' land, set-back regulations do not apply here. Architectural styles are as eclectic as in any south Delhi colony, though in this case, the jharokas and arched recesses are genuinely late Mughal. New, needle-like five-storey structures (including basements) are common, and these predominate in the lanes near the main roads. They look no different from houses in neighbouring colonies, with all the usual contemporary architectural embellishments of columns, pediments and pink sandstone. The front rooms of most houses are now shops—sometimes full-fledged shops, like a barber's, for instance—or sometimes just slits in the wall selling a medley of goods such as ribbons, asprin, biscuits, nail polish, batteries and receipt books. Because of all these shops, the old main market (a line of shops just off the dargah's chowk) has lost its distinctiveness. It begins with scattered vegetable stalls and trails off indecisively into a clutch of shops selling galvanized iron buckets, tiffin boxes and brushes.

There are many food stalls selling parathas, chole and samosas—these cater to workers in the *karkhanas* and to the very large tenant population, many of whom are single men. One casualty of the building boom has been open space. Traditional structures had a small, paved area in front as well as an *angan* inside. About 50 per cent still have one or the other type of open space. During the day, it is common to find groups of men playing cards in them, oblivious to swarming flies, and Marutis that squeeze past with centimetres to spare. The men also play seated on the village *chaupal*, or in the front verandahs of their houses and even in the dilapidated Tughlaq-era pavilion near the dargah.

Since the '60s there have been two generations engaged in non-agricultural activities. Today, for many of the inhabitants, rent is now the basic source of income. Until the drive against polluting industries, many garment-export establishments (up to some 150 sewing machines in one factory), saw mills (never entirely legal), flour mills, steel fabrication units, carpentry, shops of pottery, electronic goods repair and automobile repair units were based here. One such establishment was operating out of a many-arched, probably late Mughal, structure. Rows of hand-turned sewing machines whirred busily making burqas, and the finished garments were hung up in a neat row along the front.

A flourishing cottage industry making *rakhis* springs up each year just before the Rakshabandhan festival in which sisters tie bracelets around their brothers' wrists. People say such industries have not really closed down, though no one actually says they are still operating. Most are owned by people living outside Chiragh Delhi, who set them up in the village because of the comparatively low rents. Shops along the outer rim trade in building materials.

Saharanpur-type carving gives an antique look to bedposts and chairs—clearly, upmarket furniture makers are tapping in here. There are many steel grille workshops too—and judging by the stacks of green benches, this is possibly the beginnings of a trend favouring wrought iron garden furniture.

The settlement of Chiragh Delhi has evolved organically over 650 years. Originally, it comprised the fourteenth-century dargah of the saint Nasiruddin Mahmud, and the havelis of the families traditionally associated with the dargah. Mohammed Shah Rangila built the village walls as an act of piety to the saint. This had a decisive—if unintended—impact on the village's subsequent history. In the 1760s, the raids of the Afghan, Ahmed Shah Abdali, led the villagers of Chattarpur,Yakudpur, Raipur, Surajpur, Mehrauli and Ghitorni (this is according to the villagers; but the first four are the likely ones, with a few families from the others) to seek refuge in the fortified enclave. Land that is now Greater Kailash I and II, Kalkaji, Nehru Place and parts of Panchsheel Park, were once fields in these villages. Entire villages moved in, and this movement is still alive in the memories of the villagers today. The Delhi *Gazetteer* of 1883-84 mentions Chiragh Delhi as being one of the forty-one villages under the Ballabhgarh tehsil. Hindus and Muslims traditionally lived together in Chiragh Delhi as early as the fifteenth century: thirteen families of Ailawat Jats were among the earliest recorded as living in the settlement, other than the families associated with the dargah.

The village was defined—is still defined, in many ways— by its dargah. Roshan Chiragh-i-Dilli, a Sayyid by birth, was the fifth and last Sufi saint in India. He lived during the reign of the Delhi Sultanate ruler, Mohammad bin Tughlaq, and died in 1356, having succeeded Hazrat Nizamuddin Aulia as head of the Chisti sect. He did not bequeath his *tabarrukat* (personal insignia) to a successor, so the Chisti order ended with him. Feroze Shah Tughlaq, the Delhi Sultanate ruler who reigned from 1351 to 1388, built the dargah complex, and a small settlement grew around it. The dargah was not just a tomb, it was always a pilgrim site and a resthouse as well. The now very dilapidated tomb of the founder of the Lodi dynasty, Bahlol Lodi (1451-1488), was the monarch's summer house before it became his tomb. In 1922, Maulvi Zafar Hasan, who conducted a comprehensive survey of Delhi's medieval monuments, [2] found twenty-seven structures within the complex covering the Tughlaq-to-late-Mughal periods, successive rulers adding to the complex as acts of piety. Floral tiles, for instance, were put up within the enclosure at the behest of the Mughal emperor Aurangzeb. The daughter of Bahadur Shah Zafar (the last Mughal emperor) took refuge within the dargah after the failure of the 1857 revolt.

The dargah was always sacred to both Hindus and Muslims. Quli Khan, a noble at the Mughal court, who visited the dargah in 1739, wrote in his personal diary: 'Pilgrimage to the *mazar* (grave) is performed; large crowds gather on Sundays, particularly on the last Sunday of the month of Diwali. Visitors raise tents and pavilions near the springs . . . and bathe there. Most people with chronic problems get cured. Both Hindus and Muslims perform the same rituals of pilgrimage.'[3]

The dargah has a relaxed atmosphere even today. This is a small shrine, which has to be approached on foot through congested village lanes, and is entered by a huge arched gateway. There are only three shops in the arcade leading to it—nothing like the tangle of stalls in the gallis of Nizamuddin or even at Khwaja Qutbuddin Bhaktiar Kaki's dargah in Mehrauli. On Fridays, Id and during the Urs, it is crowded with people, but for the rest of the time it is an informal meeting place, where people come to pass the time. Shri Gautam, a teacher at the Saomi Nagar primary school, Ram Chander, a Mahanagar Telephone Nigam Limited (MTNL) linesman, Sohan Lal, an octogenarian resident of the village who comes to feed the (rather obese) resident peacocks, are among the regulars. The owner of a grille shop, who is a Jat, is another, as are the *pirzada*, Zameer Ahmad, and his brother.

It is a cool place, shaded by a huge jamun that grows in the corner of the enclosure. There are some places, particularly those that have been sacred for a long, long time, that exude an air of calm rather than excite awe. The saint was a simple man in his lifetime, and, during the 700 years after his death, he has been revered continuously, but without fuss. The pirzada complained that tour buses tended to avoid the dargah because of the narrow lanes. He even alleged that some tour groups were taken to a shrine in Jahanpannah and told it was the Chiragh Delhi dargah. He said the dargah earned very little, and even during the Urs, very little money came into the village as the visitors brought their own food. He is clearly worried about its future and his own.[4]

The pirzada (his family have been pirzadas of the shrine

for generations) said there were no incidents of communal tension in this village, not even in 1947, when several families from the Qureshi mohallah left for Pakistan, and some refugees came from Pakistan to settle there. The family of the pirzadas still lives in the old haveli which abuts the dargah. During August 1947, Zameer Ahmad's father had taken them to stay with relatives in old Delhi, fearing that there would be trouble in the village. The pirzada says—he was a child at the time—that a delegation of villagers, both Hindu and Muslim, came to his father and persuaded him to come back. They were concerned that the shine was being left untended.

In 1947, many families of Punjabi Hindu refugees came and occupied the vacant houses and lands in the village. More refugees came when, in 1953, the ministry of rehabilitation acquired land there—this is called the Kumar mohalla. Today there are about eight Muslim families left in the Qureshi mohallah. They are mainly butchers—some very prosperous. Saleem Kebab Corner on the Press Enclave Road is owned by one of them—though Saleem himself no longer lives in the village.

The dargah's unquestionable antiquity is a source of apparently genuine pride for the people of Chiragh Delhi. They know it is what puts them on the map, so to speak, and they have accurate knowledge of Roshan-i-Chiragh Dilli's history. This, even though most of them dated the time when the villages moved into the Chiragh Delhi enclosure to 1857. It actually happened a hundred years earlier. One of the reasons for the loyalty to their home is that many of the older men went to primary school under a tree in the dargah's premises, and this familiarity has bred affection, respect and sense of ownership. Most people said that they visited the dargah occasionally, and nearly all had

a story of a cure or a wish granted. The pirzada said that all
the villagers came at some time or another and that they
would allow their taps to be used by visitors during the Urs.
Only one person, a Jatav, disagreed; he said that some
upper-caste families never visited it. But this could be a
consequence of more recent tensions, that are caste-based
rather than communal, which are starting to emerge in the
village.

In Munirka village, Hindu-Muslim relationships are
cordial, but demarcated according to established rules. Shri
Jutera remembers, 'Ten or twelve people came in 1947 to
settle here. There was already a small group of Muslims
here who were butchers. The relations are good.' As another
Munirka resident, a transporter, explains, 'When they hold
their *nikkahs* (weddings) we all go, but we don't eat there.
Sometimes they have food made for us separately; then
some people eat. We also call them to weddings in our
community; they eat with us. Our village has never had any
communal tensions. We had good relations even in '47.
There are two *makbaras* (graveyards) inside the village.'

The caste system still exists—openly and formally—as a
residential principle in urban villages. In Munirka village,
an elderly woman explains: 'We all live in separate
mohallahs. Jats and Brahmins lived here first; the Harijans
came later, but the *rishta* (relationship) has always been
good. We've had a Harijan as our corporation member in
the Municipal Corporation for ten years now. Thirty years
ago, there was a lot of '*chhuya-chhut*' (untouchability). Now
there isn't any.'

In Chirag Delhi, the higher castes generally live near the
centre and the castes ranked lower in the hierarchy near the
edges of the settlement. A 1996 Indian National Trust for
Art and Cultural Heritage (INTACH) survey of castes in

Chiragh Delhi found Brahmins formed 40 per cent of the population, Jats 28, the Banias 9 per cent, the Kumhars 7 per cent, Thakurs and Sunhars accounted 3 per cent each, the Jatavs, 2 per cent, Muslims 4 per cent, and the remaining 4 per cent comprised Jains, Punjabi refugees, Balmikis and Christians. While the inhabitants said everyone mixed freely, I was told by one Jatav, that the Jats, Banias, Sunhars and Brahmins interact with each other more often and avoid contact with the Jatavs. There are two or three Christian families living in buildings that were once a school run by missionaries. The missionaries left in 1955 or 1957 and the school closed down. The families who live there don't have much contact with the villagers.

Many Jatavs are now employed in such government bodies as the MCD and the MTNL. These secure, relatively well-paid jobs for members of a community like the one in Chiragh Delhi, where some two-thirds of the population are unemployed, are resented by some sections of the higher castes. One of the villagers said, not altogether appreciatively, that a new festival in the village's social calendar was Ambedkar's birthday, which the Jatav community celebrated with much gusto, in honour of that reformer's contribution to their lot. Clearly, my (upper-caste) informant saw this as a not wholly welcome manifestation of the Jatav community's new-found self-confidence.

The Jatavs are a close-knit community in the village, and one of them, Master Khemchand, is one of the most prominent members of the community. He has a large calendar art portrait of Ambedkar hanging outside his house. Another Jatav, Harichand Gautam, the local primary schoolteacher, is a member of the Scheduled Caste/ Scheduled Tribe Welfare Board, Delhi government. Shri Gautam is an interesting and articulate man in his early fifties and spends his free time at the dargah, where I first met him. At first, his henna-ed hair and beard led me to think he was part of the pirzada's family and not till subsequent visits, when I had established my interest in *itihaas* (history), did he give me his card, inscribing it with his mobile number. He and the pirzada appeared to be great friends.

Karan Singh, late of the army, and Tatas, who has lived in Chiragh Delhi off and on all his life, paints a picture of idyllic village harmony—in the old days. 'Every community—Hindu, Muslim, Jat, Brahmin, Balmiki—were all just like a family. The Harijan would help us in the fields. My children would call those who did the *safai* (the cleaners) "Chacha", father's brother.' We would all celebrate Holi and Diwali together. These *purani rishtas* (old relationships) still have importance for those of us born in the '50s—we still have a regard for each other, whether we are Pandits or Jats.'[5]

Singh hints this is not always the case now: 'Some people feel that the younger generation should meet each other—Balmikis, Jats, whoever. But there are a few who don't. It's a pity. After all, *all* our forefathers were born and died here.' Standing in the dargah, watching the peacocks, listening to the pirzada and Shri Gautam talk, or sitting on the charpoy with Shri Jutera as he exchanges greetings with his neighbours, it seems to be that these villages are self-contained, isolated, unbothered by the ferocious metropolis just feet away. But this is deceptive. Once village lands were acquired, the villagers hurtled willy-nilly in to join the urban world.

'The lands of Munirka village were acquired in 1958. As soon as the compensation was given a year or two later, many took to gambling,' Juteraji reflects and relates a story

I was to hear many times in urban villages. It's the apocryphal story of hubris running amok, the cautionary tale mothers tell wayward sons. 'People felt they were so rich they would eat *chole* in hundred-rupee-notes and then throw the notes away.' This is the expression of the great divide between commonsensical rural thrift and urban anarchy. 'A man who was a peon at a girls' school, would go to office in a car. Many people put all the money they got as compensation in a chit fund and lost it all. Experiences like these make people look for jobs with a steady income today, even if the salary isn't very high—they long to get government jobs even now.' Shri Jutera is not opposed to affluence, but is wary of the changes it brings.

He puts it in the form of fable: 'Sixty Harijan girls (from an unnamed village) married Jats: everyone counselled the boys against it. In the Jat community, these things don't happen—*Jat me yeh sab nahi chalta*.' His tone made it clear that the unions ended badly, but chose not to specify exactly how. He ascribes the lowering of the moral tone in the village's life to the influx of tenants. It is the presence of outsiders, even more than the changeover from an agricultural life, which has, in his view, led to severe social dislocation. Tirades against 'outsiders' are the way older inhabitants of the village express their disquiet at a changing world.

The state of security within the village is a source of great pride. 'Chiragh Delhi is very safe,' Karan Singh says confidently. 'Even now you can leave your house open, go away for fifteen days and come back to find everything intact. It's not like GK (Greater Kailash). Women are safe here. There's no eve-teasing—no one even looks at girls. Our fathers used to tell us that if a girl belongs to Chiragh Delhi, she is a daughter of Chiragh Delhi, so she is your sister. Even girls from nearby villages were treated like this—Shahpur Jat, Khirkee, Madangirgaon. Some of our land was in Jamrudpur. We did not even marry into these villages.'

But here, as in Munirka, the presence of so many tenants has, in Shri Jutera's expressive metaphor, led to a lot of *'ulti pulti kaam* (anti-social behaviour).' One of the doctors in the village says there is a fairly high rate of alcoholism and gambling. He ascribes this not to unemployment or the spare leisure time after the fields were acquired, but to what he termed 'the bad influence of the tenants and the way they have lowered the tone of village life'.

Whatever the real causes, there is universal agreement on the detrimental effects of tenancy. Mourns Shri Jutera, 'My Jat brothers don't listen when they are warned about not letting their houses to unsuitable people. Earlier, the village atmosphere was very good; now it's not. People drink till they fall down. I watch them from my charpoy. The new generation gets money without having to earn it. They are not even educated. Many people are transporters. What can you do, the children won't study.'

Some women in Munirka village, employed as domestics in the surrounding colonies, speak scathingly about the way their menfolk waste money on gambling and alcohol. Many keep their wages a secret from their husbands and invest them in jewellery or utensils. Unlike village patriarchs, they are not averse to the outsiders in the village; they see them as a source of rent and as customers for the small grocery shops they (the women) have set up. Women belonging to more affluent groups are more circumspect. One, a schoolteacher from Chiragh Delhi, says the tenants were 'rowdy', but the village was by and large safer than other parts of Delhi because it was smaller and because 'everyone knows your family'.

Women are an invisible presence in villages—they are never seen sitting on the chaupals or in teashops. Young girls never lean against a car or motorbike, which is a common occupation of the village boys. Women can be glimpsed through open doorways chopping vegetables in front of the TV or chatting from and between rooftops as they hang up or take down their washing.

INTACH surveyed Chiragh Delhi to find out what the villagers most want to have. The desired objects were (in order of importance) a good school, good transport systems, a gas stove, a booster pump, the choice of shopping at proper markets instead of a usually understocked ration shop, and labour-saving household appliances. INTACH's findings were heartily endorsed by the women I spoke to, although the men dismissed them.

Chiragh Delhi was incorporated as an urban village in 1961 and its fields were swallowed up by the southward thrust of Delhi. The village panchayat was dissolved in 1977 and the settlement became part of Delhi's urban area. While the rebuilding is predominantly due to the desire to increase rentable area, some of it is also caused by the increase in the number of nuclear families and the resultant splitting up of properties. Some people estimate that nearly 100 people can live in a single haveli plot. This inevitably leads to enormous pressure on existing infrastructure. Water shortages, choked drains and flooding are common complaints. Garbage collection is irregular and the many dairies (a large number of the inhabitants keep their own livestock as well) lead to infestations of flies. These are the reasons many people cite for their desire to move out of Chiragh Delhi. Moving out of the village is a much discussed issue particularly among the younger, professional element. They say, however, that they will not sell their houses, but rent them out. An INTACH survey found 37 per cent wanted to leave, 41 per cent wanted to stay, and the rest didn't know.[6]

Karan Singh's family has lived in Chiragh Delhi for generations. We meet in a clinic owned by his brother-in-law, Dr Sunil Shandilaya, which is in a narrow street that broadens into a chaupal. The clinic is tiny—it has obviously been built onto an existing house. It was opened by Singh's father-in-law in 1958 and served people in Madangir and Khanpur. The waiting room, separated from the consultation chamber by a wooden partition, opens straight onto the street. A calendar depicting Hindu gods adorns one wall, a crucifix, another. Barely three people can fit into the consulting chamber at once. The building seems at least a hundred years old, but I am told it is about sixty. As his brother-in-law sees an endless stream of patients, Singh reveals, 'I can trace my lineage in the village. For generations our family used to farm in the area where Greater Kailash is now. Our family shrine still stands there—in W137 GK1—and we still go every Holi and cut our hair and offer it there. The place we used to live in was called Mooza Yaqudpur then.' (This is one of the settlements that relocated to Chiragh Delhi after Ahmed Shah Abdali's raids in the eighteenth century).

'There have been many changes in the last forty years,' Singh continues. The village used to be open and every home had two neem trees growing beside it. Now the trees have been cut to make way for expanding houses. All our relatives lived here. We had a sense of identity, everyone knew each other. If something happened in one house, people would come and help—in times of misery as well as happiness. The men would get together, smoke a hookah. If people didn't see you for a couple of days, they would ask about you, look for you. Now nobody asks after anyone. In the old days if someone was ill, others would take them to hospital; they would go and buy milk for them. But, you see, there was less money then. Now everyone has money. People think, "Because I have money, I have no problems. I don't need others."'

One of the interesting things I encounter is that people assume that researchers are only interested in the 'old places'. Thus, in Chiragh Delhi, you are invariably directed to the dargah or pointed toward older havelis. It's almost as if they are indulging your need for 'romance'. Yet, while the past is a source of pride, it is the images of a remembered village community that are given greater value, particularly in contrast to a not wholly satisfactory present.

After I have been to a village a few times, people tell me—unasked—the whereabouts of the person I have met on a previous visit. I stand out as a stranger and the local grapevine makes everyone aware of whom I have been talking to. Since the houses are open to the street, it is all very *unprivate*. There is no need to twitch aside a lace curtain to monitor what is going on in the street—you are a full-time, interested observer with a grandstand view. Daily life within houses takes place in full view of the street. You can look inside and see families watching television, chopping vegetables, eating or even having their siestas. Children play in the lanes and the older boys, all well-gelled hair and baseball caps worn backwards, lounge against a motorbike. Men predominate in the social gatherings in the lanes, which are basically caste-based. On Sundays, the Jatavs will gather for an early morning cup of tea at a tea shop. The Jats sit in a small park towards their end of the village on Sunday evenings.

I don't know what I expected to find in Chiragh Delhi and other villages that would have vindicated my curiosity from behind those bus windows all those years ago. I suppose I was looking for another world and what I got was, as anywhere else in the metropolis, a people preoccupied mostly with the latest episode of *Kahani Ghar Ghar Ki*. But there is one aspect that sets these urban villages apart from the rest of Delhi. We say Delhi is a town of migrants. The inhabitants of urban villages are not migrants; their families have—some of them—lived in the same spot for 200 years. Yet their loyalty is not to Delhi, for which many express contempt. It is to their land and community.

# 8

## NEWEST DELHI

IF DELHI HAS A SINGLE, UNALLOYED CHARACTERISTIC, it is an unmatched ability to reinvent herself. Her thousand universes have something for everyone; all her inhabitants carry a virtual city inside their head. On this rocky bank of the Yamuna, cities have famously come and gone; they were not taken over and re-built. From the time of the tenth-century citadel of Prithviraj Chauhan, new conquerors have always started afresh. From the eleventh century, the thrust was south to north, culminating in the seventeenth century with Shahjahanabad. Thereafter, there has been a steady southward movement which continues till today. New Delhi was built at the foot of Raisina Hill and most post-Independence construction was largely on the agricultural land south of Lodi Road—pre-Independence New Delhi's southern limit. In the last two decades, huge new townships have come up on the southern and south-eastern boundaries—Gurgaon, for instance, and NOIDA, Mayur Vihar and Patparganj. Some older towns, such as Faridabad and Ghaziabad, their proximity to Delhi finally an advantage, are also being dusted down and re-packaged as part of Greater Delhi. The new township phenomenon is not confined to Delhi alone. M.N. Buch has observed that urban development in India tends to 'degenerate into acquisition and development of new land'.[1] Buch, a former vice-chairman of the DDA, noted that time and again existing areas were left largely alone: 'The trend is to acquire new land and develop new colonies.' So whether capitals of empires or new suburbs (variously called satellite towns or townships), the invariable solution to congestion, overburdened infrastructures or new aspirations is to start afresh.

Gurgaon is but the latest—and certainly the shiniest—of the newest Delhis. It may be territorially in the state of Haryana, but a postcode does not a place define. It is Delhi's creation, a response to Delhi's insatiable needs and aspirations, an ersatz Manhattan set in the middle of the Yamuna plain. Col (Retd) Prithvi Nath, senior advisor to the DLF group which developed swathes of the mini-city, observed in 2003: 'Cities don't grow by virtue of planners, but by where people move.'[2] Gurgaon is largely the baby of the DLF, a company that was established on 18 September 1946 by Chaudhury Raghuvendra Singh (1910-2000) of the Punjab provincial civil service. Singh was one of the earliest to realize that a colossal amount of accommodation would be needed to house Delhi's population after Independence. He set about acquiring large tracts of cheap agricultural land on the southern peripheries of New Delhi, and DLF constructed some twenty-five colonies, including South Extension, the two Greater Kailashes and Green Park.

Chaudhury Raghuvendra Singh's son-in-law, K.P. Singh, oversaw the company's next stage of expansion up to this century, though its operations were restricted by the DDA

Act of 1957 which allowed private developers to develop land only in schemes which the Authority itself initiated. According to J.K. Chandra, financial director of DLF, the group was the pioneering private developer in Gurgaon and its activities there date back over two decades. The group began to acquire land in Faridabad and Ghaziabad from the early '80s, and in Gurgaon from 1985, but, as Chandra recalled, the company reasoned that given Gurgaon's accessibility to Delhi and the availability of water and electricity substations, the latter was bound to be a sound investment.[3] Today DLF owns nearly 3,000 acres in Gurgaon, of which only some 500 remain undeveloped.

An apocryphal story tells of K.P Singh sitting on a charpoy and negotiating the sale of a small piece of land with a Gurgaon farmer. A jeep breaks down nearby and while its driver repairs it, the jeep's passenger, a young man, alights and starts chatting with K.P. Singh. 'Why don't you develop these acres?' he asks. Singh explains that the laws do not allow private developers to establish new areas. 'Laws can be changed,' was the reply and three years later, so goes the story, when the young man, Rajiv Gandhi, became the prime minister, the laws were.[4]

'We had vision,' says J.K. Chandra, and through the window of his office is framed a sea of phallic skyscrapers, their glass curtain exteriors glinting in the sun; just twenty years ago crops grew here in open fields and the occasional tubewell was the most noticeable built feature of the landscape. The real fillip to the development of Gurgaon came with the opening up of the economy when multinational companies sought to establish their presence in India. Looking for office space that was sufficiently extensive, many decided to build their corporate Indian headquarters in Gurgaon, as this would allow them to prescribe the type of building they were used to: not just in the functional aspect but one which expressed the corporate signature that their clients would recognize.

Dikshu Kukreja, of C.P. Kukreja Associates, the firm responsible for the design of Gurgaon's landmark Signature Towers, explained that multi-national corporations (MNCs) bring in 'specific work ethics' such as an international management culture, office environment and new facilities, all of which require specific types of spaces. These requirements needed a scale which would not have been feasible in Delhi's expensive—and cramped—Central Business District (the area around Connaught Place). With this decision, the international corporate identity, that glitters like a gold seam through Gurgaon's many attractions for the middle classes, was firmly fixed. The extravagant, futuristic design of these buildings set the tone for the 'idea' of Gurgaon that was to emerge.

The DLF Gateway Tower, for example, which has been likened variously to a cigarette lighter, a ship's hull, as well as images less polite, is possibly the most striking feature of the showy Gurgaon skyline. The relationship between the structure and its function may be puzzling, its suitability for an Indian landscape and climate is open to question, but it is impossible to ignore. The monumental structures of the commercial complex, the DLF Corporate Park, are more conventional, but look equally expensive, metropolitan and corporate.

'Elegant, extravagant, flashy, dazzling. The new corporate architecture is changing the way Indian surburbia looks' exclaimed a 2002 article in the *Indian Express*.[5] Significantly, though the article does not say so, this is the way Indian surburbia *wants* to look; it is a departure from the erstwhile separation of suburbia and downtown. This new Indian suburbia wants both the metropolitan sophistication of downtown and the ersatz country charms of suburbia, and Gurgaon's real achievement has been to invent it—a place where you can 'walk to work'—though, in fact, Gurgaon's residents are invariably car-borne.

Previously in Delhi, offices were of two types: either the badly maintained, paan-stained look of government bhawans, or the Central Business District's highrise blocks, many built in the '70s and showing their years with chipped and greying marble frontages, small, slow lifts and leaking air conditioning systems. What Gurgaon produced were buildings with 20,000 sq. ft on average of office space, lifts activated by sensors in the lobby and the Gurgaon corporate trademark—the atrium.

The atrium has come to be more than a space; it has become the granddaddy of all metropolitan icons, symbolizing—and actualizing in steel and glass—the global aspirations of the Indian middle classes. Somehow, this concept has so captured the Indian middle-class imagination that no commercial highrise is complete without it. Malls and offices that seek to be considered prestige buildings all have a soaring, airy, plant-filled, muzak-tinkling space. It is this decade's equivalent of the mezzanine, another Latin/Italian word that captivated architects in the '70s. The atrium has become so significant in the discourse of the metropolitan landscape that a DLF building in Gurgaon is called 'The Atria', its defining feature being the six-storey atrium.

The MNCs' need to recreate a familiar work environment to express their corporate identity has created an architectural style that is internationally recognizable. As Suneet Paul, editor of *Architecture + Design* explains, 'Normally, you would relate a building to a context or a region *but Gurgaon's buildings could be anywhere—Bangkok or New York*. Global companies have brought in the international look' [emphasis mine].'[6] Indian architects have happily adapted to this trend, abandoning decades of Modernism, Brutalism, Regionalism and Revivalism. Unlike their earlier clients who would settle for pigeonhole offices, mean lobbies and compromised safety standards, corporates were not parsimonious, and were willing to pay for high-grade materials, international safety standards and ample working/parking space, leading Paul to observe that Indian architects had to change their mindsets too, habituated as they had been for decades to paring down costs for clients.

The architect whose visions have come closest to symbolize Gurgaon's metropolitan dream is Mumbai-based Hafeez Contractor, who is responsible not only for DLF's Gateway Tower, but also the Plaza Tower, the Corporate Park and DLF Square—as well as several residential complexes, such as the grand Casa Royale. Contractor has been described as a follower of Le Corbusier, though his buildings are far from the austere monumentality the public associates with the architect of Chandigarh. Contractor's structures are more dramatic, more decorative, but not quite as foreign to today's India as Le Corbusier's were when they were first built. The inescapable conclusion is that the 'foreign' is no longer foreign, a consequence perhaps of globalization, dissemination by media and travel. Contractor's designs have a visual accessibility and appeal. His architecture speaks of modernity, of affluence, of the accessibility of the world to a class which seeks to embrace these ideas and reacts adversely to what they regard as the socialist drabness of the architecture of the first four decades of Independent India.

Suneet Paul concedes that that some of the early

buildings in Gurgaon were 'direct design lifts from abroad', but maintains that subsequent structures were original. However, the point is *not* originality; rather, the fact they were copies of buildings abroad was the crux of their appeal. It is the idea or the vision that is, ultimately, the object of the exercise. Millennium Plaza, Global Business Park, Signature Towers, Plaza Tower, all—even by their names—convey the notion of being international, very contemporary and rich.

Hafeez Contractor has been quoted as saying: 'Nobody gives you the freedom to be creative,' adding it is for the architect to demonstrate to the client that better design means more productivity in the workplace. His clients in Gurgaon are certainly the high end of the blue-chip investment spectrum. They include Coke, Pepsico, GE, Hindustan Lever, Rolls-Royce, Standard Chartered, Citibank and Gillette and are, according to a *Business Today* report, estimated to bring in over Rs 50,000 crore annually to DLF in rentals (DLF does not sell land; it leases it). Gurgaon comes under the jurisdiction of the Haryana Urban Development Authority (HUDA), a public sector undertaking with which some twenty private developers are in partnership to develop the area. HUDA itself has developed 10,000 acres; about half of the remaining 6,350 acres is being developed by DLF and the rest by other private developers, the two largest being Ansals and Unitech.[7]

Developers are not only in the business of creating state-of-the-art office space; they are also engaged in Gurgaon's residential sector. This has experienced a boom in the last fifteen years, due substantially to the successful establishment of Gurgaon's corporate image. The presence of international brand names has elevated Gurgaon from an outlying suburb where affordable housing is available, to a desirable upmarket address. The population of Gurgaon, 1.35 lakh in 1991, rose to 9 lakh in the space of a decade.

While brand-consciousness has played a part, the popularity of satellite suburbs like Gurgaon and NOIDA is also, of course, a function of the spiralling price of land and rents in Delhi. Added to this is the growth of the middle class and the rapidly increasing number of middle-class migrants drawn to Delhi for professional reasons, compounded by the economic decline of many provincial towns. Yet, while Gurgaon residents wax eloquent about the pleasing absence of congestion and pollution, the landscaped green expanses and the uninterrupted supply of electricity and water, the fact is that south Delhi is still the preferred social address: DLF's owner, K.P. Singh, for instance, does not live in Gurgaon but in the heart of New Delhi in Aurangzeb Road. As Pavan Varma, author of *The Great Indian Middle Class* says, the quality of life is excellent in the private residential and affluent pockets of Delhi. 'Lutyens's Delhi,' he says succinctly, 'was built for people who rule'.[8]

The social profile of Gurgaon's residents throws light on developments in Delhi as well as the aspirations of the individual residents themselves. DLF's J.K. Chandra observes, 'Gurgaon is the choice of Delhi residents who cannot afford to buy a flat in south Delhi; so even if Pitampura (in west Delhi) is affordable, they still prefer to buy in Gurgaon as it is seen as being closer to their desired lifestyle.' Other buyers include families who sold their property in Delhi, bought a house or flat in Gurgaon and invested the remaining sum so they could have an income; still others sold property in Delhi, so as to be able to provide each of their two or three children a flat. Gurgaon, Chandra adds, is also popular with non-resident Indians (NRIs), or Indians living in other cities who want a good investment but do not want to live on the property—or not immediately. Another category—a significantly large one—is that of young professionals who are employed in the many Gurgaon-based MNCs and who are able to get loans to buy a good property. Many young professionals working in Delhi rent places in Gurgaon because they cannot afford a comparative quality of life in Delhi.

'When we first went exploring in Gurgaon it seemed much less crowded and polluted; it seemed better planned, unlike Mayur Vihar and Patparganj which seem to be bursting at the seams. The houses were also more tasteful, better built and fitted out very well,' recalls Sheema Mookherjee, cookbook writer and editor, who moved to Gurgaon from Mayur Vihar three years ago. She and her husband, both in their early forties, with two school-going children, were attracted by Gurgaon's sense of order. This image of a planned city, clean and tasteful, is reiterated in the advertisements for residential developments in Gurgaon, each invariably with a fanciful European name. All the Hamilton Courts, Beverly Parks, Regency Parks, Windsor Courts, Richmond Parks, and so on, promise the expected set of well-constructed flats or houses, reliable services and tidy, landscaped surroundings. One ad even promoted the charms of its housing scheme in a rhyming jingle: 'Amenities to Relish! A House to Cherish!'

What is significant is the frequency with which the terms 'lifestyle' and 'quality of life' are encountered, both in advertisements and as used by Gurgaon inhabitants seeking to justify their choice of residence. Both 'lifestyle' and 'quality of life' have quite specific connotations when used in this context and it is useful to deconstruct them in order to identify their individual components. Take the list that accompanies most housing scheme promotions. The ten that appear most frequently are: accessibility to Delhi; hundred per cent electricity backup; twenty-four-hour water supply; parking; lifts; round-the-clock security systems; nearness to schools and/or hospitals; a swimming pool; an adjacent golf course; a club; parks 'or 'open areas' and landscaped surroundings. Promises of a centralized supply of cooking gas, the availability of halls for special functions, gyms, post offices as well as easy financing options, also appear regularly. Interiors, too, are marketed to project a particular lifestyle. An advertisement for a residential complex aimed at 'top notch professionals' describes the wooden flooring, granite features and cutting-edge modular kitchens inside, while the exterior promises lily ponds, gentle rolling lawns and palms of many varieties, all of which together would result in a 'resort-like ambience'.

The interesting point is that apart from the basic provisions of water, power, security and clean air, the other attractions seek to accessorize elements of an idealized upper middle-class life—the club, the golf course, the green and pleasant landscape. What is on offer here is not simply accommodation at more reasonable rates than Delhi, with a couple of apparently free frills thrown in to make the offer more attractive. This is a whole pre-packaged lifestyle, and the components are recognized as such by promoters and buyers alike. These features are found in upmarket south Delhi colonies, but also include elements of American suburbia ('green', 'open', 'golf') and the order and neatness of a cantonment.

The middle classes today have well-defined expectations of what a suitable lifestyle should involve—and of what it should not. Fashion designer Suneet Verma has been quoted as saying of Delhi, 'There is so much unauthorized construction that you might spend your life's earnings building a house and then have a meat shop or a barber's shop coming up right next door. Though south of Delhi was very prestigious when I was a child, *today I equate it with Karol Bagh'* (emphasis mine).[9] This is a widely held view and one which has a clear idea of the elements that constitute a good locality. What it is not is a mess of paanwallahs, shops with goods spilling out on the pavement, dhabas extending onto the road with the detritus of potato peelings, eggshells and cigarette packs rotting between the paving stones—in other words, the elements that make up any typical Indian city.

But the absence of these elements has attendant inconveniences. Without a neighbourhood *kirana* store, or fruit and vegetable vendors, Gurgaon's residents have to drive to the market or get groceries home-delivered. A resident tells me, 'All our shopping (for groceries) has to be done with a trolley at the supermarket which is full of imported foodstuff—things like cheeses, cartons of juice, cold storage products, dog food and so on. It's expensive.'

Implicit in all this is, first, the absence of the poor, and second, the ownership of a car. Because of its newness, Gurgaon has managed to maintain the demarcation of its spaces; it manages the quite unusual combination (and segregation) of the residential and the commercial office and retail space in a comparatively small area, but it manages this because it is a suburb of Delhi, and Delhi is where all the real mechanisms of urban living exist—the municipal offices, bus terminals, the wholesale markets, the *jhuggi jhonpris* and other elements considered eyesores by many residents.

Gurgaon's population is largely middle-class with a mix of old and young: some are retired, others are middle level and senior professional, and a large group comprises young professionals and their families. Most of the last group falls in the broad MNC category—out of which an estimated 70 per cent are employed in the IT/BPO sectors. Gurgaon's many call centres make for a fairly high proportion of young, single people. There is a mix of provinces—a fairly representative all-India sample—but there are few concentrations of regional affiliations. Relations between neighbours are cordial since so many have so much in common—professionally and aspirationally. In this sense, Gurgaon has the characteristics of modern urbanization, as more social relationships are dependent on a commonality of interests—be it children's ages, work-related friendships or sheer proximity in the neighbourhood—rather than the older forms of association such as regional origins, kinship or language. Festivals, as, for instance, Holi and Diwali, are often organized by the building or residential complex; there are fewer extended families, so get-togethers are more frequently not family-centric. Durga Puja, while celebrated by Bengali associations in the area, has many non-Bengalis participating as well—this is, in fact, common to all of Delhi, where the puja has evolved to play a secular, carnival role.

Domestic services in Gurgaon are provided largely by migrants from eastern India. Maids tend to be Bengali—many directly from Malda, but local belief is that a large number are from Bangladesh; *mistris* (plumbers and carpenters) are from Orissa; security guards and drivers are from Bihar. Local Haryanvi entrepreneurs, spotting the potential profit of the situation, have built barrack-like tenements known as *pukka jhuggis* to house them. This brings in a good rental income and replaces the slum landscape that so many of the middle class have come to Gurgaon to avoid. Gurgaon's planners had sought to obviate this situation by providing servant quarters in the residential complexes, but the demand for labour—car cleaners, stall holders, *malis* etc.—outstrips how many can be accommodated and this exemplifies the middle-class conundrum: a beautiful, well-maintained cityscape needs abundant services and the providers of those services have to be accommodated somewhere; in the absence of affordable housing, this leads to the shanties and encroachments they (the middle classes) abhor. Gurgaon's ability to permanently hold off major slum areas is, therefore, uncertain.

Within Gurgaon—as anywhere else—there is a hierarchy of addresses: dwellings in multinational sponsored estates have rentals in excess of those in less prestigious complexes but a commonality of aspiration binds all of them. Gurgaon's newness gives it a sense of potential upward mobility, of the possibility of 'making good' in the near future; this also expresses itself in terms of an easy consumerism—not saving for a rainy day, like many of the younger residents' parents probably did. The economic slowdown has sapped the energy of Gurgaon and many new condominiums stand empty, waiting for a new surge of professionals who are not coming in right now because the once    less supply of new jobs has abated. But there are still many with salaries of one lakh and more, paying rents of about Rs 10,000, who still converge with their families to the malls and bowling alleys and coffee shops every weekend to spend what many other Delhi residents would earn in a month.

Gurgaon's spectacular malls showcase the leisure pursuits of its residents, their disposable incomes and their inclinations. This new Indian middle and upper classes' power stems from their possession of high-level professional and technical skills and the high incomes that these bring in. Their identities are broadly Indian, but their desires are global. Historian Sunil Khilnani analysing IT professionals in Bangalore, writes: 'The horizons of this class are certainly not constrained by the territorial frame of the nation state. They are quite prepared to forsake the shopping malls of Bangalore . . . for the real thing in Singapore (or whatever) should the opportunity arise . . . This new class too has a secessionist understanding of the idea of India.'[10]

Yet while Gurgaon has thus far managed to avoid many of the pitfalls of Indian urbanism, it is, nonetheless, incubating a whole host of them. For instance, the number of deep borewells—a new one is dug for every building under construction—has led to water shortages in buildings constructed earlier, whose borewells are shallower. Also, some five multiplexes (a total of twenty-one screens) are coming up on the Gurgaon-Mehrauli Road, which will inevitably lead to mammoth traffic jams once they are all functioning. Moreover, as S.K. Das, adviser to Delhi's Urban Arts Commission (DUAC), and a Gurgaon resident, has observed, the huge generators attached to nearly every building will eventually lead to massive pollution. In fact, many of the developments that make Gurgaon so desirable— the swimming pools, the gyms, the golf course which is lit up all night—are huge power-guzzlers.[11]

Today, most Gurgaon residents speak positively of the 'quality of life' in the suburb. This elusive idea also encompasses the non-tangible elements of Gurgaon: it is a satisfaction with the 'brand image' of the place wherein the presence of a large number of multinational offices has been cannily employed by promoters to project an artificial 'internationality' to the residential spaces—the condominiums, penthouses and villas, and the Beverly, Richmond, Windsor and all the other Parks, Courts and Plazas—they have constructed. Gurgaon's present is pleasant. The power and water situation is artificially managed and more or less independent of Haryana's state infrastructure.

Residential complexes have their own captive power plants which switch on seamlessly when the power is cut—which is not infrequently—and the arrangement is that flat or house-owners pay the electricity bill directly to the building or residential complex management and not to Haryana State Electricity Corporation. Each residential complex has its own deep tubewell, so the water supply is uninterrupted. But all this is predicated on a low population density, which, given the iron laws of Indian urbanism, will inexorably rise. Moreover, the two-car family norm (often including at least one high fuel consumption SUV), along with the frequent use of generators will lead to high levels of pollution. Over time and use the water levels will fall to dangerously low depths. These are not doomsday scenarios—they are the well established track record of older Delhi suburbs, older Delhis too, come to that. It is not difficult to see, shimmering in the not too distant future, in a not too distant part of Haryana, a New Gurgaon, which will rise with an even more dramatic skyline, and which will come packaged with new seductive visions of modernity and the same promises of a 'better quality of life'.

Gurgaon is but the latest Newer Delhi. NOIDA, Mayur Vihar and Patparganj are part of the same stratum, though about a decade or two older, as are Rohini and Dwarka. Conceptually, however, these settlements go back much earlier. By 1970, the ministry of urban development had converted pending land housing schemes into group housing schemes. While Rohini and Dwarka were schemes envisaged within the boundaries of the capital, NOIDA, Mayur Vihar and Patparganj made the emotional leap trans-Jamuna.

Before these colonies developed, 'across the river' for most Delhi residents had the feel of another country; it was certainly another state, and one of the downsides of the area was middle-class apprehension about the perceived lawlessness of Uttar Pradesh.

NOIDA had come up during the Emergency as a location for small industrial units. Over time, and given its proximity to south Delhi, it became a residential development, with today some 165 sectors of houses and flats with a population of over six lakh. Sectors 14A and 15A, because they are closest to Delhi and because of their high proportion of former senior government officials, are seen as prestigious locations. A multiplex and a cultural centre, Kala Dham, will enhance NOIDA's appeal. 'Every township needs a place which serves as a nerve centre,' says Rajiv Rautela, secretary, NOIDA Development Authority.[12] This will be the City Centre, which will have, apart from office and retail space, restaurants, hotels and (unspecified) 'socio-cultural activities'. The new six-lane highway has reduced the journey time to Delhi and has also increased the attractions of Greater NOIDA, which was slower to develop, even though the presence of several adjacent defence housing cooperatives was, according to property trend-watchers, working to its advantage. The widely held belief is the Forces, presumably because of their combat training and discipline, improve the services and the social tone of an area.

Greater NOIDA now has many new private housing developments under construction, with the standard Europeanized nomenclature—Vistas, Greens, Rivieras and even an El Deco—all promising 'elite' lifestyles. The projected population of NOIDA in 2021 is 12 lakh, nearly double what it is now. While many residents would agree—though perhaps with some qualification—that the quality of life was satisfactory, the residents of Mayur Vihar and Patparganj are considerably less enthusiastic about their own suburbs.

Mayur Vihar and Patparganj were the sites of the first mass middle-class trek across the river and large numbers of cooperative group housing societies were allotted land there. Among the societies were a group of publishers and academics, many of whom still live in Oxford Apartments, which came up in 1984 in Patparganj, though many original flat-owners have since sold their properties. The occupants are proud of its 'socialist' design: peons and other service personnel were also members of the cooperative and the cooperative put its architecture where its ideology was, and flats belonging to all income groups are distributed evenly through the blocks. It is also, therefore, one of the few complexes in the locality without a captive generator as not all the occupants can afford to contribute to its costs. 'On the other hand,' says one die-hard, liberal occupant, 'kids who go to (public schools like) Delhi Public School or Sardar Patel Vidyalaya play at home with those who go to the local *sarkari* school'. But, she added, the surrounding area was less satisfactory: 'The planning is moronic. In all of Patpargunj there is no space for a single cinema or restaurant or art gallery. There is no bookshop, nobody would be able to open one in the kind of space they'd get here. It's baffling because just next door in Mayur Vihar, the streets are wider and greener, there are parks in every block and there is space left for things other than just shelter.' Yet the residents of Mayur Vihar are no happier. 'It's groaning under the weight of its population,' says a former resident who chose to move to Gurgaon. Mayur Vihar, she feels, was ruined by its unbridled and haphazard growth.

Residents of both localities, however, aver that there is a sense of neighbourliness, perhaps because so many people who moved there were from roughly the same social background and were already acquainted when they formed housing societies. 'I enjoy knowing I have so many friends within walking distance. You can just wander across in your crumpled T-shirt for a coffee. I've lived in Gulmohar Park, Haus Khas and Defence Colony—and life in those places was ruthlessly anonymous,' says Anuradha Roy, a publisher and Patparganj resident. There is also a feeling of security: children can still play outside till late and women walk alone in the parks at least till there is daylight. The minuses are Patparganj's 'staggering ugliness', as one resident puts it. 'Perhaps,' he adds, 'because PPG is a middle-class rather than an affluent area, the differences between the folks in the shanty town and us are not as painfully obvious as in the fantasy flats of DLF'.

The Rohini and Dwarka areas are two other huge conglomerations of cooperative group housing societies that were launched in 1980. Rohini is billed (and it is difficult to assess such claims) as the 'Biggest Residential Suburb in Asia'. According to Subhas Sharma, former vice-chairman, DDA, it was planned to accommodate a staggering 1,70,000 households over three phases, but relentless pressure has led to the extension of the scheme into two more phases and another 1,58,000 residents, their homes sprawling over 3,847 hectares divided into twenty-five sectors.[13] Rohini's residents expect that the social profile and, with it, the price of land in the area, will benefit from the Metro; earlier, the CEO of Indiaproperties had observed, 'Rohini's biggest drawback is that it falls into the middle-class tag trap'.[14] This 'tag' apparently impacts adversely on real estate prices.

Unsurprisingly, a multiplex-cum-shopping centre called M2K is expected to raise the tone of the area. The developers, Unitech, are planning an amusement park as well, and a twin city centre is in the works. If Rohini is large, Dwarka is the area with the highest number of group housing societies. Yet within this area are reflections of Delhi's many worlds. Take the example of a young Tamil IT professional who came to Delhi a decade ago. He bought a flat in a Dwarka cooperative because he realized it was a sound investment and more practical than wasting money on rent. He alerted various friends and friends of friends from his community and today there is a whole group of them living in the same block. The block is *their* social space: their social interactions are largely with each other; the wives are friends, the children play together. They have made themselves a home in the diverse universe of Delhi; they will probably, most of them, not return to Tamil Nadu—though they are reluctant to actually admit it to others, possibly even to themselves.

There is recognition, especially in the newer Delhis, that residential areas need well-established associations to ensure the civic and social equilibrium necessary for healthy property values. The Federation of Cooperative Group Housing Societies Dwarka Ltd. (FCGHSDL) is one of nine set up by the Delhi government to represent the problems of each area scheme 'to promote neighbourliness, contain disputes, organize celebrations during festivals and maintain a strong managing body,' Other such federations operate in Mayur Vihar, Vikaspuri and Paschim Vihar. The rates of success differ but the initiative is an indication that there is a general consensus on the qualities that make for a desirable middle-class residential area.

Finally, another newer Delhi, but one confined to a very few, are the 'farmhouses' found in the Sainik Farms area, Chattarpur, Sultanpur and Mahipalpur. Bought by the rich in areas designated as 'agricultural', the size of the houses constructed on such land were initially set limits in the 1962 Masterplan, but, by 1981, the permitted size had been increased tenfold. All farmhouses cross these limits and are in a strict sense illegal. Sainik Farms alone has 5,000 such structures[15], but their owners' influence has halted any serious drives against them. Many (an estimated 30 per cent) of the houses were rented out as wedding venues at vast profit until such functions were halted by the MCD in January 2002 on the grounds that they were causing traffic chaos. A sanitized rural existence is part of the farmhouse credo, but they are completely urban with landscaped gardens (this is when landscape gardeners came into existence in Delhi), tasteful interiors in a mix of southern Californian and upmarket ethnic chic where a string *khattia* is as much a part of the garden décor as the Japanese rock garden. Said to be free of pollution, these are great favourites among diplomats and much of the 21st Milestone area and Mehrauli shopping complex service this segment. Farmhouses have their own captive electricity, their own tubewells and state-of-the-art security systems. They exist like fortresses, completely self-sufficient and formidably defended, ready to withstand any siege.

Newer Delhis are continually evolving out of the mother city. Chronologically, territorially, this metropolis cannot stay still—it mutates, amoeba-like. It recreates itself, but in the process also reinvents certain elements. Currently, Gurgaon is the closest approximation to the middle classes' idea of a city, yet chronic problems of congestion, water scarcity and encroachment lurk in the shadows. Syed Shafi, formerly of the Delhi School of Planning and Architecture, has observed that urbanization is keyed to a small number of large metropolitan cities. These cities suck smaller ones into their vortex, denuding older small towns and cities in

the process. In Europe and America urbanization was a
result of industrialization; in India it occurs because of the
disintegration of other activities, such as changes in
agricultural practices.[16] Economic progress witnessed in large
cities is not matched in the countryside, where
impoverishment and declining social indicators lead to an
inexorable ingress of rural migrants into cities in search of
the livelihood they cannot sustain in their village. Thus the
'city beautiful' and 'garden city' ideals that middle-class city
dwellers want so dearly that they are prepared to move to
ever newer urban areas to achieve, cannot be maintained
indefinitely. Water tables will recede from ever deepening
tubewells; mammoth generators will spew pollution and
destroy the expensive green, clean environment. The malls
and multiplexes that define metropolitan pursuits will cause
congestion and more pollution. The metropolitan middle
classes will continue to create greener pastures and build
themselves nice, spanking new enclaves, but these, too, will
be challenged. Newer Delhi is a continuing process. There
will be more.

# 9

## DELHI'S CULTURE

THE BAHADUR FAMILY'S IDEA OF A HAPPY, RELAXING way of spending a winter Sunday a few decades ago was to go on a large, elaborate picnic. Shehzade Bahadur remembers that preparations began two or three days beforehand, with generous amounts of *kachoris* and *mattris* prepared by the family's retainers under the close supervision of family matriarchs. On the day itself, the women of the household would rise even earlier than usual to ensure the complex arrangements needed to organize three al fresco meals for a gathering of fifty were in place. In the 1940s, cars were a middle-class rarity, so two or three extended families along with their servants would pack into several *tongas* and bounce their way from the Chelpuri mohalla of the old city to either Okhla, then a rural expanse, or to Mehrauli, still green and open, and, in those days, without the Ambawatta complex, farmhouses and the spreading retail outlets of the Mehrauli-Gurgaon Road.

Once the picnic spot was reached, the men would settle

down on *durrees* with bolsters or on folding chairs and the women would supervise the unpacking. If the picnic was at Okhla, the more sporty of the male element would fish in the lake, while the others listened to the wind-up gramophone playing old Sehgal 78 rpms. The younger women would look after the children and surpervise the servants who were peeling potatoes, frying purees and making tea. Kebabs were taken along for the men—the women were, by and large, vegetarian. 'Local villagers would watch us in amazement,' recalls Shehzade.

Today the whole exercise seems about as relaxing as a military operation, but that was leisure Delhi-style in the '40s and '50s. Shehzade Bahadur has a photograph taken on one such occasion—a picnic to the Qutb Minar. Some fifty members of her family are lined up in rows outside the Alai Darwaza, the men solemn in three-piece suits, the women in pastel voile sarees which had been bought in bulk by the family *munshi* and distributed among the *bahus*. The children sat crosslegged in front, the girls in frilly frocks, the boys in sailor suits.

Leisure pursuits in Delhi have changed considerably since then. Before 1947, and until perhaps the mid-'60s, leisure was family-centric, tied to festivals, weddings and seasons. That era has, like so many recollections of times past, a golden glow, a fragile, vulnerable innocence. But of course it was every bit as complex, contentious and frustrating as the present. In that sunlit photograph, the wide-eyed little girls had few choices about their own futures; today their daughters are IT specialists, biochemists and architects.

Delhi before Independence was dominated by the culture of Shahjahanabad. This was not peculiar to the Muslims alone; it was widely accepted by all communities in Delhi as the epitome of all courtly graces, the hallmark of a civilized and cultivated lifestyle. This culture continues to grip the imagination of older Delhi residents and the tone is always one of tender melancholy, a wistful anguish. Khushwant Singh recalls it vividly. 'The whole area behind Jama Masjid up to Ajmeri Gate was where courtesans, dancers and singers lived. Hijras were found in Lal Kuan. Young men of the upper classes were called *nawvas*; they dressed like fops in little cloth caps and *chikkan* kurtas; they learned manners from certain families of courtesans. It was a cultural life of *mushairas* and *mujras* in the evening.'[1] The same wistful note informs the Indian Civil Service officer, Asok Mitra's memories when he mourns the old city: 'The old enchanting paved courts with the deep stairwells of light, the chiaroscuro of Chowry Bazar, the filtered twilight on the lotus ponds of third-floor apartments on G.B. Road . . .'[2]

Nostalgia was the hallmark of this culture; an elegy for a way of life, an order, which was flattened after 1857. It was a lingering twilight when all that was left to a dispossessed nobility were the courtesies, or *tehzeeb*—in other words, the traditions and graces of a once magnificent world. It took the form of a lament not for lost riches, but for lost refinements. It was not their affluence they mourned (or so went the mythology), but the sophisticated graces it had afforded. In its absence, all that was left was dignity and a continued faithfulness to the old ways and practices of the lost world. This ethos has seeped so comprehensively into Delhi's ancestral memory, that it has become a reflexive part of the world view of certain sections of the middle class. It was from this emotional space that the old chestnut, 'vulgar display of wealth', was unleashed about upwardly mobile Punjabis. The implication is that it is not the wealth, but its 'in-your-face' display that is offensive. The Punjabi refugees' attitude to adversity was different: they collectively rejected dwelling on what they had lost; instead, they resolutely focused on the present and, by implication, the future. In doing so they effectively challenged the prevailing notion that nostalgia equalled status.

Shahjahanabad's culture had such a seductive impact on those who encountered it that in the late seventeenth and early eighteenth centuries the British adopted many of the old Mughal nobility's ways. Men like David Ochterlony, Delhi's first British Resident, dressed in kurta-pyjama, married Indian women and his evening excursions on elephantback, accompanied by his many wives, similarly mounted, is one of the favourite anecdotes of Raj mythology. Once British society was well established, that is, when there were sufficient numbers for the British to socialize among themselves and, moreover, distance themselves from Indians to establish their credentials as a ruling class, such practices largely ceased. By the early decades of the twentieth century, upwardly mobile middle classes in Delhi began to adopt anglicized modes of behaviour to indicate their modernity and progress and to identify more closely with the ruling establishment. Even so, the attitudes to wealth remained unchanged. It was part of the self-image of Delhi's vertically rising classes to reiterate their long traditions of literacy, culture and generations-old membership of elite strata.

Delhi's Kayasth community was part of the ruling establishment since the Mughal era. Raja Raghunath Das, for instance, was vazir to the emperors Shah Jahan and Aurangzeb in the seventeenth century and lived in a haveli in Shahjahanabad's Chelpuri mohallah. The Mathurs were an eminent Delhi Kayasth family with many branches. Sheila Dhar, born into the Mathur Kayasth community, once recalled dispassionately, 'They were always on the side of the powers that be.' In fact, many Mathur families had long associations with old, established Muslim families. 'They prized the culture of courtly values,' she said, recalling the world she grew up in. 'There were then six or seven leading "cultural" families in Delhi. The Shri Rams were one and the Pandits (owners of the Connaught Place shop, Pandit Brothers) were another. Lala Shri Ram used to hold *mushairas,* and this was *the* mark of the cultured Dilliwallah: the ability to feel at home in Urdu culture.' Kumkum Lal, a long-time Delhi resident, came from one such family. 'Delhi was thought of as the centre of civilization—it was *Ghalib ka sheher* (Ghalib's own city),' she explained. 'Delhi Mathurs always considered themselves better than UP Mathurs for their *tehzeeb* (refinement).'[3]

But, despite the embracing of Urdu culture, there was a formality to the Hindu-Muslim relationship in pre-Independence Delhi. 'My grandfather was a lawyer and he had many Muslim clients,' Sheila Dhar recalled. 'They sent sweets at Id and some of them would visit us then as well.' Sometimes genuine friendships existed between Hindu and Muslim men, which would be acknowledged by a visit between the wives. 'Once, when Begum Jameluddin came to visit us, great *intezam* (arrangements) were made on the verandah and my mother wore her best voile saree. The begum arrived in a buggy and was an exuberant character, laughing, wiping *paan* from her mouth as she did so. I thought she was wonderful. I sat and listened as she and my mother made conversation. The Urdu language was part of our lives—my grandmother did all her accounts in Urdu.'

The fact that the Begum did not enter the house proper, was a physical indication of the carefully maintained social distance—even if full of cordiality—between the two communities. Relations between the British and the Indian middle classes, on the other hand, were formal and a little distant. Sheila Dhar remembered, 'The British were not particularly eager to have any social contact with Indians, but Indians—let us be frank—wished for friendlier relations with the governing class. Many families regarded such contact with the English as the highest good fortune. Once, when an English lady was to visit my grandmother, such was the anxiety and excitement at home, that my grandfather actually hired a governess to teach her to say "mention not" properly.'

Shehzade Bahadur's family, another prominent Delhi Kayasth clan, lived in a haveli, the corner plot of the galli. It was a maze of rooms divided notionally among different nuclear families, and it was normal to go through the rooms of another family to get from one of your own rooms to another. The family consisted of Shehzade's grandparents, her father, his two brothers and their families. By the '40s, the custom of an extended family eating together had lapsed. 'It was just more convenient for only the immediate family to sit down to a meal at the same time,' recalls Shehzade. 'Otherwise, the men would eat first, then the children, and then (finally) the women. It took just too long.'

During summers, everyone would sleep out on charpoys on the terrace which had been liberally sprinkled with water. In the evenings, the municipal lighting man would come with his *siri* (ladder) and light each gas lamp. The streets were swept and watered by two *jamadars* (cleaners). In Shehzade's memory, the streets were always clean, and middle-class virtues were respected and upheld. 'Everyone was everyone's daughter, *chacha*, or *taiji*. Today, it's all "uncles" and "aunties".'

Shehzade Bahadur and her cousin, Rajeshwari, both

grew up in Nai Sarak, and were the first generation of Kayasth girls to be sent to school and then college. Shehzade went to Indraprastha school in the Jama Masjid area, and remembers that every area had its ayah who accompanied the children in the school bus. The ayahs were always called Mary because they were from the Christian community and—according to the Hindu stereotyping of the time— Christian women were called Mary. 'She would stand outside each house and bellow "School *chalo*" and we would rush out in our uniform frocks (we wore sarees after class nine), clutching our tiffin carriers of *alu parathas*. At my school, Mary also did a side business in *chaat* and *dal moth* during break. All Marys made wonderful *chaat*.' School was in a big haveli and for energetic games like *kho kho* the girls were taken to a park in Daryaganj called 'purdah garden' where no men were allowed. For prayers, Indraprastha being an Indian school, the pupils sang *'He Ishwar hum sab apke putriya'* at assembly. At Queen Mary's Convent, however, where the more anglicized families sent their daughters, hymns such as 'All things bright and beautiful' were rendered to the accompaniment of a wind-up gramophone. But anglicized or not, the convent fully subscribed to certain traditional values. If, for example, some men came to move the school piano, the nuns would say, 'Purdah, girls', and the girls would have to hide between two screens made of sheets held up by the ayahs.

Culture, in the sense of desired social accomplishments, was an important part of the Kayasth identity. All unmarried girls then had a music master, Sheila Dhar remembered. 'As soon as they began to sing *bhajans*, you could not only tell how long they had been learning, but even which part of the old city they came from.' Girls from 'good families' were expected to know how to supervise cooks although 'a hands-on knowledge of cooking was considered infra dig'. More importantly, they (the brides-to-be) were expected to know how to conduct themselves in society. The ability to conduct oneself with grace at dinner parties, knowledge of spoken English and general, social poise were seen as qualifications by prospective mothers-in-law. Mastery of 'keelub (club) dancing' was deemed an added qualification among the more Westernized layer. Added the irrepressible Sheila Dhar, 'Of course, it was made clear that the girl would only dance with her husband.'

Knowing how to pour a drink was also a qualification for Kayasth brides, who were expected to serve their male in-laws. The only time that the women themselves were allowed to drink was at Holi, when, so went the fiction, they were 'forced' by their husbands or *dewars* (brothers-in-law) to do so. Yet, social codes were strict and young women were allowed comparatively little freedom. Girls and boys saw little of each other. Romance, if it occurred, was what Sheila Dhar called, the *'ankhon ankhon mein* (languishing glances)' variety with, perhaps, some discreet hand-holding. At its most serious, the couple would write poems to each other. Usually, nothing came of it. Most marriages were arranged.

The inventive Kayasth community had evolved novel ways to view prospective brides which combined decorum with practicality. During the Ramlila festivities, since the procession wound its way right around the old city, families would stand out on their balconies to watch it. This provided the perfect opportunity for mothers of prospective grooms to examine a particular balcony with close attention. There, the daughter of the house stood demurely between her parents, dressed in a pretty saree with flowers in her hair, apparently engrossed in the colourful procession below. In

this sophisticated fashion, what was effectively the
elimination round (height, complexion, bearing) took place
with the dignity of all parties more or less intact.

The evolution of post-Independence middle-class Delhi
owed a great deal to the customs and values espoused by
the Kayasth community. It was as if a template had been
established defining the codes which governed the acceptable
degree of freedom for women, the centrality of the family as
the unit for social life, the importance of education and a
near courtly civility which emphasized politeness rather
than visible wealth as the sign of class. Today's Delhi has
changed a great deal, but the outlines of that way of life still
hold sway in some parts of Delhi.

Sultana Qureishi grew up in a large house in Delhi's
Sadar Bazar where several generations lived together.[4] Her
father's business interests extended as far as Bombay and
Peshawar, and Sultana Begum remembers that as many as
300 servants lived with the family at one time. Even when
times grew frugal, there were at least ten or fifteen. In 1947
her father moved to Karachi, expecting his family to join
him fairly soon after, but his mother wrote to him, '*Mei
watan me rehna chahati* (I want to live in my own country)',
so he came back to Delhi. It was an ordered life. On the
morning of Id, the whole family, including the women and
girls, went to the mosque. Sweets were sent to relatives and
to friends—both Hindu and Muslim. Most sweets were
brought from the old city's famous Ghantewala sweetshop
(so called because, legend has it, the emperor Aurangzeb's
elephant was so addicted to sweetmeats, that it stood in
front of the shop shaking the bell tied to its neck till the
owner sent out a plateful of *laddus*), though the *seviyan kheer*
would be prepared at home.

School was at the nearby St Anthony's near Sheila

Cinema and after school, Sultana and her sisters were sent to a woman who lived nearby for instruction in the Koran. Her brothers learnt from the maulvi at the mosque. Sultana Begum's family had many Hindu friends. A Sikh, who had been her father's business partner in Peshawar, lived with them for many years as he had lost everything during Partition. The friendship has survived into the third generation. Today, the house, like most buildings in Sadar, is commercial property.

Still living in Sadar Bazar is Professor Azhar, on the faculty of Jawaharlal Nehru University's Persian studies department. He lives with his family in a small part of the old house, but he is among the last of the old families to remain there. Professor Azhar is proud of the Sadar house. 'People don't really want to leave despite the pollution and the congestion,' he avers. He grew up here, in this largely Hindu locality, where all children played together. 'I've never felt scared living here,' he says. 'Muslims have always been a minority, after all, even when the Mughals ruled Delhi.'[5] He observes that in old Delhi the communities were well knit, though by and large they occupied different spaces—Ballimaran, for instance, was a Muslim locality, while Katra Neel was almost entirely Hindu. Professor Azhar's family has lived in Delhi since the 1700s. His is a solidly Delhi ancestry; his great-great-grandfather was tutor to Bahadur Shah Zafar's sons, the doomed princes who were slaughtered by Colonel Hodgson in 1857. The family lived first in the old city and then, sometime in the 1880s, shifted to Sadar. In an effort to decongest the old city, the authorities offered land at the rate of one anna per square yard in Sadar, Mallkaganj and Sabzi Mandi—then open spaces—to families willing to move out.

Twenty-eight years ago, Professor Azhar established the

English-medium Crescent School at the foot of the exquisite Ghatta or Zeenatul mosque in Daryaganj, built by Aurangzeb's daughter in 1710. Like every other public school in Delhi, the Crescent School takes the children through multiplication and précis writing to the heights of the class twelve Boards. It is a modern, well-organized school, with the typical choruses of 'Good Morning Ma'am!' emanating from cheerful classrooms decked with maps and collages. Its unique selling point is that it also teaches Urdu. A message from a former vice-chancellor of Aligarh Muslim University, Saiyid Hamid (IAS Rtd) on its 25th anniversary brochure explained its philosophy: 'The Crescent School symbolizes the effort of Delhi Muslims to lift themselves by their bootstraps.' Professor Azhar founded the school because of his commitment to the people of the old city. His affection for the world of old Delhi is profound: he speaks of the old fashioned general physicians (GPs) represented by Drs A.C. Sen and A.P. Mitra, who examined all patients unhurriedly, whose copperplate handwriting made prescriptions a pleasure to read and who charged a mere eight rupees for a consultation. He recounts how Annapurna Bhandar, a famous old Delhi sweet shop, prided itself on the exactly symmetrical pieces of potato in their samosas. It is details like these, related by an individual with pleasure and pride, which are remarkable. Delhi has assimilated all the good points of many cultures, he observes. 'It is one of the great ancient cities; it has never been destroyed; it survives.'

What survives too, are some of the traditional pastimes that made up the culture of old Delhi. Mushairas still take place, and though *kabutarbazi* is no longer the common pastime it was, there are still some places behind Jama Masjid where pigeons are bought and sold. Similarly, tonga races continue to happen occasionally, people say, and akharas are slowly becoming popular again. Kite-flying is still a common passion and there are rows of shops along Nai Sarak selling every colour and size. All through August and September the sky above the old city is alive with the flying objects.

Yet, today, the culture of the old city is no longer mainstream; it is no longer *the* culture. Sultana Begum's memories are of the '60s and '70s, and the way of life then, she felt, had changed only a little from some thirty years earlier. Things are different today. 'Delhi's culture was a Persian culture; it was soft, reserved. It was like the food, which was subtle and fragrant . . . *khushboowali*. Nowadays both the culture and the food are Punjabi.'

This is a frequent assertion made to those who are mapping Delhi's recent past. The term 'Punjabi' no longer refers simply to regional origins. It indicates a compendium of traits pertaining to behaviour, lifestyle and aspirations. What the subtext of 'Punjabi culture' usually implies is that there is no culture, in the sense of refinement or graces. A perhaps inevitable consequence of the Punjabi refugee influx into Delhi after 1947, this also coincided with Delhi's transition from a sedate imperial suburb to the capital of a new nation. More than the other migrants who flocked to the new city—the civil servants, professionals, academics, artists, labourers—who were inexorably sucked into the vortex of the new power centre, the refugees, by their numbers, had an overwhelming impact on the social surface of Delhi; the qualities of materialism, aggressive self-confidence and an impatience with old shibboleths were a product of their upheaval. The non-refugee population of Delhi reacted to the increasingly visible refugee presence by zeroing in on the regional identity. Thus 'Punjabi' has become an accusation, synonymous with nouveau riche brashness, connoting not so much an original address but a state of mind. It can be argued that this is sometimes a defensive posture; a criticism ostensibly aimed at the PUPPY—the Prosperous Urban Punjabi—made by groups who feel their own status is threatened by the rapid urban transformations of the last five decades. Now many of the new aspects of Delhi—from call centres to chilli-garlic ketchup—are deemed results of Punjabification.

Much of the angst is about the 'vulgar display of wealth', evincing the kind of shuddering refinement that antebellum southern belles would manifest in the face of Yankee carpetbaggers. But it is the increase in Delhi's disposable income—which is by no means confined to Punjabis alone—that has led to all the visible wealth, vulgar or otherwise. This *uber* affluence can be observed everywhere and manifests itself particularly during social occasions such as weddings where comparisons with an earlier, allegedly simpler, time can be made easily.

Consider, for example, this list of 'five must-haves' for a wedding trousseau which appeared in a national daily. It enumerates the indispensable items for the twenty-first-century Delhi bride: silverware, including inter alia, candle stands and tea *sets* (emphasis mine); glassware—from brandy snifters to champagne flutes; items for puja, such as Ganesh statues and *diyas* in silver and porcelain; clothes and jewellery: the former a discerning mix of Indian and Western; the latter should be 'personalized'; the final suggestion is picture frames studded with precious stones to frame the photos of the happy (and expensive) day.[6] This is a long way from the toasters and tablemat sets of twenty years ago.

But then, twenty years ago the services of Rajinder Singh Masterji would not have been required by the bride's family either. This enterprising gentleman, a former classical Kathak dancer from Lucknow, teaches choreographed dance numbers to the bride, her sisters, cousins and friends for the wedding *sangeet*. Such occasions now require special georgette and sequined outfits and the dances are usually based on popular numbers from current Bollywood hits, more robust numbers for Punjabis, more conservative dances for Bania households. The hidden special offer behind this is that the bride's unmarried sisters might get 'noticed' by prospective grooms and/or mothers-in-law. So successful is Masterji, that his fame has spread to the Indian diaspora and he is much in demand in London.

The advent of event managers into weddings is a well-tracked Delhi phenomenon and is also an indication of the many new purposes that a wedding now serves. Weddings have always been a public record of the conjugal contract itself, as well as a ceremonial reiteration of the importance of the extended family and a showcase for the bride's family's level of income and aspirations. Today, these purposes still hold good, only, some of the incomes have increased and all the aspirations have expanded. For those whose incomes will not run to an upmarket hotel, a farmhouse or the Dhaula Kuan Club—the venues of choice for the city's well bank-rolled—the public sector is striving to offer alternatives. The NDMC and the MCD are both giving their peeling-walled and *paan*-stained Baraat Ghars and community centres a makeover. They still, in this city of vast contrasts, cost about Rs 3,000, appreciably less than the one lakh rupees and over of the Page Three-type locations, and still less than the Rs 20,000 charged by the many banquet halls that have mushroomed to serve the needs of Delhi's middle-income groups.

If weddings are becoming one of the defining ways to

showcase aspirations, birthday parties are not far behind and have the added advantage of being annual, as opposed to once-in-a-lifetime (mostly), events. Today, parties can cost up to four lakh at the upper end, but these will include a master of ceremonies, and be organized round a theme, such as Jungle Book or Batman. Upmarket hotel chains are also offering Mermaid parties, or Sound of Music parties, complete with jugglers, bouncy castles and expensive 'return gifts'. The days when parents organized treasure hunts or games of passing the parcel, and provided homemade sandwiches and samosas, have gone the way of the safari suit. Less well-heeled (or less indulgent) parents can go for 'kiddie party offers' to fast food chains or bowling alleys, and various toy shops offer packages ranging from Rs 5,000 to Rs 10,000 for a turnkey job of food, 'return presents' and decoration. Such phenomena are extensively chronicled by Delhi's proliferating feature writers in search of the ultimate human interest story, thus setting the benchmark for those who read the article or watch the TV capsule.

Interestingly, leisure pursuits have become identified with spending in a way they were not when the Bahadur family went for a picnic in the '40s. It is not just the expense that is noteworthy today, but the visibility of the expense. It is as if an audience is required to witness, applaud and marvel before any rite of passage—birthdays, weddings, anniversaries—attains significance.

These personal milestones are not the only ones to have been set firmly in the public domain. Another new entrant to Delhi's social calendar is the Iftar party to mark the end of the fasting days of Ramazan. This is now a well-established way of asserting secular credentials. The first Iftar party in Delhi was given by H.N. Bahuguna in 1978 after he joined the Janata Party and the following year, Mrs Gandhi, then leader of the Opposition, invited various prominent Muslims for Iftar. Iftar had hit the social radar.[7] Previous to this, they were quiet occasions, not parties. Members of the Muslim community would without fanfare distribute *iftari* to the poor, but in recent years Iftar has become a huge affair, complete with musicians, exotic caterers and the ubiquitous presence of TV cameras, and are thrown by Arab ambassadors, journalists and politicians of every hue—a BJP leader, it is said, even held a vegetarian Iftar party.

These are accepted opportunities for being seen on TV, networking and sensing emerging alliances. The original concept of Iftar, which is the breaking of a fast together, has receded; now security concerns dictate the roping off of a VIP enclosure during many Iftar parties, while the less eminent guests foregather in the buffet tent. Iftar parties, New Year Eve parties, St Valentine's Day parties, theme parties—all of these are now commonplace. In the early decades after Independence, the few occasions celebrated were largely family affairs. Certain festivals, like Holi, Diwali and Lohri were also neighbourhood affairs, the residents of a particular colony or block coming together to set off firecrackers or throw colours. Durga Puja, too, was originally a neighbourhood affair for local Bengalis, but now, with the increasing number of *pandals*, and their complement of foodstalls, bookstalls, musical and theatrical performances, these have become public social occasions, no longer confined to Bengalis, and serving the purpose of bazaars or *melas*, often so crowded that standing space is at a premium. Yet, despite some regrets by purists, this is surely one of the benefits of urbanism—the access to the many regional cultures that flourish in a city, a blurring of boundaries whereby Durga Puja, for instance, becomes an event on the city-wide seasonal calendar.

Among the many transformations of Delhi's social landscape over the last few decades is the increasing visibility of women in positions of influence and their breaching of previous male bastions in fields as diverse as law and hotel management. Working women are commonplace in all walks of life, yet, paradoxically, Delhi consistently has India's highest rate of crimes against women.

Figures from the National Crime Records Bureau (NCRB) published in 2006 indicate that while the national average for crimes against women was 14.2 per lakh population, Delhi's was almost double, at 27.6 per lakh population. Out of 1,693 rapes that were reported from thirty-five cities with populations of over 10 lakh, Delhi accounted for 562—over a third. Delhi also scored the highest in cases of molestation: 654 to Mumbai's 385. There were ninety-four dowry deaths in the capital, the highest number in any city in the country. A total of 197 women reported being sexually harassed in Delhi, second only to Kanpur's score of 227.

Explanations for this vary from the city's lack of a single, cohesive culture to the unreconstructed male chauvinism of northern India as a whole. Delhi's rapid urbanization from small town to metropolis has meant that social codes of dress and behaviour have changed rapidly, yet very unevenly.

Moreover, the high percentage of migrants from all parts of the country makes for a diversity unique in India. All other cities have paramount regional cultures which evolve their own widely understood social codes, particularly in regard to women. In Delhi there are multiple universes, each with its own tribal loyalties. And while women may feel comparatively secure among their familiars, there is a large range of spaces and situations where women feel unsafe. While the disempowered have historically sought the vulnerable targets that women are to express their own exclusion, violence against that gender is certainly not the monopoly of this section and in fact is common to all classes. There is an apparently deeply entrenched notion of what female decorum constitutes (inside the house, modestly dressed, submissive) and the argument is that women outside this *cordon sanitaire* are regarded as legitimate objects of hostility.

In 2002, the police commissioner of Delhi's remark that sexual harassment and crimes against women would decline if women 'dressed properly' caused a citywide furore but it was a reiteration of the belief that women were responsible for the crimes against them. Women in the workplace, in public transport and on the streets are under threat, and the threat extends to female foetuses as well. The MCD released ward-wise figures for the birth sex ratios between January and June 2004. South Delhi—the most affluent zone—had the lowest ratios: 762 females to 1,000 males. Karol Bagh and Sadar had the highest: 850 and 811 respectively. The determination to have a son at all costs is therefore not lessened by education or higher incomes.

And yet the numbers of women entrepreneurs, for instance, are steadily increasing, a reflection of the city's expanding economic base as well as the growing self-confidence of women in their ability to access loans, run factories or break into hitherto unexplored niche markets. An innovative, though short-lived, venture that sought to promote this new form of female energy was the Empress Club, set up in 1999 in NOIDA. Its promotional material promised: '. . . a platform where she can meet like-minded people, form a network, exchange ideas . . .' and it offered advice on issues ranging from 'cooking tips to smart career moves to exploring potential markets', and all this for an annual membership fee of just Rs 7,500. What is significant here is the recognition of a new profile: these are first-generation women entrepreneurs, not necessarily from established business families, uncomfortable with the thought of accessing established male strongholds as, for instance, the chambers of commerce or the Lions' Club. The social transformation such initiatives indicate is that middle-class women are moving into public spaces previously accessible only to the privileged.

In the '60s and '70s, upper middle-class women were the most visible in professional situations. Their presence was relatively rare in business, legal or financial circles, but they were well established in advertising, the media, academics and in the government as well as in the non-government sector. In fact, the south Delhi woman was a recognizable breed, coming from a privileged professional background, articulate and very ready to take on a leadership role. While this is still true, the multiple universes of Delhi have generated the space for women from a variety of social classes—not necessarily English-speaking or educated abroad—to take the lead in fields both old and new.

This is a reflection of the broadening of the elite base that Delhi has witnessed in the last sixty years. Just after Independence this was a narrow category made up of civil servants, some businessmen, contractors, journalists and politicians. They lived largely in south Delhi, their children attended the same few schools: St Columba's, St Xavier's, Convent of Jesus and Mary and Modern School, and progressed to St Stephens College, Hindu College, Miranda House, Lady Shri Ram or Indraprastha College. Regional or even religious differences were ironed out by a shared nationalist ethos and a sense of class solidarity. This world held sway till the '70s when the foundation of their authority—based as it was on access to education, kinship connections and professional networks—was no longer the only source of influence. Other power bases had by then come into existence.

∽  ∽

There are today so many Delhi cultures that to hold up one and say *this* is the one true one, the rest are derivatives or mutations, is just a huge inaccuracy. While the *tehzeeb* of Shahjahanabad still lingers in ancestral memories and is regarded as Culture in its pure, authentic form by many pre-Independence residents of the city, most of Delhi's population today has absolutely no connection with it. 'This world vanished when the cream of the Muslims left the old city at Partition,' Khushwant Singh mourns. Having survived two centuries of decline, it could not survive 1947. But it was not the much maligned Punjabis that delivered the *coup de grace*; it was the transformation of Delhi once it became the political centre of Independent India, once its economy started to expand and it became a magnet for migrants from all over. The Punjabis were the largest, most visible group, but all the migrants, with their different regional origins, their defined professional ambitions and their preoccupation with making the best of the present, had little time for the old courtly graces.

The refugees, however, became the most visibly dynamic group, and so it was their culture that got the bad press. With time, any new cultural departures were labelled 'Punjabi'—any signs of obvious affluence, any aggressive pursuit of goals, was attributed to the Punjabi ethos. It was also the explanation proffered by groups on the decline—professionals whose skills were not valued by the new economy, non-refugees whose livelihoods were threatened, and in later years, by the bureaucracy who saw their absolute authority decline. Today, when people speak of the 'Punjabification' of Delhi, they refer only to its prosperity, a prosperity that was certainly catalyzed, not wholly but very substantially, by the refugee population. It speaks of a process whereby new classes were entering arenas previously accessible only to the privileged pre-Independence elite. Some were indeed Punjabi; many others were not.

In one sense, the spread of centres of social gravity from south Delhi and Connaught Place to the newer Delhis and the western suburbs is part of this movement. High-end retail marketing and the bric-a-brac of American popular culture do as well in these centres—if not better. Oddly, this manifestation of globalization is also viewed as 'Punjabi'. If the globalization of popular culture has meant the dissemination of American popular culture to all corners of the world, then globalization is, in its Indian avatar, often perceived as Punjabi. Somewhere along the way, Indianized Americana and Punjabi have merged in the popular consciousness—and it is a compliment to both as well as to Delhi, which is where it began. Punjabi is today no longer merely a regional identity; it is an attitude.

# 10

## CLASSICAL CULTURE AND HERITAGE

DELHI'S CREDENTIALS AS A CENTRE FOR CLASSICAL culture have not always been rated highly. Ajeet Caur, Punjabi poet and writer, who came to Delhi after Partition, recalls that the people of Lahore regarded Delhi as a cultural desert: 'We in Lahore thought they were *maili dhotiwalleh* (unsophisticated rustics).' Yet, such were the compulsions of history, Ajeet Caur had to make Delhi her home and she was one of the stalwarts of Delhi's own post-Independence literary circle. The Alps restaurant on Janpath became a hub for the new capital's writers, poets and artists. Later, the literary-political set shifted to the Indian Coffee House where for the price of one cup of tea, Ajeet Caur remembered, 'people could sit and talk and talk for hours . . .' The Coffee House was closed during the Emergency when it was razed to make way for Pallika Bazar.

Classical culture found a new role in post-Independence Delhi. The position of Delhi as the capital of free India led to the showcasing of classical art forms as a national priority.

Cultural patrons had not, however, been lacking in pre-Independence Delhi. The Shri Ram family of industrialists was renowned for the evenings of classical music in their house in Curzon Road. Sheila Bharat Ram, Lala Shri Ram's daughter-in-law, was a noted connoisseur of the arts and it was at her house that the young sarod player, Ali Akbar Khan, first performed to Delhi audiences. The concerts were the precursors of the Shankarlal-Murli Dhar festival (named after Lala Shri Ram's brother and son) which became an annual event sponsored by ITC. Sumitra Charat Ram, another daughter-in-law of Lala Shri Ram, was responsible for the annual Delhi institution of Ramlila. Her interest in the *Ramcharitmanas* led her to start the popular dance-drama. Once it became a regular event, the dance troupe needed a permanent place and this was the inception of the Bharatiya Kala Kendra.

The Kendra was first located in Shankar Market, but land was subsequently allotted to it in New Delhi's Copernicus Marg (formerly Lytton Road), in the Mandi House area, which later became the centre of the city's cultural scene. The Natya Ballet Centre was established by Mrs Roopa Lal, another patron of the arts. The centre's innovative *Krishnaleela* mixed folk and classical forms for the first time. Sundari K. Sridharani established Triveni on the lines of Uday Shankar's dance school at Almora. It was first located in one room at Connaught Place; the familiar Stein building on Tansen Marg did not come up till the seventies. The Connaught Place area was also home to Gandhara Mahavidyalaya which was housed in a building near the Odeon cinema hall, and to the Bharatiya Natya Sangh, which was also in Shankar Market. Kamaladevi Chattopadhyay's project on the revival of traditional craft skills had a small exhibition space in Shankar Market, until the first set of state emporia was set up in the Theatre Communications Building in Connaught Place in the '60s. The showrooms on Baba Kharak Singh Marg were not built till the '70s.

In that decade, Delhi's cultural institutions began to take on their future shape. Both classical culture and folk traditions were perceived to be critical components of the new national identity. The state, too, had got into the act of cultural promotion. In 1954, the Sangeet Natak Akademi, the Sahitya Akademi and the Lalit Kala Akademi were set up to foster the development of the performing arts, plastic arts and literature. They were autonomous institutions, funded by the ministry of culture. While their autonomy has sometimes been queried, and the objects of their cultural patronage have not always met with universal acclaim, their contribution has been important, particularly in the early decades after Independence.

One of the first tasks of the Sangeet Natak Akademi was to establish the Kathak Kendra under Pandit Birju Maharaj. With this, the headquarters of Kathak effectively shifted from Lucknow to Delhi's Bhawalpur House. Simultaneously, the revival and nurturing of folk traditions became an important part of the national cultural enterprise. There was, in the establishment, a consciousness that the plural nature of the new nation had to be celebrated for India to survive: highlighting crafts and regional and folk traditions was an expression of this. Thus it was not perceived as just an aesthetic impulse but a political necessity. The induction of folk dancers from villages all over the country (not professional troupes as they are today) into the first Republic Day celebrations in 1948 was a statement about the importance of federalism, an idea that would enter the popular consciousness as 'Unity in Diversity.' Similarly the mela held in Lodi Gardens (it later shifted to Talkatora Gardens) at Diwali was established to showcase the varieties of traditional regional handicrafts.

The National School of Drama was set up in the '60s, initially in a small flat in Kailash Colony, later moving to Mandi House. Its most famous director, Ibrahim Alkazi, was, according to Kumkum Lal, 'a towering figure who built up the institution, established professional standards and launched actors like Naseeruddin Shah and M.K. Raina, who went on to transform, along with Om Shivpuri and Sadhana Shivpuri, the theatre movement in Delhi'. Classical dance, like theatre, enjoyed a renaissance.

It was an exciting time because old, neglected styles were being revived as well. In 1954, Odissi was performed for the first time in Delhi and it so exhilarated the dance critic Charles Fabri that he hailed it as a great discovery and persuaded noted Bharat Natyam dancer, Indrani Rahman, to go to Orissa and learn the dance form from the real gurus. The Sangeet Natak Akademi formally recognized Odissi as a classical style; it also actively promoted previously neglected forms such as Kuddiattam. Chaau was first performed in Delhi in the late '50s and the amazed and delighted audience expressed their appreciation by showering 100-rupee notes on the performers. Manipuri, too, gained prominence and became one of the dance forms taught at Triveni. All India Radio was, in the '40s and '50s, in the forefront of classical vocal music, and it introduced a new generation of artistes to a national audience, while regularly sponsoring concerts of vocal music in the capital.

If theatre and dance were enjoying a revival, the literary and art scenes, too, were very active. The All India Fine Arts and Crafts Society (better known as AIFACS) was established in the '50s and was a venue for many path-breaking exhibitions. Kishen Khanna, Satish Gujral and B.S. Sanyal were establishing the new parameters of post-Independence art. In the literary scene, Hindi literature, previously confined to Benares and Allahabad, began to gain a foothold in Delhi which had earlier been a stronghold of Urdu. Writers of the stature of Vishnu Prabhakar, Harivansh Rai Bachchan, Dinkar, Sumitra Nandan Pant and Mohan Rakesh were producing original and innovative works.

The '70s were, according to many—Kumkum Lal, Lola Chatterjee and Ajeet Caur among them—the highpoint of cultural activity in Delhi. The last embers of Nehruvian socialism, the anti-Vietnam war protests, the anti-colonial, anti-American imperialism, liberation struggles in Africa and Latin America and the Cultural Revolution in China together heightened political consciousness, and one of the more violent ways in which this was expressed was in Delhi's colleges by an involvement—active or armchair—in the ongoing Naxalite movement, an underground revolutionary movement which sought to bring about social change, based on the doctrines of Marxism-Leninism.

For all these reasons, three decades after Independence cultural activity in the capital had reached a kind of critical mass, the performing arts and painting were flourishing and the NSD was staging avant-garde plays while the other institutions of Mandi House prospered as well. The direction of Delhi's cultural activity changed during the '80s. The greater participation by the State in mega-melas such as the Festivals of India, the rise of cultural czars and czarinas as, for instance, Pupul Jayakar and Rajiv Sethi, enhanced the professionalism with which Indian civilization was projected abroad, but also increased the role of the Department of Culture, the Indian Council of Cultural Relations (ICCR) and other government institutions, and resulted in Delhi's art scene being totally appropriated by the capital's establishment. State patronage is undoubtedly useful in supporting artists and performers, as well as providing venues and sustaining art forms in danger of disappearing, but by its very nature, establishment patronage discourages iconoclasm and irreverence. Instead, it tends to promote the safe, the acceptable, the popular.

But if State support is problematic, commercial sponsorship has its downsides as well. In the '60s and '70s, Dhoomi Mal in Connaught Place was the best-known commercial gallery in Delhi. Today, the list would fill pages— both private and, especially, corporate—testifying to the enormous interest in art among the mobile middle classes, but not necessarily to the growth of the innovative or the experimental. Some art critics have described the popularity of Raja Ravi Varma or Tanjore glass painting or the revival of interest in the Nathadwara school as the rise of an 'art as décor' phenomenon, which enterprising art entrepreneurs have successfully made into a flourishing business. The undeniable upside is, however, that there is growing space for artists to exhibit and sell their work.

While painting and dance have benefited from the plethora of art galleries and the establishment of institutions such as the India International Centre and Habitat, drama, both in Hindi and English, has lost some of its earlier momentum. Lola Chatterjee, Delhi University professor and long time observer of Delhi's art scene, notes that the high cost of renting auditoriums—up to Rs 18,000, sometimes, for one evening—makes English plays prohibitively expensive to stage. When corporate sponsorship is at all available, the preference is for popular bedroom-farce type plays over contemporary or experimental theatre. Joy Michael's Yatrik and Barry John's Theatre Action Group had, through the

'50, '60s and '70s, presented plays by Jean Anouilh, Tom Stoppard and Anton Chekov, but now find the costs too high and the audience too small.

There has been no decline in interest in crafts, however. Dilli Haat (built over a covered nalla on Aurobindo Marg) is an enormous success in showcasing traditional handicrafts to a new generation of Delhi residents. The state emporia on Baba Kharak Singh Marg were once the flagship stores for state handicrafts. Initially successful, they have fallen prey to all the predictable ailments that dog state enterprises— shoddy goods, indifferent staff, no market research or contemporary design. The one exception was the Gujarat State Emporium—Gurjari. The handicrafts movement had been pioneered by Kamladevi Chattopadhay in the '50s and she was responsible for the establishment of Cottage Industries, first set up in barracks on Janpath. Gurjari's success was the handiwork of Jaya Jaitly, who explored the crafts of remote Gujarati villages and mediated traditional designs with contemporary taste. The popularity that Gurjari products—bags, kurtas, file covers, furnishings, *jootis*— enjoyed in the '70s and '80s was phenomenal and changed the aesthetics of an entire generation. Ethnic chic thrived in the social atmosphere of the revolutionary '70s, the ethnic idea itself became an identity, a radical, nationalist alternative to the aesthetics of polyester, plastic and pyrex. It became fashionable to wear khadi, *bandhni* and traditional block prints. If it was all skilful marketing, it was so skilful that no one realized that.

Later, private organizations would join the trend, extending the look to a readymade garment sector, to table linen and bed linen. In time, these spread to the mass market, as shops in Lajpat Nagar and Sarojini Nagar began to move stocks of mass-produced textiles in traditional designs; through this, ethnic entered the popular consciousness. Previously, fashion was defined by imported goods—American jeans, French chiffon sarees, English suitings and the like; the 'Gurjari' phenomenon brought the indigenous into the fashion mainstream. It was an ideological as well as an aesthetic revolution, a logical conclusion, in many ways, of the conscious revival of handicrafts and the significance accorded to regional folk forms. Jaitly moved on from Gujarati handicrafts to national politics, and even though today there are other 'looks'—for instance the popularity of Western clothes for women working in multinational offices—the traditional look remains a well-established part of the popular aesthetic.

～  ～

If Delhi has been the centre of the country's cultural politics, a new battleground in the capital is the politics of heritage. All cities have histories; even today's new suburbs like Patparganj have had calamitous events take place on the soil on which they stand. The battle of Patparganj took place almost exactly 200 years ago and—who knows—just feet below the asphalt and concrete may lie the remains of heroic soldiers and fragments of their halberds, helmets and swords. Certainly, the detritus of Delhi's chequered history—the tombs, the forts, the gateways, the mosques, walls and dargahs—lie scattered, almost casually, all around. The relationship that Delhi's dwellers have had with these vestiges of the past has often been critiqued; stigmatized as at best indifferent, at worst destructive, and consistently philistine. Delhi for the last half century has been a city of migrants, birds of passage, whose roots—and therefore pasts—lie elsewhere.

Moreover, the past itself is not just—as is often said—another country, but thousands of countries, as different groups spotlight different sets of images, vocabularies and icons which they see as defining their identities. Two people sitting next to each other on a DTC bus will claim totally different histories and even if they are Delhi-based, those pasts are not likely to include the monuments designated as such by their blue Archeological Survey of India (ASI) plaques that are of concern to the conservation-heritage lobby.

It is said that the pilgrimages people undertake reveal where they locate their identity: pilgrim sites are often religious centres, but they could equally be film stars' houses, or rocks or graves; rarely, in India, are they historical buildings. The pleasures of the past—in the sense of the physical remnants of a previous time—are not universally revered. The idea that whatever is old should be respected and, therefore, protected because it tells us about how we came to be who we are, is not universal, perhaps not even indigenous, nor has it been around a long time. In was only in the nineteenth century in Britain, for instance, that the landed classes, having accumulated both income and education, embarked on Grand Tours which took them to the classical sites of Greece and Rome and instilled in them an admiration for crumbling, moss-laden ruins.

Significantly, the decay and the antiquity of the ruins were intrinsic to the appreciation. They were far removed from the vigorous newness of the Industrial Revolution at home, a revolution which was inexorably changing the physical and social landscape, even challenging the social security of the ruling class. Therefore, notions of what was regarded as 'picturesque' came to be defined by the antiquity, air of melancholy, the sadness of the decay. This was reinforced by the emphasis on nature and natural surroundings that was advocated by the Romantic poets— a reaction to the Industrial Revolution. This appreciation of the past was part of the self-definition of a landed class that sought to distinguish itself from newer affluent groups that had come up then. To venerate the origins of European civilization was projected as a mark of refinement, a symbol of established ancestry. This perception had an impact on how Indians view their heritage even today.

In India, if attitudes to the past are complex, views on which past to preserve, and how to preserve it, are equally contested. Delhi's role as the national capital has meant the active promotion by the State of nationalist iconography. The manifestations of this, building-wise, were the Red Fort, the India Gate, Parliament House, the Secretariats and Rashtrapati Bhavan. The annual institution of 'Beating the Retreat', for instance, a thoroughly colonial ritual against a matching backdrop, has come to be seen as a continuation of Republic Day celebrations, while the Republic Day parade itself has established the association of Vijay Chowk, Janpath and Rajpath firmly within the nationalist agenda. Some popular pilgrimage sites for the public are the *samadhis* (cremation sites) of former leaders, Gandhi Smriti, Shantivan, Shaktishal, and Rajiv Gandhi's samadhi. These, along with Teen Murti Bhavan, 30 January Marg and 1 Safdarjang Road are now secular dargahs, places where people pay their respects, not just to national icons but also to the nationalist agenda itself.

Significantly, it is not the structures or buildings that are being venerated, but the personalities they represent. Mahatma Gandhi, Jawaharlal Nehru, Indira Gandhi and Rajiv Gandhi have moved beyond party and politics to take their place in the sacred pan-Indian pantheon. While there is consensus on the sacred nature of these locations, the move to declare the whole of what some call the Lutyens's Bungalow zone as a heritage area has met with some public resistance not least because the area is not hallowed by death or sacrifice or martyrdom, but seen as an effort by a privileged section to perpetuate its privileges—in this case, in the form of subsidized premium housing.

Thus the move for a specific location to become a sacred spot in the public mind is a complex process, and not achieved by simply designating a monument as one. Most of Delhi's 151 ASI-designated monuments, and the multitude of other structures which are over 300 years old scattered round the city, do not evoke all that much popular interest. Heritage means different things to different groups and people will rally to protect what they regard as sacred, but this is often directed at structures which are not necessarily historic or architecturally noteworthy. In the protection of Delhi's historical buildings, several groups are involved.

The restoration of Delhi's oldest church, St James (built in 1836), was funded jointly by the the Government of Delhi, INTACH and the Skinner family in Britain—descendants of the Anglo-Indian cavalryman, James Skinner, of Skinner's Horse regiment who built the church. The repair and development of the eleventh-century Qila Rai Pithora, citadel of the Rajput king, Prithviraj Chauhan, was taken up by Jagmohan, then urban development minister in the Bharatiya Janata Party (BJP) government. He spelt out his vision of conservation as being '. . . to weave history and heritage in the new urban fabric that is presently being spun in Delhi and develop a large park around the complex and create a glorious backdrop of the Rajput style of garden it deserves'[1]. His plans included an eighteen-metre-high statue of the great warrior to be placed atop a four-metre pedestal. The government changed before this could happen.

Delhi's chief minister, Sheila Dixit, has unveiled plans to restore Coronation Durbar in north Delhi to its former glory. It was here, in 1911, that King George V announced plans to transfer the capital from Calcutta to Delhi. Today, the place where 80,000 people, 'governors, princes and peoples of India gave their dutiful homage and allegiance' to the King in a fabulous tented township, is a dusty park on the outskirts of Mukherjee Nagar. The chipped and eroded statues, including that of the King Emperor himself, removed from its perch in India Gate, are just lying around. It is not the glories of history that come to mind, but its ironies. The restoration is with an eye to the Commonwealth Games in 2010. Explaining the decision, Dixit said: 'We could think of (the coronation) as negative—200 Indian princes came to pay their respects to the king as emperor of India—but that was the politics of the time. History is history and now we're talking of today; tourism, cultural ties and common links.'[2]

History may be history, but it is one of the most fiercely contested battlegrounds in India; the multiple groups that seek to define what it is, also disagree, sometimes violently, on how it should be preserved. The proper 'look' and function of a historic building is open to several interpretations. There are those—and perhaps this is the majority—who feel that monuments should be restored, set in tidy parks with paved paths and serried rows of bougainvillea. This is the approach advocated by Jagmohan, for instance. Others, and in this category one could possibly include Sheila Dixit, prefer to delve into the history of the site itself and promote that for purposes of tourism. This has sometimes been called 'themeparkification' and involves tidying up the site but in some accordance with its period authenticity. Such an approach includes providing a substantial tourist 'package', that is, making it worthwhile for tourists to visit the site, and also to use the site to stage dance or music festivals.

It has been suggested, for instance, that giant screens should be installed in the Qutb Minar, which would project views recorded by cameras placed on top of the minar as the public is no longer allowed to climb the tower after a fatal stampede took place some decades ago. Whether this would increase its appeal is open to doubt. Meanwhile the Qutb has also been the venue of classical dance festivals and is one of Delhi's most visited sites by domestic and foreign tourists.

The third, very minority view of conservation prefers to see monuments in a state of slight, genteel decay to emphasize their lost, melancholy aspect—a legacy of the British colonialists' view of India. This is the past as Orientalist romance, influenced, perhaps unconsciously, by the crumbling, vegetation-covered ruins that Thomas Daniell and his nephew, Willam Daniell, painted so successfully in the 1780s. This vision of India as picturesque, as decayed, of a great civilization in ruins, was ultimately a political statement. Reprinted in the illustrated papers of the day, the British public saw India as not just a mysterious, exotic, romantic 'other', but also as irredeemably backward and ruined, and this went a long way in consolidating public support for the idea of Empire. This vision of the Indian landscape as exotic, Gothic and crumbling persists among promoters of upmarket tourism which, like the immensely successful transformation of a Rohilla fort in Haryana into a luxury hotel, appreciates the past best when it is slightly rough-edged, rustic, and other-worldly. But it also has adherents among a certain small section of Indians who find this vision irresistibly seductive and it is this section that opposes the transformation of monuments into neatened-up, well-labelled, mass tourism sites.

The increasing popularity of the idea of conservation in some quarters, the seriousness and respect with which it is now regarded, has led to the entrance of corporates to the conservation field. The Oberoi Hotel group, for instance, has entered into a partnership with the ASI and the Aga Khan Trust for the lighting of Humayun's tomb, erected in 1571. The Trust has donated Rs 2.5 crore towards relaying the tomb's garden. The tomb is the burial place not only of the emperor Humayun, but also of Shah Jahan's doomed son, the liberal, gifted Dara Shikoh, defeated in the war of succession with Aurangzeb. The last Mughal emperor, Bahadur Shah Zafar, fled there with his sons when the British recaptured Delhi, hoping the shades of his ancestors would save him from retribution for the uprising in 1857. They did not and two of his sons were captured and later killed by Colonel Hodson. These and other historical details will be recounted on laminated boards spread over the grounds; an authentic Mughal garden will be planted and an information centre established on the site. Corporates are eligible for 100 per cent tax deduction for their forays into conservation and this, together with an appreciation of history, has prompted others, notably the Apeejay Group, to look after the site of Jantar Mantar, an eighteenth-century observatory which could accurately measure eclipses and planetary positions, in front of their hotel, Capital Park.

Preserving historic buildings is often a matter of contention; it is frequently seen as the esoteric interest of a minority, standing in the way of what is regarded as progress. In Mehrauli village, for instance, a site so picturesque for outsiders with its curving lanes and occasional jharoka doorway, fully 70 per cent of the residents want to move out, preferring the surroundings of a typical middle-class colony. In Chiragh Delhi village, residents resent attempts to prevent them from pulling down their old houses so that they can build large multistorey buildings which can then be rented out, substantially increasing their incomes. Hauz Khas village, a favourite tourist destination, sells itself as an upmarket shopping area which also provides the opportunity to eat out in allegedly authentic 'rustic' surroundings. The 'rusticity' is made up of some Rajasthani carved doors, some Moorish archways, some Mexican adobe frontages and other elements of unidentifiable origin.

The residents of Hauz Khas village had already lost the agricultural lands they had acquired during the rapid expansion of south Delhi for fairly modest amounts of compensation. They now receive substantial income in rent from the owners of boutiques, restaurants and antique shops that mushroomed in the village. Removed from their traditional occupation, while many residents have set up businesses in construction, trucking and taxi services, the sudden increase in disposable income has also led to increases in alcohol consumption, gambling and anti-social behaviour.

A resident of Munirka village, which has not been gentrified in the same way, explained to me that to live in surroundings that are familiar, but have been taken over for purposes you have absolutely no understanding of and, frankly no interest in, is, at best, disconcerting. But to be exposed day after day to people who see you as part of the scenery, who take pictures of you as you sit on your charpoy or ask you to pose with your buffaloes, robs you of *izzat*, dignity. The villagers were prosperous farmers. They are literate and shrewd and they have prospered from the forces of urbanization that makeovers like Haus Khas village represent. The village embodies not just the varied pace of urbanization, but the cosmically contradictory cultures it can manifest.

The conflicting views about conservation were brought out most clearly during the ASI's clearing of illegal constructions in Tughlaqabad Fort. In the '80s, land within the precincts of the fourteenth-century fort was illegally sold to gullible buyers by unscrupulous real estate agents in collusion with local political interests. Plots of 50 sq. metres were sold for Rs 5,000. Pucca constructions, even some commercial structures, came up and the ASI's protests that this was a protected monument fell on deaf ears. The buyers, with political backing, insisted that they were part of a village that had existed for centuries within the Fort. The ASI maintained that the 1905 Revenue Survey made it quite clear that the village's land covered only 327 bighas of the Fort's area. A report by Delhi's then finance commissioner, Madan Jha, made public in 1997, mentioned 'active and sustained collusion between (the) departmental representatives concerned and (the) political powers that be in the area'. Despite this, no action was taken until 9 April 2001, when, under orders from Jagmohan, then urban development minister, thirty-five bulldozers moved into the Fort area and demolished over 300 jhuggis and other structures. In all, some fifteen acres were recovered. The residents resisted and teargas had to be used, ten people were injured and eight detained. Political scores were being settled; the victims were those who had bought the land. One of them, seventy-year-old Chaudhury Balbir Singh, said angrily, 'It is clear that the police are ready to render us homeless at all costs to make the place a tourist attraction. We are not going to give up our hearth and home without a fight.'[3] Another said the demolitions were carried out 'just to attract a handful of tourists from abroad'.

Their argument, then, is framed in the following terms

and cuts to the heart of any debate about conservation in a developing society. Those who have an interest in heritage are outsiders, so their interests should not come before locals. Secondly, only a few tourists will come anyway, so the revenues generated will be negligible; yet the people being uprooted stand to lose everything. On the other hand, while it is true that the value of a fourteenth-century fort cannot be quantified, nor can its 'utility' be explained outside a particular historical paradigm, nonetheless its antiquity, the purpose for which it was built, the techniques used and the sheer drama of its location give it an undeniable significance. Between those who view the Tughlaqabad Fort as an invaluable example of medieval architecture and those who see it as standing on valuable real estate, is a virtually unbridgeable chasm. Yet, without a broad consensus on its significance, conservation cannot work. Architect Abhimanyu Dalal observes, 'Restoration should not be antiseptic and the area converted into a showcase . . . (conservation) has to work with traders and owners. Only then will the plan be viable.'[4] The idea that history is of value to a whole society, that it belongs to everyone, that it has an intrinsic worth—these are ideas that have to be widely accepted before conservation takes place.

Delhi's disparate groups are a long way from agreeing on the past, let alone on its preservation. Ajeet Caur's reflections in 1947 on Delhi's lack of 'culture', are not, even today, absolutely disproved. The State's conscious promotion of a national classical culture has succeeded in establishing institutions where that culture is nurtured, cosseted even. Projects such as the Society for the Promotion of Indian Classical Music and Culture Among Youth (SPICMACAY), a non-profit organization, which began on a small scale staging classical music and dance performances in Delhi's schools and colleges in 1977—now with chapters all over

India and abroad—did a great deal to spread awareness of classical forms. Similarly, INTACH has contributed not only to preserving heritage but also raising and disseminating awareness of its significance. Walks organized by the Habitat centre, exploring Delhi's monuments or Delhi's ecology, draw enthusiastic response. Yet Delhi's journey to such a popular, citywide consensus on the significance of both classical culture and conservation is a long one. Here, too, the city's lack of a single regional identity works against it. Unlike other cities, neither the culture nor the past resonate as a basis for primordial identity. The wide sections of the middle class that throng classical cultural events in Chennai, Mumbai or Kolkata are not found in Delhi. It is not that Delhi does not possess a critical mass of residents who subscribe to a classical cultural ethos—the well-attended classical dance and music classes and performances attest to that. Equally evidently, it is not that Delhi has not possessed a classical tradition of its own or a past that it celebrates— the traditions of Shahjahanabad, the memories of its poetry, its music, the strong support for conservation of Chandni Chowk and surviving havelis—but the broader consensus on preserving the culture is still incubating because the city's disparate groups remain viscerally connected to disparate cultures.

# 11

## DELHI'S SOCIAL SPACES

THE PARLOUR WAS A '70S INSTITUTION. IT WAS MORE than a Connaught Place (CP) restaurant. If, in the '50s, Delhi's middle classes flocked to 'Alps', and the '60s generation frequented the dimly lit 'La Boheme', the '70s were all about sitting at diabolically uncomfortable low tables and stools, under graffiti-covered walls, eating ham steak with pineapple. Downstairs, the Cellar thrummed to the sounds of Crosby, Stills and Nash, but the Parlour was where, while sizzlers were produced on oval wooden trays, intense conversations about Life took place. CP was still the centre of the Delhi social universe. 'Going for a loaf' in CP meant cold coffee at Depauls in Indian Oil Bhavan, shopping for Kolapuri *chappals* on Janpath and browsing among the serried rows of glossy Penguin Modern Masters at the Bookworm. Nostalgia is always softly lit, and doubtless decades hence people will be recalling Ansal Plaza or the Basant Lok complex the same way. Yet, in many ways the history of Connaught Place mirrors the changing social geography of Delhi. The city's changing fortunes reflect the shifts in Delhi's centres of gravity, the transformed ideas of leisure, the development of niche markets and the overwhelming popularity of malls as shopping destinations.

CP went through a period of decline in the '80s and '90s, struggling to find a contemporary profile, to repackage its attractions so as to draw the local middle classes which had almost completely deserted it for the siren calls of malls and more accessible local shopping complexes. Connaught Place's unlikely saviour was the Metro, which brought it back onto the leisure map. Today the crowds have returned to its restaurants, bars and shops; but it was a close thing.

The decision to have a circular shopping plaza to serve the needs of the British residents of New Delhi (Indian babus were to shop separately at Gol Market) had come as early as 1917, mooted by John Nicholls, member of the New Delhi Planning Committee. Connaught Place was named after the Duke of Connaught, uncle of the King Emperor George V. It is not clear why this particular unremarkable royal was chosen to be so honoured, and though Connaught Place and Connaught Circus have been renamed Rajiv Chowk and Indira Chowk respectively, CP it remains in the public discourse. The actual design was by Robert T. Russell, the architect who designed Flagstaff House (Teen Murti Bhavan), the Eastern and Western Courts and many senior officials' bungalows. Nicholls had suggested the design of matching, curving blocks pierced by radial roads. Russell executed the scheme with classical colonnades and a dazzling white facade. The aesthetics of the scheme, however, did not translate into a rush to buy property in the area, even though it was being offered at Rs 2 a sq. yard.

Connaught Place had been a jungle of keekar trees and most Indians connected with the project were deeply skeptical of its ever rivalling Chandi Chowk as a market. One of the main contractors of Connaught Circus was Sir Sobha Singh. His eldest son, Bhagwant Singh, recalled that his family's role in the construction business began in Sargoda (now in Pakistan) where they constructed several factories and civic buildings in Multan, Lyallpur (now Faislabad) and in Sargoda itself. Bhagwant Singh's grandfather, Sardar Sujan Singh, was sent by Malcolm Hailey, then commissioner, Sargoda, and later chief commissioner, Delhi, to attend the 1911 Durbar in Delhi on behalf of the district. Sir Sobha Singh, Bhagwant Singh recalled proudly, was the only contractor to build Connaught Circus, all the others built Connaught Place—referring to the outer and inner circles respectively.

In the original design, the inner circle had only six blocks which had 585 pillars, with 1021 pillars in the outer circle. Sir Sobha Singh was responsible for the construction of A Block and one of the first buildings to come up was the Regal Theatre, which he subsequently bought at Rs 48 a sq. yard. 'My father ran it himself,'[1] Bhagwant Singh remembered, adding that in the early years the theatre's clientele was so sparse that sometimes the night show's entire audience consisted of only three or four people. The surrounding areas, too, were not regarded as particularly good investments. C.S. Gupte, then a young member of the Town Planning Organization, recollects that his uncle bought a plot in Babar Road for the even then minimal Rs 2 a sq. yard, but sold it again almost immediately, unnerved by the jackals which howled through the night.[2] Bhagwant Singh recalls that Scindia House was originally allotted to the Maharaja of Gwalior as a base for Gwalior Potteries; but the Maharaja felt it was a bad investment and asked Sir Sobha Singh to buy it. It was not possible under the original sale deed to change the name of the building for ten years; so it has remained Scindia House till today, and in real estate terms, it is priceless.

It was the Second World War that dramatically changed Connaught Place's fortunes. The large numbers of American servicemen stationed in New Delhi provided a ready pool of free spending customers for the fledgling market. The cinemas—Odeon opened in early 1944—and the restaurants, too, benefited enormously. Kwality's ice cream, in particular, was enthusiastically spooned up by the soldiers and helped to establish Kwality as one of New Delhi's leading restaurants and the ice cream as one of the country's leading brands.

Manish Sahai has lived in Connaught Place since he was a child. His parents bought a flat there in 1932 and he says proudly that the structure is so sound that even today, seventy years later, no repairs have been needed in the plumbing or construction.[3] While the living accommodation in Connaught Place was initially intended for the shop owners, few were inclined to live there, preferring their homes in the old city. The flats were bought by Indian professionals looking for a base in New Delhi. Servants' quarters and garages were located in the Middle Circle and the living, as Sahai remembers it today, was good. A bagpipers' band played twice a week in the flowery central park and the Sahai family, along with many others, took their folding chairs and packets of thin-cut sandwiches to listen to the laments and reels. Sahai played cricket there with his friends, and his parents would dine and dance at the restaurants—Davico's was famous for its teas, Wenger's for its Italian cook.

In the early years of the market's existence, many of the cinemas doubled as theatres. Sahai recalls watching Prithviraj Kapoor perform at the Regal Theatre as well as at the Rivoli.

The latter, along with Odeon and Plaza was owned by the Peshawar-based Roshanlal Sawhaney. The shops of note were the Army & Navy Stores for household goods and clothes, Empire Stores for provisions, M.R. Stores for hardware, J.B. Mangaram for biscuits and chocolate, and Keventer's for dairy products, while A.N. John was the barber and hairdresser. Today, apart from Keventer's, they have all disappeared. Other survivors include Har Narayan Gopi Nath which still sells pickles, Nath Chemists still dispense drugs, Cook and & Kelvey still trades in silverware, and Balujas, the shoe shop. Photography studios have managed to survive—and thrive. Mahatta was established in 1923 and is still running, though under different ownership. Kinsey Brothers, another studio, is even older, having been established in 1905; it even made the annual (summer) migration to Shimla along with the government and is today owned by the famous Dilwali family of photographers who were associated with Kinsey from the early years. Another famous name in Indian photography, Avinash Pasricha, still owns Delhi Photo Company, established in 1938.

Partition and the events leading up to it caused a lot of damage in Connaught Place. The shops were broken into and plundered by mobs, but after Independence, Connaught Place retained it popularity as the new capital's premier marketplace. While new markets, allotted to refugees, sprang up all over the expanding city, their appeal was purely local—sophisticated or upmarket goods were to be had in Connaught Place. This continued till the '70s, with new book shops and restaurants opening frequently. But then several circumstances incubating since Independence emerged to usurp Connaught Place's position. Ownership patterns had not changed since before 1947. It is estimated that the whole of Connaught Place is owned by just six or seven people; over 75 per cent of the properties are tenanted, some rented at amounts fixed decades ago.

Though attempts have been made to change this situation, notably the Delhi Rent Amendment Bill of 1997 which sought to increase rentals, this was opposed strongly by tenants of commercial properties all over Delhi. The end result is predictable: few tenants are willing, or perhaps able, to invest in the maintenance of their properties, and the impact on Connaught Place is all too sadly visible. Encroachment on to pavements and staircases, a complete laissez-faire in signboards and a parking system which is both chaotic and inadequate have combined to diminish Connaught Place's attraction for motorists. The one-way system, introduced in 1990, led to serpentine traffic snarls with enterprising motorists attempting to beat the system by zipping down the Middle Circle, which was never meant for heavy traffic.

Moreover, retailers are divided among several rival associations, each with a different agenda, and their perceptions of where Connaught Place should be headed also differ widely. Retailers with outlets in both Connaught Place and other south Delhi markets, Snowhite and Deepsons, for example, admitted—ruefully—that sales in the latter were better through the '80s and '90s, not least because the showrooms there were larger as well. Many retailers had to resort to frequent 'sales' to boost trade, but despite this tactic, numbers dropped in those decades by as much as 50 per cent.

In many ways, Connaught Place is still fixated on its past. Jagmohan Gupta of Young Friends and Co., another old Connaught Place shop, laments: 'We have turned the exclusive Connaught Place market where only high-income groups could come, into Karol Baghs and Kamla Nagars.'[4] In fact, Karol Bagh and Kamla Nagar markets have never stopped booming. Moreover, smaller markets such as Pallika Bazar, Mohan Singh Market, Janpath and Shankar Market, on the edges of Connaught Place, have become rival retail outlets—and increased traffic congestion. Suggestions on pedestrianization, extending opening hours and Sunday shopping have been opposed by many traders, unwilling to venture into the unknown. Before the Metro magically restored CP's fortunes, tourists from outside Delhi were the one group to frequent Connaught Place in numbers; locals were unimpressed by the often tacky items, the old-fashioned nature of the displays and the uncompetitive pricing. The Barista generation was clearly impervious to CP's rather forlorn charms.

Connaught Place's loss to local markets was exacerbated by its transformation into a business address. Known as the Central Business District, office space expanded through the '70s and '80s, especially on the approach roads of Kasturba Gandhi Marg and Barakhamba Road, where nearly all the old bungalows were pulled down to accommodate new commercial highrises. One of the first casualties of the increased numbers of office-goers, and the consequent traffic and parking congestion, was the old-fashioned provision store—few customers were going to confront the traffic snarls of the Inner Circle when their local markets could amply supply their needs. Empire Stores, with its mingled scents of coffee and bacon, its wooden floors and counters, its high ceiling and long-poled ceiling fans which moved as slowly as the ancient staff, was among the last to go, replaced by the three-floor Bata shoe shop. The recent burgeoning of new office complexes at District Centres such as Rajendra Place, Nehru Place and Janak Place as well as those in Gurgaon and NOIDA have also affected CP's status as a desirable business address. The newer centres offer new constructions with larger floor spaces and plentiful parking, which are tailor-made for contemporary businesses. The rents are also lower.

Then, Connaught Place staged a recovery. New commercial highrises, such as Ambadeep, the DLF Centre and Statesman House have added some 60,000 sq. ft of space to the Central Business District. The transformation of Odeon, Plaza and Rivoli into multiplexes—the contemporary staples of any successful market complex—has re-ignited CP's attractions. Also, as a leading property analyst points out, 'CP is ultimately a global address and companies are willing to pay for that.'[5]

Yet, while Connaught Place always lurked somewhere in the public's consciousness because of its heritage site status—as a heritage site it is, in its own way, in as bad shape as any medieval monument occupied by squatters. Patwant Singh, a prominent Delhi architect, has remarked: 'Connaught Place is remarkable for its proportions and its dazzling white facades. We have ruined something beautiful.'[6] Ultimately, Connaught Place became a victim of its own antiquity and prestige. Antediluvian tenancy laws, a wistful yearning for past glories, the unthinking concentration of businesses and spaces designed for a less motorized era, alongside the rapid growth of local, niche markets, all contributed to its decline in the capital's shopping stakes. The same forces that had transformed Delhi from a sleepy government city to a twenty-first-century megapolis, marginalized CP.

Through the '80s and '90s it had the look of a seedy, provincial marketplace, its once elegant colonnades plastered with posters for IT coaching classes; gaudy bedcovers and tourist souvenir tack spread on its pavements. Even today, Metro notwithstanding, it looks shabby and down-at-heel, with just a few brand outlets smartening up their own frontages with incongruous marble and tiles. Whether it can swing a successful renovation is still uncertain. Till then, the ghosts of the golden couples of the '30s who danced till dawn in the restaurants still linger in the colonnades, but are probably rather disconcerted by the tides of shoppers and sightseers that throng the area today.

Connaught Place's association with restaurants is a long one: Delhi's earliest restaurants—that is Western-style eating places, as opposed to, say, the small eateries in areas like Parathewali Galli or the *chaat* shops of old Delhi—were all in Connaught Place. A social history of India's gastronomic impulses was charted by Lalit Nirula, head of the famous Nirula's chain (which has recently sold some of its stock to a foreign company), at a talk he gave in Mumbai some years ago. Giving a witty, informed, insider view of eating trends, he identified the large numbers of American servicemen billeted in Delhi during the Second World War as the start of the restaurant trend.[7] They triggered the first Western-style restaurants—the 'Continental' menus, the band with a 'crooner' and a dance floor; the whole ambience of starched white tablecloths, dim lighting and art deco interiors that we see in Delhi's older restaurants dates from then. Kwality followed up its success at selling ice creams to servicemen by adding snacks to its menu, then becoming a full-fledged restaurant. Standard and Gaylord were two other popular restaurants which came up in the decade after Independence.

The Nirulas set up Hotel India in 1934 in Connaught Place's D block and opened Nirula's restaurant in L Block in 1939 which 'introduced ballroom dancing and cabaret'. Three years after Independence, this was transformed into the

Brasserie—a self-service cafeteria—and the same year the group opened the Chinese Room, a first for Delhi since Chinese eateries previously existed only in Kolkata and Mumbai, a function of their large Chinese population. The real, wholly Delhi gastronomic invention was tandoori chicken, and Moti Mahal in Daryaganj—which specialized in that Indian ambrosia—opened its doors in 1947. Meanwhile, the delights of expresso coffee and central air conditioning (restaurants were air-cooled before) were also introduced to Delhi by Nirula's. While the cheeseballs at Wenger's were a huge draw, La Boheme, set up by Nirula's in 1960, introduced Dilliwallahs to Hungarian cuisine. It was enormously popular with AWOL students of Delhi University who appreciated the privacy of the semi-darkness.

The Delhi literati favoured Alps, a restaurant situated where the Lufthansa offices now are. Subsequently, when the Alps waiters were refused a wage hike and walked out to found the Coffee House, the intellectuals followed suit and the speculations on life, death and revolution took place there. Manish Sahai remembers that the house *piece de resistance*—apart from the coffee—was coffee jelly. Both the jelly and the discussions came to an end when the Coffee House was demolished during the Emergency and Pallika Bazar came up in its stead. The action was said to be at the behest of then prime minister Mrs Indira Gandhi's son, Sanjay Gandhi. Tradition has it that it was felt that the place was a hotbed of anti-establishment discourse. Perhaps the authorities of the time calculated—correctly—that most Dilliwallahs would prefer shopping to subversion. At any rate, Pallika Bazar still stands and a new, antiseptic Coffee House has come up in between the emporia on Baba Kharak Singh Marg.

Delhi's first luxury hotel, the Ashoka, opened its doors

in 1950. The ersatz Rajput/Mughal/CPWD structure was much admired, though Naipaul was famously unimpressed by its air of smug, pink self-consequence and wrote scathingly of its 'comic little cupolas'[8] The Oberoi Intercontinental (as it was first called) came up in the '60s and introduced the coffee shop concept to New Delhi (the Oberoi Maidens Hotel in Civil Lines was rarely visited by people living south of Daryaganj). Today, Delhi brims with luxury hotels. Several came up in 1982, the year both the Non-Aligned Conference and the Asiad Games took place, and it has been a steady, sometimes steep, increase. It is hard to imagine today the awe with which the term 'five star' was regarded in a city cut off from imports and officially wedded to a cult of Gandhian austerity. Unlike the present, when well-heeled locals visit hotels routinely for the restaurants and coffee shops, earlier, the city's older hotels, Claridges, say, impinged little on the consciousness of most Dilliwallahs. Fonseca's, another old hotel, was renowned for its Tibetan momos, but it was pulled down and the Taj Mansingh came up at the same site. Its coffee shop, Machaan, was immediately popular. The '60s also saw Delhi's first discotheque—the Ghungroo at the Maurya.

All this time, eating out in Delhi meant basically Mughlai, Chinese or what was known as 'continental'—which comprised such staples as Chicken a la Kiev (unknown in Kiev), Russian Salad (unknown in Russia) and Mixed Grill (unknown in origin). Authenticity, however, does not constitute a very significant part of cuisine—after all, pizzas in America and curries in Britain would not necessarily be recognized as such by Italians and Indians respectively. South Indian food began its conquest of north India through restaurants like Dasaprakasa in the Ambassador Hotel, although less expensive south Indian 'tiffin' was available at

Bengali Market, along with local items like *chaat* and *gulabjamuns*. The older restaurants, such as Gaylord, continued to proffer solid, old-fashioned menus which suited their clientele. Gaylord in the '60s played an important social role: 'Here, boy met girl over cona coffee and chicken patties . . .'[9] and several million litres of cold coffee were consumed by ladies' kitty parties.

The fast food revolution in Delhi began with the opening of the Hot Shoppe by the Nirula group in 1977, when an entire generation was introduced to the delights of sloppy joes. The Nirulas' '21 flavours' ice cream parlour opened in 1978 and again revealed to Dilliwallahs that there was more to ice cream than vanilla and tutti frutti. Potpourri, Delhi's first salad bar, opened the following year, above the ice cream palour. Today, Nirula's has outlets all over Delhi, but it is no longer the only fast food operation in the capital. The American Dominos pizza chain has, for instance, tied up with the Indian Oil Corporation to provide motorists with chicken and *paneer makhani* pizzas while their cars are being refuelled. The popularity of fast food also reveals both the adaptability and the independence of the Delhi palate—the willingness to try new things and then mould them into the familiar—pizza, for instance. An amazing statistic revealed that in 2002, some 20,000 to 30,000 pizzas were being consumed *every day* in Delhi. There has been a significant boom in the number of new restaurants serving 'speciality' cuisines: Thai, Italian, Mexican, Japanese, Korean and 'non-Punjabi' Chinese. The last is a departure from chow mien (which has enthusiastically entered the *dhaba* repertoire) and sweet and sour pork—the previous universal favourites. Furthermore, the last two decades have witnessed the rise of regional Indian cuisines as the marker of real sophistication, the proliferating outlets serving Chettinad food, for instance.

Meanwhile, 'Punjabi' is no longer a pejorative when it comes to taste. One socially significant restaurant venture is even called 'Punjabi by Nature', specializing in such treats as Tandoori Broccoli and pepper-flavoured vodka. This is the coming of age of the Punjabi in Delhi, where Punjabi no longer means refugee or pushy or new-rich. It has been calculated that a new pub opens in the city every six days. Saket market has a total of twenty-two; the Basant Lok complex boasts twelve. The rise of the pub has been accompanied by the death of the disco. Discos were admittedly never very plentiful and confined to hotels (dancing needs a special licence), but their ready transition into pubs indicates that their demise was caused by the fact that they were too noisy and too young, and that disposable incomes are still largely in the hands of those who want to sit down and chat without shouting.

This desire to sit and chat is one of the causes behind the explosion of coffee-and-dessert-type restaurants which offer a limited menu of the quiche, pasta and salads variety. Barista and Cafe Coffee Day outlets proliferate—clearly, Delhi's middle classes wish to frequent places which are not mealtime-specific. Art cafes, where genuine art hangs on the walls to be bought by customers, and health food cafes are also new in this decade. The ambience is ever more important and other things being usually equal, restaurants strive with each other to provide a different 'experience'. The new Nirula's outlet in Shushant Lok has paintings by such established artists as Anjolie Ela Menon and Arpita Singh on its walls: 'Since this is an upmarket area, we opened with a different profile.'[10] The days of the local Bengali Sweet House, with rexine banquettes and stainless steel plates, have been left very, very far behind.

Takeaway custom has increased exponentially, with

Waiters on Wheels doing good business through the '90s. Lalit Nirula has spoken of the rise of a 'pan-Indian cuisine' comprising south Indian masala dosa and vada, north Indian tandoori chicken and curry, and Bengali rasgulla; this can now be had in any small city, but in Delhi there is a significant increase in eating out. This shows not only the enormous rise in disposable income, but also the fundamental shift in the idea of eating itself. Lalit Nirula has concluded that factors such as the increase in the number of working women, the scarcity of domestic help and the enthusiasm of children for 'ordering out' are behind this trend. Equally important is the tectonic shift which sees eating out as leisure and the perception of restaurant food as more interesting and appetizing. Large sections of middle-class Delhi do not want *tinda sabzi* anymore.

But the ultimate entertainment in Delhi today is derived from window shopping. It would be no exaggeration to say that Delhi has a patent on that exercise. Shopping is a pastime, a pursuit which does not always involve a commercial transaction. There is something almost metaphysical in this idea, strange though it might seem: malls are the new temples; they evoke a sense of awe, they are places visited for fun or consolation. When good Dilliwallahs die, they will probably go to malls.

But though malls are the newest and most popular elements in the shopping experience, Delhi's older markets are still in the running. In the last three decades, there has been a general 'sorting out' of shopping destinations. These decades saw CP's decline, the rise of some local markets and the petering out of others. It is not so much that markets serve very specific needs—most retain a variety of shops and some specialized outlets. Kotla Mubarakpur is one of the rare exceptions: the entire market is devoted to hardware and house construction ancillaries. Partly, it is a result of its location in the middle of south Delhi; but partly it is one of the mysteries why some markets take off and others do not. Malaviya Nagar Market is bustling with its complement of restaurants and boutiques; Haus Khas Market, on the other hand, retains the slightly sleepy, slightly seedy air it had in the '60s.

One of the major transformations is that of Sarojini Nagar Market. It began as a few vegetable *khokas* set up by refugees near the railway track. The market itself was built in 1950 and the shops were allotted to refugees. Initially, it consisted of vegetable and provision stores, with one or two saree and shoe shops. The rent for a shop in those days was Rs 45 a month. In 1979, the shopkeepers appealed to Sikander Bakht, then minister for urban development, to allow them to become owners, and subsequently the shops in Sarojini Nagar and nine other markets were transferred to the allottees. Most shops in Sarojini Nagar are still with the original owners. The market attracts customers from all over Delhi and has—most remarkably—retained its reputation as a place where branded goods as well as inexpensive items are available. A big draw for the younger crowd is the amazingly inexpensive export-reject clothes shops. Sarojini Nagar Market has succeeded because it appeals to both ends of the economic spectrum. For instance, the vegetable stalls stock celery, broccoli and avocadoes as well as everyday tinda and *gobi*; the electronic goods shops keep locally made desert coolers as well as branded split-level air conditioners, and the saree shops display a zardozi range as well as cotton or polyester varieties.

If Sarojini Nagar Market is one type of successful makeover, Khan Market is another. This market began as a couple of provision stores which came up to service the barracks of Lodi Estate, themselves built as 'temporary constructions' to house the many allied servicemen who were based in Delhi during the Second World War. After 1947, the market was constructed and shops allotted to refugees. It was named after the brother of the legendary NWFP leader, Khan Abdul Gaffar Khan, who was known in India as the 'Frontier Gandhi'. Meher Chand Khanna, the Congress politician from NWFP and a staunch supporter of the Frontier Gandhi's Awami National Party, named the market after Gaffar Khan's brother, Khan Abdul Jaffar Khan, who was always called 'Dr Khan Sahib', and who was assassinated by political rivals in NWFP in 1958.

At that time the market was a small row of stores, including Sovereign Dairies (which has since closed), Anand Dairy (still functioning), a shoe shop, a chemist and two book shops—Bahri Sons and Faqir Chand. Today, only 25 to 30 per cent of the shops are still with the original owners— these include the books shops, the Crockery Emporium, Bunty and Modi Stores. Its popularity is a function of its location in the heart of affluent south Delhi, despite sometimes chaotic traffic snarls—a range of new ventures, notably the Neemrana shop, Benetton, Fabindia and others, reflects its high-end retail position. Yet customers have remained loyal. Mr Bahri of Bahri Sons recalls with pride that an army officer, who first came to his bookshop as a young captain, continued to come regularly through the years, and was still a loyal customer when he became a general.

One of the secrets of Khan Market's success is that shop owners have kept pace with changing tastes: Nirmal Narain Mehra, for instance, was allotted a shop in the market by the refugee rehabilitation ministry. He first sold dairy products, then, looking at changing consumption patterns, his became a party supplies shop; today the venture is looked after by his son and grandsons, supplying everything from turnkey theme parties to streamers, hats and goody bags. Similarly, B.K. Marwah first set up a general goods store in 1975, but changed it into the Music Shop, which his son, Ashok Marwah, is in charge of now. Nearby, Pandara Market, comprising twenty-one shops and five restaurants, has moved decisively upmarket since its early days when customers of Pindi restaurant would eat the famed tandoori chicken sitting on charpoys outside the kitchen. Today the restaurant has marble and mirrored interiors and the whole market has been smartened up and pedestrianized with fountains and retro-Victoriana street lamps. And it is still hugely popular.

To hold the fickle fancy of the public is no mean task. The state government emporia have lost custom to Dilli Haat, and CP in its low decades lost out to South Extension and other local markets, and now these are in turn taking a back seat to malls. Malls have Delhi enthralled, but with increasing numbers opening frequently, it is not unlikely that malls, too, will give way to the next new thing— whatever that may be. Ansal Plaza was Delhi's first mall and its mix of eating places, bars and branded retail outlets was immediately popular, but larger malls in Gurgaon and other newer Delhi areas have outstripped it in size and facilities. One estimate has it that by 2013 over 75 per cent of the retail space in the National Capital region would be dedicated to malls.[11]

The malls' mix of shopping and entertainment—whether cinema multiplexes and/or restaurants within a single building, with ample parking levels—has proved popular with the middle classes and demonstrates quite clearly the changes in the perceptions of shopping. Shopping is no longer a simple transaction: it is an experience. In Gurgaon today, few residents have the option of running down to a *kirana* (corner) shop (as most colonies in Delhi have in profusion) if they have run out of *haldi*; nor do fruit and vegetable vendors push their trolleys into residential areas, causing traffic jams and spreading a detritus of peelings and rotten tomatoes. Fresh produce is available at hygienic Safal booths and customers apparently prefer to trundle trolleys round supermarket aisles than be served personally at old-style kiranas. If buying groceries for the middle classes needs to be a first-world experience, malls are almost like amusement parks, where the entire family can enjoy a day's outing.

The potential retail space of present and planned malls is around 2,205,00 sq. ft, while the demand is projected at 18,000 sq. ft.[12] Half the space in existing new malls in the NCR is still to be sold or rented. NOIDA entered the mall business marginally later than Delhi or Gurgaon, so its rentals were higher: Rs 80 to 175 per sq. ft, as opposed to Delhi's Rs 90 to 140 per sq. ft. Gurgaon, with the largest number of malls (some two dozen functioning in 2006 and, according to a popular Gurgaon website, there are over a hundred more in the pipeline, showed the lowest: Rs 40-65 per sq. ft. Therefore, newer malls will increasingly be catering to local customers or will have to evolve niche attractions to continue to pull in custom. Ultimately, malls will have to compete with each other by upping their attractions—maintenance, security, parking, as well as the appeal of the goods on sale. But the mall phenomenon also has a trigger apart from the retail explosion. Observed one expert on property trends, 'Mall development is purely driven by real estate. Most mall developers assume that if they can convert idle real estate into a mall, it is bound to succeed.'[13]

As malls have changed the shopping experience in Delhi, multiplexes have transformed the watching of films. Single cinema houses, apart from a very, very few, are no longer viable concerns in Delhi. Watching a film at one of these is a dispiriting experience. The once smart art deco facades are peeling and unpainted, the foyers are seedy and at the ticket office a terminal weariness struggles with disbelief that you actually want a ticket. The dog-eared tickets themselves look recycled and the hall is unbelievably grubby. The air smells musty, the seats are torn and an entire row looks as if it has been forcibly uprooted. There are a handful of people in the hall, all of whom look extremely doubtful about the prospect of the next two and-a-half hours. The film may unreel without incident, but nearly half the audience melts away at the intermission, and when we get up to leave, there are only about ten people in the entire hall.

Before the video and DVD revolution, before the Uphaar tragedy in 1997, when a fire engulfed the hall, killing fifty-nine people, including infants and children, before Anupam PVR unveiled to Dilliwallahs the ancillary pleasures of popcorn and hamburgers, going to the movies was uncomplicated by anything except the worry that tickets might not be available. Today, the multiplex experience is as much about the surroundings as it is about the film itself.

Films today are expensive to screen and small, independent theatres cannot afford the big box-office hits. Nor can they raise ticket prices too steeply as people will simply not pay too much to see a film in an 'ordinary' theatre. Multiplexes charge upwards of Rs 150 for their seats, but people pay willingly for the ambience, the excellence of the sound system, and the brand-new box-office smash hit. Journalist Ziya us Salam wrote a heartrending elegy for the once grand talkies that provided an entire generation with the stuff of its dreams.[14] Minerva, once owned by Sohrab Modi (he sold it when he became a star) was the first to show Dilliwallahs *Kashmir ki Kali*. Jagat, near the Jama Masjid, founded by Lala Jagat Narain in 1937, screened *Chaudhavi ki Chand* and had full houses for *Mere Mehboob* till its silver jubilee.

Jagat has closed because Narain's family, although still in the film distribution business, cannot afford the big hits anymore. Similarly, New Amar, near Ajmeri Gate (a stone's throw from the house where Saira Banoo grew up), which was initially a theatre where Prithviraj Kapoor trod the boards, has been pulled down to make way for a Metro station. Excelsior, which screened the first Hindi talkie, *Alam Ara*, is still open, but the clientele it once attracted because of its boxes does not go there anymore. Majestic (owned by the family of banker to the Mughals, Lala Chunna Mal), Jubilee, Novelty, Ritz, Naaz, Grandala and Kamal have all closed down. Radhu in east Delhi is still running, but barely; West End survives, but Delite, where entire classes of Delhi University students would bunk college to catch the morning shows, no longer reverberates to Amitabh Bachchan's fury or Lata Mangeshkar's high-pitched warbles. Instead, three-screen-or-more multiplexes are opening all over Delhi. Many are remodelled cinema houses since the Masterplan decrees that original uses cannot be changed. Sonia cinema in Vikaspuri, west Delhi, is now a full-fledged three-screen PVR multiplex, with retail outlets of Archies, Benneton and McDonalds within its halls—a development that 'had transformed a sleepy suburb into a major social hub'.[15] Savitri in south Delhi, owned by the DLF group, has been reinvented as a four-screen Family Entertainment Centre.

Also in south Delhi, Alankar has undergone a transformation, as have Nataraj in Kirti Nagar, Paras in Nehru Place and Vishal in north Delhi. The Golcha management spent two crore to redo the lobby and increase capacity. In the newer Delhis, the DI Cinema in Gurgaon, the M2K (this stands for Movie Masti Komplex) in Rohini, Pitampura, the four-screen Satyam in West Patel Nagar and many more have come up. Fundamentally, this is a response both to the ever more sophisticated technology, the higher safety standards after the Uphaar disaster, easily available pirated versions of newly released films, satellite television and private cable operators who screen new films within hours of their release, as well as the accelerating rate of box-office flops from Bollywood (sometimes, films run for just four days). Theatre owners cannot afford to screen a movie to nearly empty halls, hence the smaller halls, a choice of English and Hindi films, a choice of timings and high ticket prices—though these vary with shows—so customer satisfaction becomes paramount. Dhruv Jalan of the Filmistan group, which owns 500 cinemas all over India, put it thus: 'The movie business is not just about ticket sales. It needs to create the right kind of image.'

The right kind of image has specific components: multiplexes are coming adorned with glass lifts, food counters, multi-cuisine restaurants and escalators, plus branded retail outlets, pubs and so on. Movie seats are now specially contoured to allow audiences to rest more snugly— and the popcorn/cold drink interval has been mandatory for a decade. Today, eating out is not only about food, nor shopping wholly about goods, and taking in a movie is not entirely related to the film. At every point, the 'experience' has a significance which is independent of the immediate goal: say, buying a pair of shoes is not simply getting a reasonably well-fitting, long-lasting, moderately priced piece of footwear. The surrounding accompaniments of the muzak, the lift and the interior décor of the outlet apparently count for as much, if not more.

Yet, how far this is a middle-class need for the ultimate purchasing event, and how far this is a bid by retailers to increase their sales as much as possible, is open to question. The investment in every possible seduction is to induce members of the public who have come to buy a pair of socks/watch a film/eat a *kathi* roll, to buy a television set *as well*, is part of a rational marketing strategy. The increase in disposal income in Delhi, and the increasingly sophisticated understanding of retailing, have given birth to the encompassing fulfilment of the shopping/eating out/film viewing experience. Arguably, this can be called progress; at any rate this is where post-millennium Delhi is.

If consumerism is the new leisure and malls are the new 'temples', then the temples themselves are by no means immune to these new trends. Religious activity has not decreased in Delhi. If anything, newer, more elaborate places of worship are being built regularly. The giant marble mansions of the gods in Chattarpur, or the new temple at Friends Colony are but the latest, grandest additions to the nearly constant tradition of temple-building in the city. The main structure of the Kakaji temple was built in the eighteenth century by Raja Kedarnath, prime minister to Emperor Akbar II. Countless later additions by rich, pious merchants have made it a conglomeration of styles and clashing colours. The legend is that the temple was built by a farmer who discovered that one of his cows was regularly offering milk to the goddess Kalka. In gratitude for this honour, he built the goddess a small shrine. Today in the temple, the goddess, draped in silks, sits under a silver umbrella, the whole crowned by a marble canopy. It is not clean and is crowded at all times of day: beribboned schoolgirls come to offer fervent prayers before their board exams, young men, old women throng the courtyard—this is Hinduism in bustling, popular, everyday practice.

Somewhat different is the atmosphere at the Lakshmi Narayan Temple, better known as the Birla Mandir. Built by industrialist B.D. Birla in 1938, it is a cluster of ochre and chocolate spires atop large, well-lit, spotless shrines to Lakshmi, Narayan, Hanuman and Radha-Krishna. The walls are adorned with scenes from the epics in calendar-art style, the place is spotlessly clean and the movement of worshippers well organized. On a non-festival weekday morning that I visited the temple, there were hardly any people there. The row of temples on Lodi Road causes traffic jams on Thursdays but on most other days, while there is a steady stream of the devout, there are no crowds.

But the relaxed nonchalance to religious spaces in Delhi is not irreverent; on the contrary, the seamlessness of the sacred and the profane is one of the most positive aspects of religion in India. When not stirred up by sectarian elements, religion is an ordinary part of daily life. Delhi has largely followed this tradition, though with glaring lapses in 1947 and 1984. At the eighteenth-century Ghatta or Zeenatul Masjid in Daryaganj, for instance, the children's voices rise upwards from the Crescent School immediately below. A knot of youths talks causally at the gateway; two women hold a low-voiced conversation near the rack for shoes. Similarly, at the thirteenth-century dargah of Chiragh Dilli, two retired men sit motionless under a tree and the owner of a metal grille shop in the village pauses to share some news before prayers begin; outside the church on Lodi Road on Sunday mornings, maids from Ranchi meet each other after the service. This is the social highlight of their week; they look happy, animated.

Even at the imposing Jama Masjid, the grand steps leading to the entrance are milling with ear cleaners, food vendors and toy sellers, and entire families can be found sitting in the cool of the colonnade. Religious spaces posses a sociability of their own; they are rarely awesome or forbidding.

Clubs are playing a decreasingly important role in Delhi life. The India International Centre (IIC) was established in 1966. It was intended to be a forum where people could meet to discuss foreign affairs. It has retained its gravitas by holding seminars and staging classical music performances regularly, but it is also the favoured meeting ground for the liberal south Delhi set—government, NGOs, academics, journalists, think-tankers and some politicians. It is the temple to Nehruvian values, quite possibly its last bastion, and this despite the fact that it is also favoured by the younger BJP set. The library is where retired civil servants have a home away from home, its dining room is where serious establishment networking takes place, its lounge the place where the now ageing post-Independence generation—some still carrying *jholas*, the identity badge of anti-establishmentism—congregate. IIC is a serious temple.

The Habitat Centre is the favoured hunting-ground of the upwardly mobile, corporate-business category. Habitat has its own cultural credentials: plays, concerts and a heritage sites' walking group that is now becoming seriously engaged in conservation. Its restaurants are crowded, its 'olde English' décor bar full of the influential and well-heeled.

Other Delhi clubs, however, are showing some symptoms of decline, an exception being the Press Club, which, though not a monument to spit and polish, thrives because of the largely professional homogeneity of its membership and the popularity of its bar. The Delhi Gymkhana was set up in 1931 and was one of the first clubs to admit Indians. Its membership is divided equally between corporate/business and the civil service and army, but senior civil servants having muted conversations about their ministries are more likely to be found today in the IIC. The Gymkhana is poised undecidedly between the old Raj traditions that its architecture and its history conjure, and the newer 'Punjabi' generation that makes up much of its active membership. The preponderance of marble, the slight neglect of the library, the vibrance of its card rooms and the noise of its bar, all indicate new directions. The Chelmsford Club, too, has seen better days, while the Roshanara Club set up in 1922 by R.E. Grant Gowan as a cricket club for the British, seems to belong to another, lost world. While cricket still brings members together, the change in values became evident when the wooden dance floor was replaced by marble.

≈  ≈

The Garden of the Five Senses in Mehrauli is spread over twenty acres and enfolds a flower garden, a lotus pond, a rock and boulder section and works of art. The garden is the creation of architect Pradeep Sachdeva, who also designed Dilli Haat. A member of his design team explains the rationale behind the area: 'The park . . . is not just a place for sitting and walking in for one's enjoyment, but demands more active participation.'[16] Few things so exemplify the differences between Delhi's various universes than the reactions to open green space. The notion that a park has to have a purpose other than to provide access to fresh air and exercise is a well entrenched one among some sections of the middle classes in Delhi who need a structured environment even to relax.

Lodi Gardens, for instance, is for power walking. So is Nehru Park, which also has the occasional concert and art show. Green space is certainly the magic mantra that all new housing developments trumpet when selling their desirability, but it is as a suitably ornamental backdrop. A resident of one of south Delhi's prestigious apartment complexes confesses that none of the residents ever sat in the elegant, exposed brick-lined space in front of the flats. It is a lovely spot: the sunlight filters gently through carefully positioned creepers and pot plants, casting dappled shadows on amphitheatre-like steps, and it is cool even on hot summer afternoons—all a hundred yards from the front door. Yet families are never seen there and the children of the flats prefer to play cricket in the parking lot. The space is, however, carefully tended by community-paid malis, and an elaborate system of water recycling is used to keep it green. It is, effectively, an exquisite backdrop and doubtless nudges the value of the apartments up by a couple of lakh at least.

But go to India Gate on a hot summer evening, and the scene is absolutely different. The lawns are packed with families, some on durries, some on folding chairs, each group just inches apart, inches that are navigated agilely by balloon sellers, chanachur vendors and urchins hawking cold drinks. The green neon lights of a hundred ice cream carts light up the scene as *alu parathas*, *rajma chawal* or *luchee tarkari* are unpacked from insulated tiffin carriers, or pizzas unfolded from their cardboard packs. Here is unselfconscious enjoyment, by people enjoying the city, the open air, the family outing; but each group remains intact, within its own private bubble. It is one of the most engaging sights in Delhi and one that accurately mirrors the city's extraordinary but unique temper.

# NOTES

## 1. IN THE EYE OF THE BEHOLDER

1. Pavan.K. Varma: *The Great Indian Middle Class,* Page 187; Penguin 1998
2. Khushwant Singh: 'A Historical Sketch' in B.P. Singh and Pavan K Varma's (eds) *Millennium Book of New Delhi,* Page 41; OUP 2001
3. Madhu Jain: 'The Happening City', Page 138 *op cit*
4. Sheila Dhar: *Here's Someone I'd Like You to Meet;* OUP 1999
5. Interview
6. Interview
7. Interview
8. David Halberstam: *The Fifties,* Preface Page *x;* Villard Books 1993
9. Khushwant Singh: *Delhi, A Novel;* Penguin India 1990
10. Ahmed Ali: *Twilight in Delhi,* Page 66; OUP 1991
11. William Dalrymple: *City of Djinns;* Flamingo 1994
12. Percival Spear: 'Delhi—The 'Stop-Go' Capital' in R E Frykenberg (ed): *Delhi Through the Ages: Selected Essays in Urban History, Culture and Society;* The Delhi Omnibus (Gupta, Spear and Frykenberg) Page 323; OUP 2002

13. Narayani Gupta: 'Delhi: The Nineteenth and Early Twentieth Centuries' in R E Frykenberg (ed): *Delhi Through the Ages: Selected Essays in Urban History, Culture and Society*; The Delhi Omnibus *op-cit* Page 139

14. H.K. Kaul (ed): *Historic Delhi*, Page 413; OUP 1985

15. Nazir Ahmad: *The Bride's Mirror*; Permanent Black 2001

16. Sabina Sehgal Saikia: '1911: It's Yesterday Once More'; *Times of India*, 6.1.01

17. M.M. Kaye: *The Golden Afternoon*; Viking 1997

18. Urvashi Butalia: *The Other Side of Silence*; Viking 1998

19. Anita Desai: *Clear Light of Day*; Heinemann 1980

20. Prabhat Patnaik: article in *D. School: Reflections on the Delhi School of Economics*; OUP 1995

21. James Cameron: *Indian Summer: A Personal Experience of India*, Page 104; Penguin 1987

22. V.S. Naipaul: *An Area of Darkness*; Andre Deutsch 1964

23. Jan Morris: 'Mrs. Gupta Never Rang' in *City Improbable*, Page 126; Khushwant Singh (ed); Viking 2001

24. Ruth Prawer Jhabvala: 'Development and Progress': *East into Upper East*; John Murray 1998

25. Sargarika Ghose: *The Gin Drinkers*, Page 37; Harper Collins 2000

26. Anjana Appachana: *Listening Now*; IndiaInk 1998

27. Susan Vishwanathan: *The Visiting Moon*; IndiaInk 2002

28. Gautam Bhatia: *Punjabi Baroque and Other Memories of Architecture*, Page 56; Penguin 1994

29. Khushwant Singh: *Delhi, A Novel*; Penguin 1990

30. 'The Alchemy of an Unloved City' in Denis Vidal, Veronique Dupont and Emma Tarlo (eds): *Delhi, Urban Space and Human Destinies*, Page 16, Manohar/ Centre de Sciences Humaines 2000

## 2. THE IDEA OF NEW DELHI

1. Kostov, Spiro: *The City Shaped: Urban Patterns and Meanings through History* Bulfinch Press, 1991

2. Kostov, Spiro: *ibid*
3. Letter to Valentine Cirol; quoted in H.Y. Sharada Prasad's article on Rashtrapati Bhavan
4. Lord Hardinge of Penshurst: *My Indian Years 1910-1916;* Page 224; John Murray 1948
5. Robert Grant Irving: *Indian Summer: Lutyens, Baker and Imperial Delhi;* Page 83; Yale University Press 1981
6. Kostov, Spiro: *op cit*
7. M.M. Kaye: *The Golden Afternoon* Page 71; Viking 1997

## 3. THE MAKING OF NEWER DELHI

1. Sunil Khilnani: *The Idea of India*, Page 109; Hamish Hamilton 1997
2. Interview
3. Delhi Administration: *Gazetteer of India*, Page 756; Delhi 1976
4. Interview
5. Delhi Administration: *Gazetteer of India*; Page 757; Delhi 1976
6. It was called 'Saracenic' because the ancient Greeks referred to all tribes east of the Euphrates as 'saracens'. In time the term came to be loosely identified with Islam.
7. Gautam Bhatia: *Punjabi Baroque and Other Memories of Architecture*; Penguin India, 1994
8. A plaque at the entrance has the words: 'To the Glory of God and for the advancement of sound learning and religious education. St Stephen's College Delhi. This stone was laid by Sir Charles A. Elliot, K.C.S.I. on Friday 11th April 1890'.
9. Bryan Appleyard: 'The Look We Love' *The Sunday Times* (London) 26. 3. 06
10. Jon Lang: *A Concise History of Modern Architecture in India*; Page 58; Permanent Black, 2002
11. Tom Dyckhoff: 'Hooray for Carbuncles', *The Times Review* (London) 4.9.04
12. Interview 8.3.03

13. *Sunday Express Newsline* 1.2.03
14. Peter Ackroyd: *London The Biography*; Page 755; Vintage 2001

## 4. REFUGEES: DELHI'S LAST CONQUERORS

1. Interview 23.7.01
2. Quoted in Tai Yong Tan and Gyanesh Kudaisya: 'Capital Landscapes' in *The Aftermath of Partition* in *South Asia*; Page 197; Routledge 2000
3. *ibid*; Page 198
4. Interview 8.12.2002
5. Interview 14.5.2002
6. Delhi Administration: *Gazetteer of India 1976*, Page 112; Delhi, Publications Division
7. M.K. Gandhi: *Delhi Diary: Prayer Speeches 1947-1948*; Navajivan 1948
8. Tai Yong Tan and Gyanesh Kudaisya Page 199 *op cit*
9. Interview 12.12.03; Islamabad
10. *The Hindustan Times*, April 22, 1948
11. Interview 2002
12. Interview 23.7.01
13. Interview
14. Naveen Kulshreshtha 1993: unpublished master's thesis, T.V.B. School of Habitat Studies
15. Prakash Tandon: *Punjabi Saga 1857-1987*; Page 220; Viking 1988
16. Interview 11.4.05; Islamabad
17. V.N. Dutta 'Punjabi Refugees and Greater Delhi' in R.E. Frykenberd (ed) *Delhi Through the Ages* (Spear, Gupta, Frykenberg) Delhi Omnibus Page 298; Oxford University Press 2002
18. V. N. Dutta *op cit* Page 295
19. Interview
20. Christophe Jaffrelot: 'The Hindu Nationalist Movement in Delhi: From Locals to Refugees and Towards Peripheral

Groups?' in Dupont, Tarlo and Vidal (eds) *Delhi, Urban Spaces and Human Destinies;* Page 198; Mahohar/ Centre de Sciences Humaines 2000

## 5. GOVERNMENT DELHI

1. Interview
2. David C. Potter: *India's Political Administrators 1919-1983;* Page 160; Clarendon Press 1986
3. Quoted in Jon Lang, Madhavi Desai and Miki Desai: *Architecture and Independence: The Search for Identity—India 1880 to 1980;* Page 59; Oxford University Press 1997

## 6. COLONIES: THE SHAPING OF MIDDLE-CLASS LIFE

1. Narayani Gupta: 'Delhi: The Nineteenth and Early Twentieth Centuries' in R.E. Frykenberg (ed) *Delhi Through The Ages.* The Delhi Omnibus (Spear, Gupta and Frykenberg) Page 149, OUP 2002
2. Interview
3. Colony comes from the Latin *coloniae,* used by the Romans for permanent military settlements in Italy, which guarded strategic points such as rivers and passes.
4. Prakash Tandon: *Punjabi Saga 1857-1987;* Page 215; Viking 1988

## 7. REMEMBERED VILLAGES

1. Interview
2. Interview
3. *Gazetteer of Delhi 1883-1884*
4. Interview
5. Interview
6. Indian National Trust for Art and Cultural Heritage: *Process*

*for Historic Site Development: Chiragh Delhi, A Case Study;*
INTACH, Delhi 1996

## 8. NEWEST DELHI

1. M.N. Buch: *Rationalising Management of post-Independent India*
2. Quoted in *HT Estates* 22.2.03
3. Interview 8..3.03
4. R. Sridharan in *Business Today,* 1.2.02
5. *Indian Express* Sunday Magazine, 8.12.02
6. Quoted in the *Indian Express* Sunday Magazine, 8.12.02
7. Interview with HUDA administrator, Anurag Aggarwal; *Hindustan Times* 1.6.02
8. Quoted in *Sunday Times of India* 8.4.01
9. Quoted in 'Satellite towns are better if you don't miss the glamour' *Sunday Times of India* 6.4.01
10. Sunil Khilnani: *The Idea of India,* Page 148; Hamish Hamilton 1997
11. Quoted in 'Southward Ho' by Sutirtho Patranobis; *Sunday Hindustan Times* 9.3.02
12. Quoted in *HT Estates* 2.11.02
13. Quoted in *HT Estates* 1.3.03
14. Naresh Malkani quoted in *HT Estates* 1.3.03
15. *HT Estates* 11.8.01
16. Interview 21.3.01

## 9. DELHI'S CULTURE

1. Interview 11.8.00
2. Asok Mitra: *Delhi Capital City* Publications Division 1970
3. Interview 23.3.03
4. Interview 22.9.05
5. Interview 10.1.05
6. Deepak Whorra: *The Hindustan Times* 8.1.03
7. Arati Jerath: *Indian Express* 4.12.00

## 10. CLASSICAL CULTURE AND HERITAGE

1. Report in the *Times of India* 22.12.00
2. Report in *The Sunday Times* (London ) 30.10.05
3. Quoted in the *Asian Age* 10.4.01
4. Quoted in *The Hindustan Times* 23.12.00

## 11. DELHI'S SOCIAL SPACES

1. Interview 16.5.02
2. Interview 23.7.01
3. Interview 14.5.02
4. Quoted in Prarthana Gahilote's article, 'The Fall of CP: From Hip to Has Been', *Express Newsline* 24.11.02
5. H.K. Verma, VP of Ansals Properties quoted in *HT Estates* 21.9.02
6. Quoted in *Express Newsline* 24.11.02
7. Lalit Nirula: speech given to a hospitality summit in Mumbai 28.01.99
8. V.S. Naipaul: *An Area of Darkness*
9. Gauri Bhatia: 'Somethings Never Change', *The Pioneer* 26.6.94
10. The group's GM Operations, Gurjeet Singh, quoted in *Express Newsline* 7.8.02
11. *HT Estates* 22.6.02.
12. Naresh Malkani, CEO Indiaproperties quoted in *HT Estates* 2.6.02
13. Hemant Mathur, Senior Consultant, KSA Technopak, quoted in *HT Estates* 22.6.02
14. Ziya us Salam: 'Few Takers Now for Dream Merchants', *Hindu Metro Plus* 19.3.01
15. *HT Estates* 21.9.02
16. Vidya Tongbram quoted in Ella Datta: 'Making Sense of Cities', *HT Sunday Magazine* 9.3.03